MEXICAN MIGRATION AND THE U.S. ECONOMIC CRISIS

CCIS Anthologies, 7

CENTER FOR COMPARATIVE IMMIGRATION STUDIES, UCSD

Mexican Migration and the U.S. Economic Crisis

A Transnational Perspective

edited by

Wayne A. Cornelius

David Fitzgerald

Pedro Lewin Fischer and

Leah Muse-Orlinoff

Center for Comparative Immigration Studies

University of California, San Diego

Printed in the United States of America

Cover design by Debra B. Topping.

Cover photograph courtesy of the *North County Times*.

Except where otherwise noted, photographs in this volume are by
David Fitzgerald, Wayne Cornelius, Lauren Harris, Georgia Hartman,
Jorge Narvaez, and Alpha Martell.

ISBN–13: 978-0-9800560-4-4 (cloth)
ISBN–13: 978-0-9800560-5-1 (paper)

Library of Congress Cataloging-in-Publication Data

Mexican migration and the U.S. economic crisis : a transnational
perspective / edited by Wayne A. Cornelius . . . [et al.].
    p. cm. — (CCIS anthologies ; 7)
  Includes bibliographical references.
  ISBN 978-0-9800560-4-4 (cloth) — ISBN 978-0-9800560-5-1 (pbk.)
  1. United States—Emigration and immigration—Economic aspects. 2.
Mexico—Emigration and immigration—Economic aspects. 3. Mexicans—
United States. I. Cornelius, Wayne A., 1945– II. Title. III. Series.

JV6471.M49 2010
  304.8'73072—dc22

2009035400

CONTENTS

PREFACE

WAYNE A. CORNELIUS, DAVID FITZGERALD, PEDRO LEWIN FISCHER, LEAH MUSE-ORLINOFF, AND MICAH GELL-REDMAN

This volume is the fifth in a series based on the annual research projects of the Mexican Migration Field Research and Training Program (MMFRP), based in the Center for Comparative Immigration Studies, University of California, San Diego, with the participation of Mexican partner institutions.[1] The fieldwork on which this volume is based took shape in the fall of 2008, when the United States was plunging into a deep economic crisis. There were ample indications that the crisis could have significant impacts on flows of Mexican migrants to and from the United States. In 2008, remittances sent home by Mexicans working in the United States declined in absolute terms, for the first time in the thirteen years for which comprehensive official statistics had been compiled. The stock of Mexicans residing in the United States was no longer growing, and apprehensions of undocumented Mexicans by the U.S. Border Patrol were falling at a rate not seen since the U.S. recession of 2001–2002 (Passel and Cohn 2008, 2009; Pew Hispanic Center 2007).

While the macro-level trends in migration were obvious, the explanation for them was less straightforward. Beyond the economic crisis itself, several potentially confounding and countervailing factors needed to be considered. Beginning in 2007, after the latest failure of comprehensive immigration reform legislation in Congress, the U.S. government had embarked on a markedly more aggressive immigration enforcement regime, including both border and interior enforcement activities as well as regulatory changes that made life for undocumented immigrants more precarious. The economic crisis in the United States, which might have

---

1. Previously published volumes include Cornelius and Lewis 2007; Cornelius, Fitzgerald, and Lewin Fischer 2007; Cornelius, Fitzgerald, and Borger 2009; and Cornelius, Fitzgerald, Hernández-Díaz, and Borger 2009. All can be ordered from http://www.rienner.com/.

been expected to push Mexicans out of the U.S. labor market, was also dragging the Mexican economy into a severe recession, increasing incentives for emigration and limiting options for would-be return migrants.

These conditions set up an intriguing opportunity to use the MMFRP's 2008–2009 field research to advance our understanding of how economic shocks affect population movements, a notably under-examined subject in international migration studies.[2] We were extremely curious about how people were faring on the ground, in both migrant-sending and receiving communities. How were individual decisions to migrate, to stay at home, or to stay in the United States being influenced by the economic crisis? How important was the crisis relative to tougher U.S. immigration enforcement—both at the border and in workplaces and neighborhoods—in discouraging new emigration and encouraging settlement in the United States? How was the crisis affecting the economies of migrant households and communities?

A common narrative in U.S. media coverage in late 2008 and early 2009 was that the U.S. economic crisis was provoking a mass return migration of Mexicans to their places of origin. "Reverse Migration Rocks Mexico" was the headline of a typical article, appearing in the influential journal *Foreign Policy* (Beith 2009), which predicted that up to three million Mexicans would soon become economic refugees from the United States, swamping the capabilities of state and local governments in the areas to which they were returning. While some Mexican scholars had begun to question the evidence for such claims (see, for example, Alarcón et al. 2008), there were no systematic, recently collected, individual- and community-level data to contradict them.

METHODS

To gather such data, we returned to Tunkás, an indigenous community in rural Yucatán that the MMFRP first studied in 2006, when the U.S. economic boom was at its peak, and the Tunkaseño satellite communities in Southern California. The principal fieldwork in Tunkás was conducted in January–February 2009; the California fieldwork was conducted in February–March 2009. A binational team of thirty-eight researchers, comprising undergraduate and graduate students from U.S .and Mexican institutions,

---

2. Exceptions include Borger 2009 and Hanson and Spilimbergo 2001.

conducted a total of 1,031 in-home survey interviews on both sides of the border.

The universe for standardized survey interviews in our Mexican research site was every person aged fifteen to sixty-five living in Tunkás at the time of our fieldwork. Every household in Tunkás was visited at least once by our field interviewers, and in many cases all eligible household members were interviewed. A total of 881 Tunkaseños who reside in Tunkás or, in a few cases, other parts of the Yucatán Peninsula were interviewed. Since we sought to interview the town's entire adult population, there was no sampling procedure and therefore no sampling error. We make no claim that the survey sample is statistically representative of larger universes of Mexican migrants and potential migrants. However, Tunkás is broadly representative of indigenous communities of emigration in southern Mexico, as documented in numerous survey and ethnographic studies conducted in such communities since the late 1980s.[3]

On the U.S. side, "snowball" samples consisting of a total of 151 migrants originating in Tunkás were interviewed in the most important U.S. destinations for Tunkaseños, that is, Los Angeles and Orange County, California. Contact information provided by relatives interviewed in Tunkás was used to locate most U.S.-based interviewees. The average duration of the standardized interviews, on both sides of the border, was forty-five minutes. The refusal rate for interviews attempted in Tunkás was 8 percent. The snowball sampling technique used for our California interviews makes it impossible to calculate a precise refusal rate, but refusals were more frequent there, due to the climate of suspicion and fear engendered by the intense U.S. immigration policy debate since 2006 and increased immigration enforcement activities in neighborhoods and worksites.

In addition to survey interviews, our research team conducted more than five hundred hours of in-depth, unstructured interviews, which were digitally recorded and transcribed for analysis. These interviews, exploring a very broad range of topics, sought to elicit more fine-grained information that would be useful in interpreting the standardized survey interview data. Throughout this book we have attempted to interweave evidence from our ethnographic and survey interviews to create the most

---

3. See, for example, Cohen 2004; Cordero Díaz 2007; Fox and Rivera-Salgado 2004; Hellman 2008; Hulshof 1991; Klaver 1997; Smith 2006; Stephen 2007; Velasco Ortiz 2005; Whiteside 2007.

complete and revealing portrait of *los migrantes de la crisis* attempting to survive and adjust in a turbulent economic environment.

KEY FINDINGS

The global economic contraction of 2008 served as a striking reminder of the ties that bind the world's nations—an interconnectedness particularly apparent in international migratory movements. When our research team returned to Yucatán and Southern California for its second round of fieldwork with the people of Tunkás, intimate links between the sending and receiving communities were readily apparent (chapter 1). These links permeated every sphere of Tunkaseños' lives, from kitchen to workplace, classroom to cornfield. Perhaps the most striking discovery of the 2009 field study is that Tunkaseños on *both* sides of the border face the same risky choice: to maintain a precarious existence at home, or to embark on a costly and difficult journey with uncertain outcomes.

Chapter 2 focuses directly on the consequences of the economic crisis for Tunkaseños living in Yucatán and California, documenting the strategies that they have devised for coping with *la crisis*. The macro-level numbers are striking. Economic output in the United States shrank more in 2008 than in any year since the 1930s. Months before the recession officially began in December 2007, employment in the construction sector, which had been one of the heaviest users of Mexican migrant labor in recent years, had contracted sharply as the U.S. housing bubble burst. To make matters worse, Mexico was not immune to the disease afflicting its northern neighbor, suffering an even more precipitous decline in output and a sharp increase in unemployment. Tunkaseños found themselves scrambling to cope with the aftereffects.

Among those living in the Southern California communities of Anaheim and Inglewood, where Tunkaseño migrants are clustered, most have seen their work hours cut back and overtime eliminated. Nevertheless, we found that the economic crisis has not spurred substantial return migration. Depending more heavily on family support networks, reducing their living expenses, and sending less money back to relatives in Tunkás, the vast majority of Tunkaseño migrants were choosing to weather the storm rather than return to Mexico.

Meanwhile, Tunkás found itself caught in a perfect economic storm, buffeted by a weak economy at home, fewer remittances from abroad, and a drought that decimated agricultural production. Rather than intensify northward migration, the crisis has put the plans of many potential international migrants on hold. Prior to 2008, the vast majority of would-be Tunkaseño migrants had a job waiting for them in the United States before they even left home, usually arranged by relatives and friends already working there. But with many fewer jobs available—unemployment in California shot up to 11.6 percent in the first half of 2009—the United States currently holds much less appeal. Now, a multi-week job search is often required, and the employment opportunities still available are more unstable than they used to be. However, for most potential migrants, the decision to stay home is only temporary. We found Tunkaseños eagerly awaiting improvement in the U.S. economy that would permit them to follow through on their plans to go north. Meanwhile, some were migrating internally, seeking work in the Yucatán Peninsula's tourist destinations.

That Tunkaseños, facing a freefalling U.S. (and local) economy, would choose to remain where they are rather than migrate internationally is partly a consequence of U.S. border enforcement efforts, which discourage unauthorized migration mainly by making it costlier to hire a people-smuggler. As the border enforcement buildup begun by the Clinton administration in 1993 continues to evolve—with additional billions of dollars being invested each year in pedestrian fencing, vehicle barriers, a nascent "virtual" fence, and more Border Patrol agents—the probability of being apprehended at the border and the physical risks of unassisted crossings have risen significantly. Nine out of ten undocumented Tunkaseños whom we interviewed in 2009 had felt compelled to hire a people-smuggler to assist their most recent border crossing. Most get what they pay for; while nearly half of the most recent cohort of unauthorized Tunkaseño migrants were apprehended at least once on their way into the United States, all ultimately succeeded in crossing the border. Tunkaseños already living in the United States are acutely aware of the costs and dangers of migrating without papers, which are powerful incentives to wait out the current downturn rather than make a temporary journey back to Tunkás followed by an attempted reentry into the United States.

The heavily fortified border is one of a number of factors that have induced undocumented Mexican migrants to remain in the United States for longer periods, breaking earlier patterns of circular migration. But while their sojourns have grown longer, settling has not gotten easier. U.S. government enforcement activities aimed at immigrants living in the United States have become more aggressive since 2006. In 2009 we found surprisingly large proportions of Tunkaseños who had experienced immigration raids at their workplace (or had heard about such raids from relatives and friends) and traffic stops by local police who asked about their immigration status. But we found no evidence that U.S. interior enforcement efforts were actually discouraging Tunkaseños from going north.

The confluence of economic pressures and changing border enforcement tactics poses an analytic challenge for researchers: Which of these two factors is most influential in a decision to migrate or stay at home? As shown in chapter 4, enforcement and economics interact in complex ways. For example, diminished income-earning opportunities in the faltering U.S. economy reduce the capacity of some would-be migrants to go north because their U.S.-based relatives—the most common source of financing to hire a people-smuggler—have less disposable income. Moreover, with highly uncertain job prospects in the United States, it is less rational for would-be migrants to invest thousands of dollars to hire a people-smuggler and risk their lives in the desert or the mountains to migrate illegally.

Our multi-year field research in Tunkás shows a sharp decline in Tunkaseños' propensity to migrate to the United States from 2006 to 2009. The year-to-year decline coincides perfectly with the unfolding of the U.S. economic crisis, with the steepest drop occurring between 2008 and 2009. While border enforcement continued to intensify from 2006 to 2009, the greatest discontinuity in the environment for migration decisions during this period was the contraction of the U.S. job market. We hypothesize that it is the *combination* of higher costs of migration (mainly, "*pollero*" fees, pushed upward by border enforcement) and a lack of jobs in the United States that has reduced the propensity to migrate clandestinely in recent years. If so, a sustained economic recovery in the United States is likely to cause illegal flows to rebound, as has happened after every U.S. recession since 1990.

The multivariate analysis reported in chapter 4 does not enable us to conclude that U.S. economic conditions are, in fact, more influential than border enforcement in deterring new migration, because our sample of Tunkaseños does not contain sufficient numbers of documented migrants (the control group for this analysis). However, it shows that even Tunkaseños who are legally entitled to enter the United States were less likely to go north in 2009 than in previous years—a clear indication that the lack of an assured job in the United States is discouraging would-be migrants, regardless of legal status.

In responding to changes both economic and policy-related, Tunkaseños are forced to renegotiate their position in a transnational labor market (chapter 5). In Tunkás this may mean augmenting the precarious livelihood provided by agriculture with activities in the informal economy or seeking employment in the urban centers and tourist destinations of southern Mexico. Tunkaseños in the United States have also looked to the informal sector, while adapting quickly to whatever wage-earning opportunities present themselves. In pursuing this flexible strategy, Tunkaseño migrants are surprisingly unhindered by laws intended to prevent employment of those unauthorized to work in the United States. Most U.S. employers continue to accept false or borrowed documentation, even if they "know for sure" that the worker is unauthorized.

Whether in Tunkás or in the job magnets of Southern California and southern Mexico, Tunkaseños with more experience in the labor market and higher levels of education find these investments in "human capital" rewarded by higher wages. By asking about the relative value of education in different geographical contexts, chapter 6 explores the connections that Tunkaseños make between labor market opportunities, educational attainment, and upward mobility. Our data reveal that most Tunkaseños are aware of the potential payoffs from education. Prevailing opinion in the town holds that youths should complete at least their middle school education before migrating to the United States. Educational attainment has improved dramatically over the past two decades, though major obstacles remain. Few Tunkaseños complete high school and still fewer attend college, primarily because the cost of doing so is too high. Young women still lag behind their male counterparts, and may not be well served by the secondary education available to them in Tunkás. In the

United States, the steepest barrier to achievement facing the children of Tunkaseño migrants is legal status, without which the dream of pursuing a college education remains largely out of reach.

As Tunkás becomes a more established community of emigration, certain attitudes, values, and beliefs permeating the town are informing the choice that young people make to remain at home or seek their fortunes abroad. As reported in chapter 7, our qualitative interviews revealed the influence of this culture of migration especially on young men, who often see the intrinsic value of migration for adventure before they perceive the instrumental value of migration for economic advancement. Young women are also swayed by the culture of migration, though for them the importance of family ties and responsibilities often trumps pressures to earn wages—one reason why young females prefer internal migration over going to the United States.

Just as cultural values linked to migration have been woven into the fabric of the community, it has become typical for Tunkaseño families to face some form of disruption due to migration. Our observations of Tunkaseño families (chapter 8) revealed that the economic benefits of international migration are often counterbalanced by familial instability—a cost that may be ameliorated if family members migrate within Mexico rather than to the United States. At the same time, migration does not necessarily mean that Tunkaseños abandon the forms of community participation that serve to build social capital. Our fieldwork (chapter 10) reveals that three main forms of community participation—associations known as *gremios* that support the town festival, traditional dance troupes, and team sports—are all alive and well in the town and in the Tunkaseño migrant diaspora. The analysis points to the highly politicized nature of these activities, and poses the question of whether they help or hinder the development of formal, transnational organizations.

Finally, this volume continues our effort to use the MMFRP's annual field studies to illuminate significant aspects of the health status of migrants as well as nonmigrants in our research communities. This year's project focused on nutrition-related health problems. Chapter 9 reports that Tunkaseños living in Tunkás lack fresh produce and other essential sources of nutrition; as a result they are more often afflicted by nutrition-related diseases than their migrant counterparts. Surprisingly, members of Tunkaseño families receiving remittances from their U.S.-based relatives are more likely to have been diagnosed with high cholesterol and diabetes, perhaps because they consume unhealthy levels of meat. On the other hand, medical care is more readily available to those living in Tunkás than to Tunkaseño migrants living in the United States. This difference is due in part to the wider availability of publicly subsidized care in Tunkás, but it also reflects the barriers to health service delivery common in U.S. migrant communities, including high costs and, for the undocumented, fears of detection and deportation.

ACKNOWLEDGMENTS

This study was made possible by generous grants from the Ford Foundation, the Fundación BBVA, and the Foundation for Population, Migration, and Environment (PME), as well as support for the MMFRP from the UC Office of the President and the following units of the University of California, San Diego: the Office of the Senior Vice Chancellor for Academic Affairs, the Division of Humanities, the California Cultures in Comparative Perspective Program, the Center for the Study of Race and Ethnicity, Eleanor Roosevelt College, John Muir College, Revelle College, and Sixth College. Essential administrative support and limitless good cheer were provided by Ana Minvielle, Management Services Officer of UCSD's Center for Comparative Immigration Studies.

In Mexico, we are indebted to Tunkás's Municipal President, Juan Gabriel Sulub Cabrera, and his entire team for their hospitality and support for our field research, as well as to the teachers and administrators in all of Tunkás's public schools. The study benefited from data on the economy of Tunkás and Yucatán provided by the state's Planning and Budget Secretariat. Our partner institution in Yucatán, the Center INAH Yucatán/Instituto Nacional de Antropología e Historia, provided essential administrative and logistical support. Professor Debra Cornelius of Shippensburg University played a key role in the fieldwork supervision. As always, our greatest debt is to the people of Tunkás, on both sides of the border, who graciously welcomed us into their homes and shared with us their experiences, hopes, and fears at a time of exceptional stress in their lives.

REFERENCES

Alarcón, Rafael, Rodolfo Cruz, Alejandro Díaz-Bautista, Gabriel González-Konig, Antonio Izquierdo, Guillermo Yrizar, and René Zenteno. 2008. "La crisis financiera en Estados Unidos y su impacto en la migración mexicana." Tijuana, Baja California: El Colegio de la Frontera Norte. Unpublished paper, December.

Beith, Malcolm. 2009. "Reverse Migration Rocks Mexico," *Foreign Policy*, February.

Borger, Scott C. 2009. "Estimates of the Cyclical Inflow of Undocumented Migrants to the United States." CCIS Working Paper No. 181. La Jolla, CA: Center for Comparative Immigration Studies, University of California, San Diego, http://ccis-ucsd.org/publications/wrkg181.pdf.

Cohen, Jeffrey H. 2004. *The Culture of Migration in Southern Mexico*. Austin, TX: University of Texas Press.

Cordero Díaz, Blanca Laura. 2007. *Ser trabajador transnacional: Clase, hegemonía y cultura en un circuito migratorio internacional*. Puebla, Mexico: CONACYT/ Benemérita Universidad Autónoma de Puebla.

Cornelius, Wayne A., David Fitzgerald, and Scott Borger, eds. 2009. *Four Generations of Norteños: New Research from the Cradle of Mexican Migration*. La Jolla, CA: Center for Comparative Immigration Studies, University of California, San Diego.

Cornelius, Wayne A., David Fitzgerald, Jorge Hernández-Díaz, and Scott Borger, eds. 2009. *Migration from the Mexican Mixteca: A Transnational Community in Oaxaca and California*. La Jolla, CA: Center for Comparative Immigration Studies, University of California, San Diego.

Cornelius, Wayne A., David Fitzgerald, and Pedro Lewin Fischer, eds. 2007. *Mayan Journeys: The New Migration from Yucatán to the United States*. La Jolla, CA: Center for Comparative Immigration Studies, University of California, San Diego.

Cornelius, Wayne A., and Jessa M. Lewis, eds. 2007. *Impacts of Border Enforcement on Mexican Migration: The View from Sending Communities*. La Jolla, CA: Center for Comparative Immigration Studies, University of California, San Diego.

Fox, Jonathan, and Gaspar Rivera-Salgado, eds. 2004. *Indigenous Mexican Migrants in the United States*. La Jolla, CA: Center for U.S.-Mexican Studies and Center for Comparative Immigration Studies, University of California, San Diego.

Hanson, Gordon H., and Antonio Spilimbergo. 2001. "Political Economy, Sectoral Shocks, and Border Enforcement." CCIS Working Paper No. 44. La Jolla, CA: Center for Comparative Immigration Studies, University of California, San Diego, http://ccis-ucsd.org/publications/wrkg44.pdf

Hellman, Judith Adler. 2008. *The World of Mexican Migrants.* New York: New Press.

Hulshof, Marije. 1991. *Zapotec Moves: Networks and Remittances of U.S.-Bound Migrants from Oaxaca, Mexico.* Nederlandse Geografische Studies, no. 128. Amsterdam, Netherlands: Instituut Voor Sociale Geografie, Universiteit Van Amsterdam.

Klaver, Jeanine. 1997. *From the Land of the Sun to the City of Angels: The Migration Process of Zapotec Indians from Oaxaca, Mexico, to Los Angeles, California.* Netherlands Geographical Studies, no. 228. Utrecht/Amsterdam, Netherlands: Dutch Geographical Society, University of Amsterdam.

Passel, Jeffrey S., and D'Vera Cohn. 2008. "Trends in Unauthorized Immigration: Undocumented Inflow Now Trails Legal Inflow." Pew Hispanic Center Report. Washington, DC: Pew Hispanic Center, October 2.

———. 2009. "Mexican Immigrants: How Many Come? How Many Leave?" Pew Hispanic Center Report. Washington, DC: Pew Hispanic Center, July 22.

Pew Hispanic Center. 2007. "Indicators of Recent Migration Flows from Mexico." Pew Hispanic Center Fact Sheet. Washington, DC: Pew Hispanic Center, May 30.

Smith, Robert C. 2006. *Mexican New York: Transnational Lives of New Immigrants.* Berkeley, CA: University of California Press.

Stephen, Lynn. 2007. *Transborder Lives: Indigenous Oaxacans in Mexico, California, and Oregon.* Durham, NC: Duke University Press.

Velasco Ortiz, Laura. 2005. *Mixtec Transnational Identity.* Tucson, AZ: University of Arizona Press.

Whiteside, Anne. 2007. "Transnational Yucatecans and Language Practices in San Francisco, California: Results from a Participatory Research Survey," *Kroeber Anthropological Society Papers* 96: 80–105.

A transnational family based in Tunkás and Anaheim, California.

1 Introduction

LEAH MUSE-ORLINOFF AND PEDRO LEWIN FISCHER

Tunkás, a Maya-speaking town of approximately 2,600 inhabitants, is located ninety minutes from Mérida, in Yucatán's north-central region. Tunkaseños have been migrating to the United States in substantial numbers only since the late 1990s, but for many decades they have been moving to Mérida and the tourist destinations of the Mayan Riviera (Cancún, Playa del Carmen) in search of employment. Initially studied in 2006 by the Mexican Migration Field Research and Training Program (MMFRP), Tunkás was revisited in 2009 to discover what had changed in Tunkaseños' migration patterns and in the effects of migration on the community.

We found that, in some ways, little had changed since 2006: A few new houses had been built, and many more were under construction. These new homes, often funded by remittances sent from the United States, are bigger and more eye-catching than those built without *migradólares*. A cyber-café now draws a steady stream of students who use the computers for their school assignments and to play on-line games or message their friends. New stores, including small clothing shops and hardware stores, have sprung up, while other businesses, such as the supermarket on the edge of town, have expanded. However, these stores struggle to stay open; their owners report that the economic crisis and declining remittances from the United States are hurting Tunkaseños' purchasing power.

In February 2009, recently returned migrants from the United States were conspicuous by their absence, reflecting the gravity of the economic crisis that has threatened the livelihoods of Tunkaseños working in the United States. The adult migrants who had returned to the town for the annual fiesta noted the "changing mentality" of Tunkaseño youths and grumbled about their clothing styles, their music, and their irreverence. Yet in many cases the consumption patterns of the young people of Tunkás can be attributed partly to the influence and presence of these returning migrants, who show up wearing American clothes, listening to American music, and driving American cars. These are the chronic growing pains of a town recently arrived to international migration, one that is still coming to grips with the fact that it has become a community of emigration, pervasively linked to the United States.

The overriding change that we encountered in our most recent fieldwork is that Tunkaseño families on both sides of the border were under much greater pressure to make ends meet, and their feelings of insecurity were notably stronger than in 2006. Tunkaseños in 2009 were being buffeted by a global economic crisis, a sustained decline in U.S. and local job prospects, severe climatic conditions, the increasing militarization of the U.S. border, and a series of U.S. government policies designed to make life more difficult for undocumented migrants living in the United States.

We begin this chapter with a brief overview of the patterns of emigration from Tunkás to the rest of the Yucatán Peninsula and to the United States, with particular attention to the sociodemographic characteristics of migrants. We then discuss the specific economic, ecological, and political challenges currently confronting Tunkaseño communities in Mexico and the United States, highlighting the changes observable since 2006.

TUNKASEÑO MIGRATION PATTERNS

There are two major patterns of emigration from Tunkás. The first is internal migration within Mexico. Tunkaseños live and work throughout Mexico, but most internal migrants live in two principal areas: Mérida, the capital of the state of Yucatán, and the Mayan Riviera, a series of tourist destinations along the northeastern coast of the Yucatán Peninsula, in the state of Quintana Roo. Nearly half (43 percent) of the Tunkaseños whom we interviewed in 2009 had lived or worked in another part of Mexico at some point; 12 percent of interviewees currently reside outside of Tunkás in another part of Mexico. As shown in figure 1.1, there has been a steady, though moderate, increase in the density of internal migration since 1975. Many Tunkaseño internal migrants return regularly to their hometown. As reported in chapter 8 of this volume, many internal migrants retain a house and even a household in Tunkás, returning nearly every weekend to be with their families.

Figure 1.1. Density of Internal Migration from Tunkás, 1975–2009
(percentage of Tunkaseños living elsewhere in Mexico)

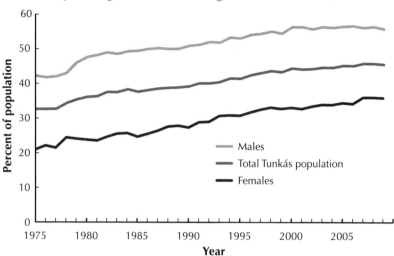

The Mayan Riviera's seemingly unending need for construction and service workers began in the late 1960s. The labor market on the coast grew dramatically in the 1980s and 1990s as cities like Cancún and Playa del Carmen received substantial development assistance from the Mexican government and became some of the most important international tourist destinations in Mexico. Mérida, the other major destination for internal Tunkaseño migrants, is also an important tourist destination, and offers service sector, white collar, and construction jobs. Previous MMFRP research (Rodríguez, Wittlinger, and Manzanero Rodríguez 2007) has demonstrated the importance of labor migration to these domestic destination areas as preparation for Tunkaseños' eventual migration to the United States. Stints in Mexican tourist cities gave Tunkás's first international migrants the financial and human capital necessary to facilitate their move into the U.S. labor market.

The second major Tunkaseño emigration pattern is international migration, principally to Southern California.[1] The first international migrants

---

1. In recent years, two Tunkaseño men have worked for six months each year in Canada. The men are registered with Canada's guestworker program for Mexican farmworkers and are employed as seasonal beekeepers on a medium-sized farm outside of Toronto. For a description of the program, see Verduzco Igartúa 2004.

from Tunkás traveled to the United States as part of the Bracero program of contract labor importation in the late 1950s and early 1960s. For the next thirty years there was slow but steady growth in circular migration between Tunkás and Southern California. In the late 1990s, however, the number of Tunkaseños migrating to the United States rose substantially (figure 1.2). Several factors, including stronger demand for migrant labor in the rapidly growing U.S. economy, the saturation of the domestic labor market in the Mayan Riviera and Mérida, and the relatively low cost and low physical risk of clandestine entry into the United States, converged to drive this increase. Initially, migrants from Tunkás to the United States were men who migrated without their wives or children. However, as shown in figure 1.2, women have also been well represented in post-1990 migration to the United States.

Figure 1.2. Density of International Migration from Tunkás, 1975–2009
(percentage of Tunkaseños living in the United States)

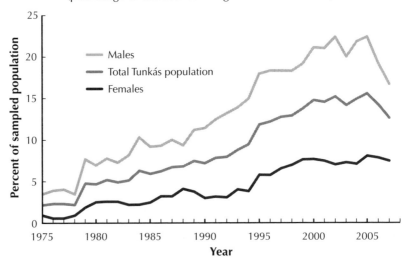

In early 2009, the modal Tunkaseño migrant was a 36-year-old married male with at least one child (table 1.1). The average migrant had completed nine years of school and spoke Maya well or moderately well. Prior to migrating, the average Tunkaseño living in the United States in 2009 had worked in agriculture or had been a student, which reflects the relative youth of many Tunkaseño international migrants.

Table 1.1. Sociodemographic Characteristics of Tunakseño Migrants

Characteristic	Percent
Gender	64% male
Marital status	66% married
Children	69% at least one child
Documentation status	76% undocumented
Maya speaker	80% speak Maya
Average age	36 years
Educational attainment	9.32 years

The modal Tunkaseño migrant to the United States now works in the service sector, likely in one of the many car washes that ring Los Angeles International Airport. Most U.S.-based Tunkaseños also live near the airport, in the Inglewood section of Los Angeles. The second and third most important clusters of Tunkaseños can be found in the cities of Anaheim and Santa Ana, in Orange County.

Tunkaseños overwhelmingly migrate without papers. Seventy-six percent of Tunkaseño migrants living in California at the time of our 2009 fieldwork were undocumented, and only 21 percent of Tunkaseños who had *ever* been to the United States migrated legally. Many of the documented Tunkaseño migrants whom we interviewed in 2009 were able to legalize their status under provisions in the 1986 Immigration Reform and Control Act (IRCA), although a few older residents obtained their "green cards" during or shortly after their participation in the Bracero program and were able to arrange papers for their children. Tunkaseños who migrated to the United States subsequent to IRCA have had a much harder time legalizing their presence in the United States. The lack of a generalized legalization process in the last twenty-three years has made it virtually impossible for Tunkaseño migrants to regularize their legal status if they entered the United States clandestinely.

Most Tunkaseños migrate for one of two reasons: to find a job in the United States, or to be reunited with family members already living there. Men tend to migrate for the first reason, and women for the second. As shown in figure 1.3, nearly two-thirds of male Tunkaseño migrants (61 percent) reported that employment opportunities such as the greater availability of jobs and the higher wages in the United States were the primary motivating factor for international migration. In contrast, only 35 percent of women indicated that job prospects were the most important reason for having migrated to the United States. Two out of five female migrants went to the United States to join family members already living there, while family reunification was the most important reason for migration for only one in ten male migrants.

Figure 1.3. Primary Reason for Migrating to the United States (weighted responses)

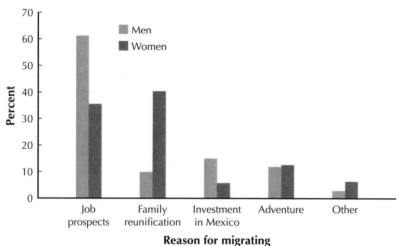

Note: Up to three responses to our question about reasons for the most recent migration were recorded. In this tabulation of results, the reasons were weighted according to the order in which they were mentioned by the interviewee.

Relatively more Tunkaseño migrants to the United States are now settling there permanently than at the beginning of the town's international migration flow. This higher incidence of settlement responds to the maturation of the U.S.-based migrant community, including the birth of children in the United States and ongoing incorporation into U.S. social and labor contexts, but it also reflects the effects of U.S. immigration control policies that have "bottled up" undocumented migrants within the United States (see chapter 3, this volume). While in previous decades Mexican migrants circulated seasonally between job opportunities in the United States and their home communities, tougher border enforcement since the late 1990s has discouraged migrants from returning home. As a consequence, many undocumented Tunkaseños in the United States remain there continuously for five or more years, often without returning to visit their relatives in Tunkás.

THE LOCAL POLITICAL CONTEXT

At the time of our 2009 fieldwork, Tunkás was experiencing a period of high political tension.[2] The proximate roots of this tension lie in the 2007 local elections, in which the mayor was not eligible for reelection and a new administration took over the *municipio*. However, the outgoing mayor continued to lead a strongly vocal opposition group. Shortly after the election the newly elected mayor, a man in his early thirties, proposed a local development initiative using resources from the state government to create an ecotourism park centered on several of the local *cenotes*.[3] The plan would have created a tourist destination in Tunkás, one that complemented rather than competed with the many tourist attractions in the nearby town of Izamal. According to the mayor, income from the park would have been used to support elderly town residents, pay a salary to the thirty-two *ejido* members who were participating in the project, and cover the operational costs of both the ecotourism park and the *ejido*. However, building an ecotourism park on ejidal lands was unthinkable to many *ejido* members, who, under the leadership of the ex-mayor, mounted a strong opposition to the mayor's proposal. The project was ultimately voted down, and at the time of our 2009 fieldwork the incumbent mayor remained an unpopular leader among many members of the *ejido*.[4] The conflict over the ecotourism park reactivated a long-standing conflict between the municipal government and the *ejido*—a conflict that, if not unique to Tunkás, is manifested there with considerable vehemence.

---

2. For further information on the political and economic history of Tunkás, see Silva, Niño, and Solís Lizama 2007.

3. *Cenotes* are deep holes in the limestone that underlies much of the northern part of the Yucatán Peninsula. Fed over centuries by rainfall and water seeping through the porous land, *cenotes* are often full of water and are impressive natural formations.

4. The ongoing conflict over the ecotourism project may have been at least partly responsible for the higher than expected interview refusal rate (8 percent) that we experienced in our 2009 survey in Tunkás, which was roughly twice as high as we had encountered in our 2006 survey. We hypothesize that some *ejidatarios* opposed to the ecotourism project declined to cooperate with our study because they assumed that it was somehow connected to the incumbent mayor.

The local political conflict in Tunkás does not end at the boundaries of the *municipio*, but also extends to the Tunkaseño community in California. Many Tunkaseño migrants believe that their hometown's political leaders do not pay enough attention to them, and few U.S.-based Tunkaseños feel connected to the governance of their place of origin. As a consequence, by early 2009 there was little if any coordinated, transnational political action involving Tunkaseños in the United States and those in Tunkás.

In our 2006 field study we documented the participation of the town government in the Tres por Uno program, a development initiative coordinated at that time by the Institute for the Development of Mayan Culture in the State of Yucatán (Instituto para el Desarrollo de la Cultura Maya del Estado de Yucatán, INDEMAYA). Tres por Uno funds came from U.S.-based migrants, the municipal government, and state and federal agencies. The monies were used to build softball and soccer fields in Tunkás. However, as explained in chapter 10 of this volume, political tensions in Tunkás play out even in these ostensibly nonpolitical arenas, and at the time of our 2009 fieldwork the softball fields built with Tres por Uno funds had been closed for use by the mayor.

Table 1.2. Federal Economic Assistance to Tunkás and Yucatán (in pesos)

	2006	2007	2008
Tunkás			
Participations	6,042,223	6,056,710	7,287,809
Contributions	2,906,814	3,184,004	3,843,023
Total	8,949,037	9,240,714	11,130,832
Yucatán			
Participations	1,571,686,063	1,640,922,139	1,979,153,963
Contributions	1,016,996,334	1,170,380,785	1,412,385,750
Total	2,588,682,398	2,811,302,924	3,391,539,713

Sources: Cuenta Pública 2006, 2007, and 2008, Gobierno del Estado de Yucatán.

The complicated political circumstances of Tunkás are reflected in the town's budget and resource allocation processes. For all intents and purposes, Tunkás does not generate any resources from local sources (less than 50,000 pesos, or roughly US$3,500 per year). Consequently, the town depends almost entirely on money earned elsewhere. Table 1.2 shows the

Playground in Tunkas's central plaza, built in 2009 by the municipal government. *Photograph by Rolando Euán*

total economic transfers made to Tunkás between 2006 and 2008, as well as those made to the state of Yucatán. Funds in the first category, known as "participations" (*participaciones*), are assigned according to demographic criteria. The second category, called contributions (*aportaciones*), can only be used to alleviate local problems through infrastructure development or other public works projects. Between 2006 and 2008, net state allocations grew by approximately 20 percent, but if inflation is taken into account the increase is closer to 10 percent.

In addition to the resources identified in table 1.2, the *municipio* received around 11.5 million pesos (a little under US$825,000) in general assistance from the federal government in 2008, as well as 4 million pesos (US$292,000) for social and community initiatives. The *municipio*'s total budget for 2008 was 26.8 million pesos (US$1.84 million). Most of the funds the *municipio* receives are for infrastructure projects. During 2008 these funds financed the expansion of the potable water system, several recreational facilities, eight kilometers of street paving, and a water purification facility. Funds from the "community strengthening" category were used for public safety, lighting, and telephone services. Because most of Tunkás's budget is destined for public assistance and basic infrastructure needs, very little is left over for economic development initiatives that might alleviate the town's persisting poverty. Tunkás is one of 69 *municipios* in Yucatán (out of 106) that have been classified by the federal government as "highly marginalized." The few jobs generated in the town through public financing are temporary and not an important source of employment for local residents. At the time of our fieldwork, for example, the town government had hired about a dozen Tunkaseño construction workers who had been laid off from their jobs in the Mayan Riviera to help build a Community Development Center, including a library and computer center. The project was completed by mid-summer 2009 and the workers were dismissed.

THE EFFECTS OF THE "GREAT RECESSION" ON TUNKASEÑO COMMUNITIES

The conditions of deprivation and scarcity that many Tunkaseño families routinely confront were compounded by the onset of the global economic convulsion that sent the U.S. and Mexican economies into a tailspin in late 2008. What Tunkaseños call the "great recession" of 2008–2009 actually began in 2007 when the U.S. housing bubble burst, the credit market collapsed, and companies began massive layoffs. Mexico swiftly followed the United States into recession, and by late 2008 the Mexican year-over-year GDP had fallen by over 8 percent (Luhnow and Harrup 2009). The plunge continued in 2009; Mexico's economy shrank by more than 10 percent in the first half of the year. The export-manufacturing, service, and tourism sectors experienced the sharpest declines. All three are important for the regional Yucatecan economy: 70 percent of the workforce in the state of Yucatán works in manufacturing, and the tourism industry of Mérida and the Mayan Riviera employ hundreds of thousands of workers. Declines in Mexican tourism driven by the economic crisis and, subsequently, the outbreak of "swine flu" in the second quarter of 2009 caused a sharp contraction of employment opportunities in the tourist areas of Yucatán and Quintana Roo.

The economic crisis also had a substantial effect on employment in the United States, and Hispanic workers experienced disproportionately high job losses (Kochhar 2008). Many of these layoffs resulted from the collapse of housing prices. The decrease in home construction activity (a primary employment sector for Mexican migrants) led to high unemployment rates for Hispanic workers. California was particularly hard hit, and in parts of the state, like the Los Angeles area, unemployment surpassed 10 percent in early 2009. For the Tunkaseños who live in the United States, job losses were certainly a worry. However, given the concentration of U.S.-based Tunkaseños in service occupations and their relatively low participation in the construction industry, many were shielded from the first rounds of layoffs in 2008 and 2009. They were not, however, insulated from cuts in working hours, which reduced family incomes significantly for many members of the Tunkás community in California (see chapter 3, this volume, for further information).

Tunkaseños living in Yucatán were immediately affected by this drop in their U.S.-based relatives' earnings, which translated into smaller and less frequent remittances. In mid-2009 the Banco de México reported that remittances to the state of Yucatán declined by 12 percent between the first quarter of 2008 and the first quarter of 2009—a significant change, since for many years the rate of growth in migrant remittances sent to Yucatán was among the highest among Mexican states. An additional complicating economic factor for Tunkaseño families in 2008 and 2009 was the drop in the value of the peso relative to the dollar. When the exchange rate changed from 10 pesos per dollar in August 2008 to 13.50 pesos to the dollar in October 2008, it immediately became more expensive to purchase imported goods and food in Mexico. However, the new exchange rate benefited families that receive remittances, because the dollars arriving from the United States yielded more pesos. In some cases, the new exchange rate helped to offset the declines in net dollars remitted by U.S.-based migrants.

ECOLOGICAL CHALLENGES

Tunkás, like much of the northern Yucatán Peninsula, lies in an ecologically fragile zone. The land is rocky and the topsoil thin, and rainwater seeps rapidly through the limestone surface. Local farmers are dependent on seasonal rains to nourish their crops, and when the rains do not arrive the farmers have little recourse, given that there is no irrigation system nor any way to pump water from the deep underground *cenotes* to the fields around the town. In Tunkás, the 2008 rainy season simply failed to materialize, and as a result most of the town's small-scale farmers lost some or all of their harvest for the year.

As an additional challenge, the drought, combined with an unseasonably cold winter, meant that the small yellow flowers known as *xukul* did not blossom. These flowers are the primary source of sustenance for the millions of bees kept by Tunkaseños, and since the *xukul* did not bloom, the bees began to starve. Beekeepers had to feed the bees a mixture of sugar and water, an expensive proposition. The beekeepers, many of whom also have small parcels of land on which they depend for their family's food supply, were thus hit on every front. The drought ruined their crops; the bees required expensive feeding and did not produce honey, so there was no honey to sell; remittances from children or other relatives in the United States decreased; and family members who used to work in the Mayan Riviera or Mérida not only stopped sending money back but returned to Tunkás and became yet another mouth to feed.

CONCLUSION

The economic, political, and ecological disturbances of 2008–2009 meant that the circumstances of life for Tunkaseños in their hometown as well as in the Tunkaseño diaspora in the United States had changed markedly between the first and second MMFRP field studies—thus illustrating the importance of multi-year field research in migrant-sending and receiving communities. Between 2006 and 2009, there had been an obvious decline in new migration from Tunkás to the United States, mostly but not entirely attributable to dismal economic conditions in the United States; but return migration from the United States had also dwindled to a trickle. Tunkaseño families on both sides of the border had changed their spending habits, attempted to increase their participation in both the formal and the informal labor markets, and adopted a range of other strategies to help make ends meet.

The challenge for the transnational Tunkaseño community is to make it through the current hard times until economic growth can be restored and, hopefully, access to the U.S. labor market can be made easier and less costly through reforms to the U.S. immigration system. Barack Obama had been inaugurated only a few days before we arrived for our 2009 fieldwork, and among many migrants and their relatives there was a sense of optimism that perhaps this new administration would both end the "great recession" and usher in an era of liberalized immigration policies.

REFERENCES

Kochhar, Rakesh. 2008. "Latino Labor Report, 2008: Construction Reverses Growth for Latinos." Pew Hispanic Center Report. Washington, DC: Pew Hispanic Center, June 4.

Luhnow, David, and Anthony Harrup. 2009. "Mexico's Economy Slumps, Dragged Down by U.S.," *Wall Street Journal*, May 21.

Rodríguez, Andrea, Jennifer Wittlinger, and Luis Manzanero Rodríguez. 2007. "The Interface between Internal and International Migration." In *Mayan Journeys: The New Migration from Yucatán to the United States*, ed. Wayne A. Cornelius, David Fitzgerald, and Pedro Lewin Fischer. La Jolla, CA: Center for Comparative Immigration Studies, University of California, San Diego.

Silva, Travis, Amérika Niño, and Marian Solís Lizama. 2007. "Tunkás: A New Community of Emigration." In *Mayan Journeys: The New Migration from Yucatán to the United States*, ed. Wayne A. Cornelius, David Fitzgerald, and Pedro Lewin Fischer. La Jolla, CA: Center for Comparative Immigration Studies, University of California, San Diego.

Verduzco Igartúa, Gustavo. 2004. "The Temporary Mexican Migrant Labor Program in Canadian Agriculture." CCIS Working Paper No. 90. La Jolla, CA: Center for Comparative Immigration Studies, University of California, San Diego, http://ccis-ucsd.org/publications/wrkg90.pdf.

Empty chairs at a temporary bullring exemplify the effects of the U.S. economic crisis on Tunkás's annual fiesta in February 2009, where returnees from the United States were conspicuous by their absence.

2   Coping with *La Crisis*

ARTURO AGUILAR, GEORGIA HARTMAN, DAVID KEYES,
LISA MARKMAN, AND MAX MATUS

> *I work fewer hours and it affects me a lot. I can't spend as much as I used to spend. I'm looking for another job but it's very difficult. I only buy what I need. I don't spend on things that aren't necessary.*—Jorge, a Tunkaseño migrant in the United States

December 2007 marked the beginning of a period of economic decline in the United States. A little over a year later, the downturn was recognized as a full-fledged economic crisis. Unemployment rates reached twenty-year highs, and Latinos were losing their jobs faster than any other group (Kochhar 2009). In Mexico, the simultaneous drop in tourism and remittances began to affect families' purchasing power, and both migrants and nonmigrants began seeking ways to make less money go further. In this chapter, we seek to explain how Tunkaseños in the United States and those still in Tunkás have adjusted in response to *la crisis*.

We found that nearly every Tunkaseño migrant interviewed had been affected by the crisis in some way. More than half of U.S.-based Tunkaseño migrants had seen their work hours reduced. Some were able to get second jobs to compensate for the lost income, but employment opportunities were scarce. Most Tunkaseños were looking for ways to reduce expenses, either by not returning to Tunkás for their yearly visit or by reducing the remittances they send to family members in Mexico. Importantly, and in contrast to widespread reports in the U.S. and Mexican media, the economic crisis was not causing migrants based in the United States to "give up" and return to their hometowns. The continued draw of U.S. wages convinced Tunkaseño migrants, regardless of their documentation status, to look for ways to ride out the crisis in the United States. In this chapter, we document the strategies they employed.

The U.S. economic downturn was not the only reason that Tunkaseños based in the United States saw staying put as a better economic option than going home. Indeed, in 2008 and 2009 Tunkás experienced a "perfect storm" of economic shocks: simultaneous decreases in remittances across the hometown population; reduced employment opportunities in the tourist meccas of the Mayan Riviera and the state capital, Mérida; and a combination of drought and freezes that devastated Tunkás agriculture, especially honey production. Most Tunkaseños involved in agriculture lost all or part of their harvests in the 2008 growing season. As a result, food prices soared and job opportunities virtually disappeared. U.S.-based Tunkaseño migrants received reports that family members were reining in household expenses by postponing purchases, selling livestock, or significantly restricting their diets. Migrants living in the United States knew that returning to Tunkás during the economic crisis would not only lower their families' incomes by ending their remittances, it would complicate matters further by adding another consumer to the household.

We begin our exploration of the impacts of the crisis on Tunkaseños on both sides of the border by offering a brief history of the crisis and explaining how it has played out in Southern California and the Yucatán Peninsula. We then draw on quantitative and qualitative data to describe how Tunkaseño migrants in the United States have experienced the crisis and to identify their economic strategies for making it through the hard times. We next turn to the ways in which Tunkaseños in Tunkás have adjusted their behavior in response to the crisis. We conclude by describing how the economic crisis has affected Tunkaseños' migration decisions, finding that most Tunkaseños are choosing to stay where they are—whether in the United States or in Mexico—for the time being. However, qualitative data suggest that migration plans are not being abandoned altogether but merely postponed until the U.S. economy recovers.

A BRIEF HISTORY OF THE CRISIS

According to the National Bureau of Economic Research (2008), the U.S. recession began in December 2007. The recession was not restricted to the United States but was part of a worldwide crisis, reflecting the interconnected nature of national economies in the era of globalization. Mexico felt the echoes of the U.S. recession almost immediately and went into recession shortly after the United States, the second time in thirty years that the two countries experienced simultaneous recessions. However, as measured by the growth of real GDP, the current recession has had much more serious impacts on both countries' economies than previous ones (see figure 2.1), leaving economic migrants like Tunkaseños without a "refuge" from the crisis, given that opportunities are limited in both their sending and receiving communities.

Figure 2.1. Real GDP Growth in the United States and Mexico

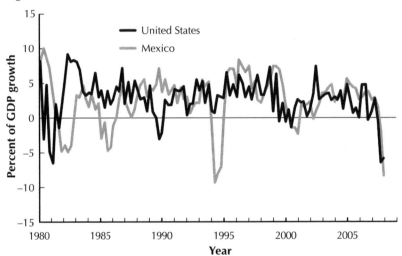

Sources: Data from INEGI and Bureau of Economic Analysis.

Even before the downturn was officially designated as a recession, Latino workers in the United States were being laid off in high numbers; the unemployment rate for foreign-born Hispanics leapt from 4.9 percent to 6.2 percent during 2007 (figure 2.2).[1] These layoffs came primarily in the imploding construction sector, which employed large numbers of Latinos, both migrants and U.S.-born. The construction sector accounted for 54.2 percent of all jobs lost by Latinos in 2007 (Kochhar 2008). The

1. The non-Hispanic unemployment rate increased from 4.6 to 5.0 percent during the same period (Kochhar 2008, 5).

unemployment rate of foreign-born Hispanic workers continued to rise in all sectors, and by the end of 2008 their unemployment rate reached 9.2 percent, two percentage points above the overall unemployment rate (figure 2.2). By early 2009, unemployment in California, home to the nation's largest Latino population, was running well above the national average. In Los Angeles, Long Beach, and Santa Ana—areas where U.S.-based Tunkaseños are concentrated—the unemployment rate reached 10.1 percent in April 2009, and at the time of writing, in May 2009, the unemployment rate among the Hispanic population was 12.7 percent.

Figure 2.2. Unemployment Rates among all U.S. Workers and Hispanic Workers

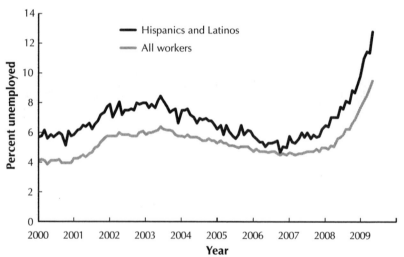

Source: Data from the Bureau of Labor Statistics.

As a result of job losses they suffered beginning in 2007, Mexican migrants in the United States began reducing the amount of their remittances to Mexico. The growth in remittances to Yucatán began to slow and continued to do so through 2008 (with the exception of a small spike in the second quarter). Figure 2.3 illustrates the sharp slowdown in remittances, which in 2004 had risen more than 30 percent over the preceding period but by 2009 were actually decreasing (as measured in U.S. dollars).

Figure 2.3. Rate of Growth of Remittances to Yucatán

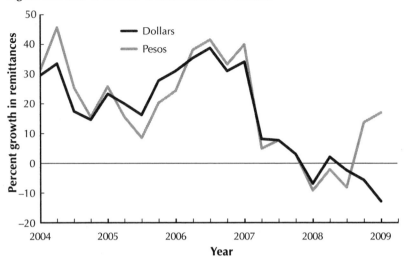

Source: Banco de México data.

However, we should note that dramatic fluctuations in the value of the Mexican peso relative to the dollar also had an important impact on remittances. The exchange rate went from just under 10 pesos to the dollar in August 2008 to 13.50 pesos per dollar only two months later, expanding the purchasing power of remitted dollars. So even though fewer dollars were being remitted, the actual amount of money that households received rose because of the fluctuating exchange rate (see figure 2.3).

As the dollar amount of remittances was falling in Mexico, unemployment rates were on the rise. National unemployment rates reached 5.1 percent in the first quarter of 2009,[2] 1.1 percentage points higher than the previous year. Even Quintana Roo, a state where the unemployment rate consistently fell below the national average, has seen unemployment rise in recent years. Unemployment in Quintana Roo is of particular relevance

2. Unemployment figures are drawn from the National Employment Survey conducted by Mexico's National Statistics Institute (INEGI). Unemployment levels in Mexico are often underestimated in official reports because employment in the informal labor sector is typically reported as self-employment rather than unemployment. For instance, the percentage of people employed in the informal sector in Quintana Roo increased by 40 percent from December 2007 to December 2008, suggesting that formal and stable jobs became scarcer during that period and migrants were forced to find alternatives for survival on their own.

for Tunkaseño migrants because the tourist destinations along the state's Mayan Riviera are their principal destinations within Mexico.[3]

Overall, it is clear that the economic crisis has had a significant impact on Tunkaseños. U.S.-based Tunkaseño immigrants have been hit hard by the crisis but so, too, their family members who have remained at home and witnessed their country's fall into recession along with its northern neighbor. The only bright spot is the rising peso-to-dollar exchange rate, which has helped protect remittance recipients somewhat from the effects of the downturn.

IMPACTS OF THE CRISIS ON TUNKASEÑO MIGRANTS IN THE UNITED STATES

In this section we discuss how Tunkaseños in the United States have experienced the economic crisis. In terms of their employment patterns, we find that many have been laid off or had their work hours cut back. However, because they are concentrated in the service sector, Tunkaseños seem to have been somewhat insulated from the worst effects of the recession. We also discuss U.S.-based Tunkaseños' coping strategies to withstand job losses and other economic hardships. We find that they are reducing their expenditures and relying on migrant networks to help minimize their living costs. We conclude the section with an analysis of the resulting change in migrants' remittance-sending behavior.

Employment

Tunkaseños working in the United States are largely clustered in the service sector (see figure 2.4). Interviews with Tunkaseño migrants revealed that a significant proportion of these service workers are employed in car washes in Inglewood and Anaheim, California.[4] Others report working in restaurants, hotels, and factories.

---

3. At the time of writing, however, the regional tourist industry was not yet showing signs of collapsing. Data from the Mexican Department of Tourism showed little variation in the hotel occupancy level in Cancún, and international tourist arrivals increased in 2009. A probable explanation is that the rise in the value of the dollar relative to the peso made destinations such as Cancún more attractive to bargain-seeking tourists.

4. See chapter 5 for a detailed analysis of the labor market patterns of Tunkaseños in the United States and Mexico.

Figure 2.4. Occupations of Tunkaseño Migrants Living in the
United States, 2009

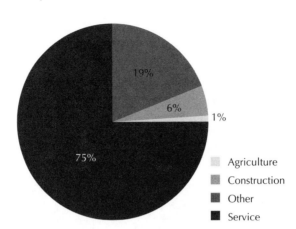

The percentages total more than 100 percent because of rounding.

Tunkaseños typically rely on friends and family already present in the United States for help in obtaining employment. These social network effects are very clear in our survey data. As shown in figure 2.5, 67 percent of Tunkaseños who planned to migrate to the United States reported that they expected to work in the service sector, while 66 percent of our respondents report finding their most recent job in the United States through referrals from relatives, friends, or neighbors. Tunkaseños' concentration in services, a pattern at odds with the overall population of Mexican migrants to the United States, who tend to cluster in the construction sector, may reflect their reliance on migrant networks that channel them into the service sector.

Some U.S.-based Tunkaseño migrants have lost their jobs, and others report significant decreases in the hours they work each week. Many of the latter have sought to supplement their reduced income by taking second jobs. In our survey interviews, 52.8 percent of Tunkaseños in the United States reported working fewer hours in early 2009 (thirty-seven hours per week on average) than in the previous year (figure 2.6). The fact that 10 percent reported working more hours may indicate that these interviewees have taken second jobs.

Figure 2.5. Expected Employment Sector of Potential Tunkaseño Migrants

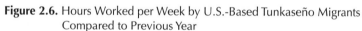

2006, *N* = 67; 2009, *N* = 39

Figure 2.6. Hours Worked per Week by U.S.-Based Tunkaseño Migrants
Compared to Previous Year

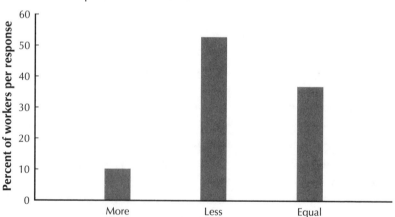

N = 106

We had expected some variation between documented and undocumented migrants, with the latter being more susceptible to layoffs, yet
roughly the same percentage of both groups reported working fewer hours
per week in early 2009 than in the previous year (figure 2.7), suggesting

that undocumented and documented workers are equally vulnerable to the effects of the economic crisis. However, we did find variation in the average number of hours worked, with undocumented migrants reporting an average of forty-two hours per week and legal migrants reporting an average of thirty-five hours.

Figure 2.7. Hours Worked by U.S.-Based Tunkaseño Migrants per Week Compared to Previous Year, by Legal Status

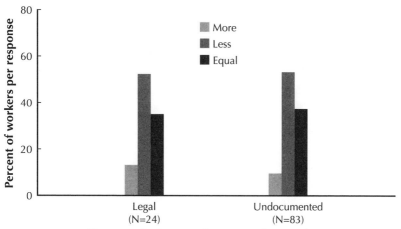

Hours worked per week compared to previous year

Mauro, a migrant living in Anaheim, exemplifies many of the patterns discussed above. He had worked in a rubber factory for twelve years, ever since first arriving in the United States. When we spoke with him in January 2009, he reported that his regular forty-hour workweek was being cut to thirty hours or less. When we returned to interview him again in May, he had been laid off. Over the next month he submitted fifty job applications at local businesses but did not receive a single callback. Finally, he spoke to an older Tunkaseño who was tired of his job at a local restaurant and recommended Mauro for his position. Mauro now works at the restaurant eleven hours a day, with a day off every two weeks. Like many Tunkaseños, Mauro relied on social networks to find his new job, though it represented a change in employment sector. Although Mauro is working more hours at the restaurant than in his previous job, he is earning less than at the rubber factory.

Coping Strategies

As the economic crisis has deepened, U.S.-based Tunkaseños have coped with job losses and reductions in income by taking second jobs and reducing daily household expenditures, sharing meals and consolidating households. They are generally not using government assistance programs, preferring to rely on their social networks to get them through the crisis.

Like most migration from Mexico to the United States, Tunkaseño migration is channeled through social networks (Massey 1999; Massey et al. 1987, 1993). The building of transnational links usually begins far in advance of a decision to migrate, as evidenced by the fact that Tunkaseño migrants have an average of five family members already living in the United States at the time of their first trip north. Migrants' social networks not only lower the cost of migration and settlement, but they can also serve as safety nets during hard times. For example, sharing meals and combining households to save money has become more common, especially among "unattached" male migrants in California. Mauro, the migrant who lost his factory job, described his relationship with the Tunkaseño community:

> We help each other. I set aside the little money I had saved, and everybody bought food and invited me to eat with them so that I wouldn't have to spend my money. That's how it works here. The ones who are out of a job, they are supported by the community.

Besides inviting out-of-work migrants to share a meal with them, some Tunkaseño families prepare extra food to sell to their Tunkaseño neighbors at low prices. Juanita, a Tunkaseña living in Anaheim, has begun doing this. While we were interviewing her, several people came to her house to purchase the inexpensive *tortas de cochinita* (Yucatecan-style sandwiches) she had made earlier that day.

Tunkaseños in the United States also benefit from the support of large extended families. Larger household sizes mean that Tunkaseños are better able to pool their resources when needed. Though the average size of Tunkaseño households in the United States (5.07) and Tunkás (5.09) are very similar (see table 2.1), there is a notable difference in household composition. In Tunkás, individuals report living with a larger number of close relatives than their counterparts in the United States; U.S.-based Tunkaseños report living with a significant number of distant relatives. Thus Tunkaseños replicate large household sizes in the United States, though, because of the constraints of the migratory process, the U.S.-based households often extend beyond the immediate family. This strategy constitutes a form of risk diversification; with multiple incomes contributing to the economic survival of the household, economic security is increased (Massey 1999; Massey et al. 1993). If one individual becomes unemployed, the reduction in income is buffered by the income of other household members. Thus the same social networks that help Tunkaseños make the decision to migrate and help them find a job once they arrive in the United States are now serving the essential purpose of an informal safety net to get people through the economic crisis.

Table 2.1. Characteristics of Tunkaseño Households in Tunkás and the United States, 2009

Average household size in Tunkás	5.09
Average number of close relatives[a]	3.11
Average number of more distant relatives[b]	0.98
Average household size in United States	5.07
Average number of close relatives	2.63
Average number of more distant relatives	1.44

[a] Close relatives are husband/wife, father/mother, son/daughter, brother/sister.

[b] Distant relatives are all remaining classifications, such as grandparents, aunts/ uncles, cousins, and so on.

Tunkaseños are *not* trying to survive in a tough economy by abusing government assistance programs. We found that welfare, Food Stamps, and unemployment benefits show a current participation rate of roughly 2 percent or less; participation in WIC[5] and medical assistance programs is higher (see table 2.2). There are several reasons why Tunkaseños may

5. The WIC program (Women, Infants, and Children) aims to safeguard the health of low-income women, infants, and children up to age five who are at nutritional risk. WIC provides nutritious foods to supplement diets, information on healthy eating, and referrals to health care. http://www.fns.usda.gov/wic/aboutwic.

avoid using cash assistance programs. Some may choose not to participate in order to avoid the stigma attached to receiving government assistance; others may be ineligible due to their documentation status. Those
undocumented respondents who did report receiving public benefits
were able to do so because at least one member of their family is a legal
resident of the United States, usually a U.S.-born child.

Table 2.2. Reported Current Use of U.S. Government Assistance Programs
by Respondent or Any Member of Respondent's Family, by Legal
Status in the United States

	Undocumented	Documented
Welfare	1.0%	2.9%
Medical[a]	17.0%	20.6%
Food Stamps	1.0%	2.9%
WIC	15.2%	11.8%
Unemployment benefits	1.0%	2.8%

[a] Includes Medicare, Medicaid, and Medi-Cal.

Remittances

Remittances from the United States are a crucial source of income for
many Tunkaseño households. In our 2009 survey, 77 percent of U.S.-based
Tunkaseños reported sending money to their family in Tunkás. However, under economic pressure, many have been forced to cut back on the
amount they are able to send. Figure 2.8 shows the change in remittance
sending by Tunkaseño migrants based in the United States. Nearly half
reported that they sent less in remittances in 2009 than the previous year.
Of this group, 46 percent attributed the drop to a job loss or reduction in
work hours, while 26 percent said they remitted less because of a decrease
in earnings and/or the loss of overtime pay.

Figure 2.9 presents a kernel density estimation[6] of the change in remittances. In this case, the density estimation supports the previous finding:
remittance sending has declined over the last year. The negative range has
a higher mass than the positive range, which suggests a higher proportion of individuals decreasing the amount of money they send to family
members in Mexico than of individuals who increased their remittances.

---

6. For further information on kernel density estimation, see Silverman 1984.

The mean change in remittances sent per week is –$34.88, meaning that in early 2009 Tunkaseño migrants were sending about $140 less per month than a year before. While this clearly has a strong deleterious impact on their families in Tunkás, the devaluation of the peso has partially mitigated the effect.

Figure 2.8. Reported Change in Remittances by U.S.-Based Tunkaseños

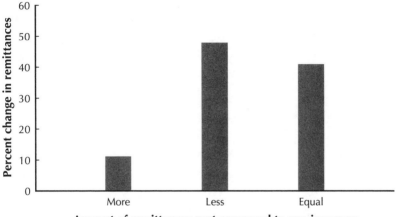

Amount of remittances sent compared to previous year

Figure 2.9. Estimation of Change in Remittances by Tunkaseño Migrants

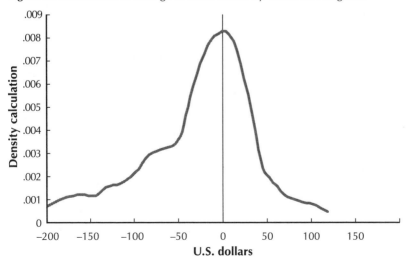

Juan, a Tunkaseño living in Inglewood, California, exemplifies this trend. His work hours have been reduced considerably, and he has been forced to restrict spending to bare necessities. Despite cutting back on "luxuries" such as a meal out on Sundays, Juan has also been compelled to decrease the amount of money he sends to his wife and children in Tunkás. He migrated to the United States in order to feed his family and send his daughter Carmina to school. He is worried that the reduced amount he can send his family is affecting their nutritional status. Thus, while the economic crisis has led many Tunkaseño migrants living in the United States to increase their reliance on their social networks, the effects of the downturn in the U.S. economy are also felt in Tunkás with the decline in remittances. We now turn to the experiences of Tunkaseños in Mexico.

EFFECTS ON TUNKASEÑOS IN TUNKÁS

In early 2009, it seemed that almost all Tunkaseños in Tunkás were being affected by the economic crisis. Some had seen a decrease in their own earned income, while others had lost remittances. The most unfortunate of them had experienced both types of income loss. Many Tunkaseños were forced to develop new coping strategies to deal with the crisis, including entering the informal economy, using informal credit systems, and reducing expenses.

Employment

Though the Tunkás labor market is discussed in depth in chapter 5 of this volume, a brief overview of employment patterns is needed to understand the particulars of economic crisis management in Tunkás. Simply put, employment options in Tunkás are extremely limited. The town's few family-owned businesses provide very limited employment opportunities for nonrelatives. A plurality of the economically active population (43 percent) work in agriculture, followed by services, at 23 percent (see figure 2.10).

Because of the high concentration of Tunkaseños in agriculture, the local economy is extremely vulnerable to weather conditions. In 2008 a drought devastated the harvest, leaving many Tunkaseños without their usual source of income and food. That year, almost everyone who had planted a crop reported a total or partial loss at harvest time, and very few received any type of government aid to help offset this hardship (see figure 2.11). Indeed, when Tunkaseños speak of *la crisis*, they are often referring to both the macroeconomic crisis and the crisis in local agriculture.

Figure 2.10. Main Employment Sectors of Economically Active Tunkaseños Residing in Tunkás

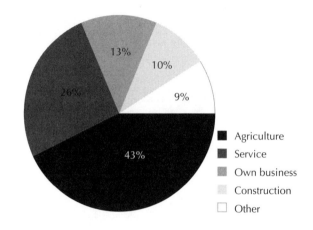

Figure 2.11. 2008 Crop Losses in Tunkás and Receipt of Government Aid

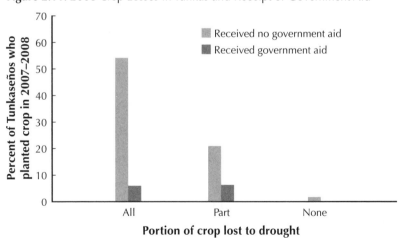

N = 89

Significant numbers of Tunkaseños also work in the informal sector. These jobs, which include selling food from one's house, producing handicrafts, and similar tasks, have helped offset income losses attributable to the drought and the drop in remittances from the United States. For example, Yolanda used to receive 1,500 pesos (about US$115) every two or three weeks from her son in California, but when he lost his job in October 2008 he was no longer able to send any money. Yolanda's two sons who live in Tunkás work in agriculture, but since the drought they are only finding work one or two days a week and earning only about 800 pesos per month (US$62). Yolanda's family has been forced to resort to informal work to supplement the household's income. Every two or three weeks Yolanda produces two handmade hammocks, for which she is paid 15 pesos (just over US$1) each. Her husband earns 200 pesos a month (US$15) repairing clothing in their home, but this type of employment cannot support their day-to-day household needs, leaving them in a very vulnerable position.

Remittances

Money sent from the United States is a key source of income in Tunkás. Almost one in four respondents (23 percent) said that someone in their household receives this type of financial support. The vast majority of remittances go to close relatives who are household heads in Tunkás, usually the sender's parents (43 percent) or spouse (37 percent) (see figure 2.12).

The degree to which people in Tunkás are affected by a decline in remittances depends on their level of dependence on this money to survive. Money sent from the United States is used to cover a variety of expenses, which can be grouped in three categories: (1) recurring subsistence expenses, such as food, clothing, school supplies, and medicines; (2) occasional voluntary expenses, including costs related to community participation and religious celebrations; and (3) infrequent investment expenses, such as construction of a house or business, improvements to agricultural projects, or a vehicle purchase. When Tunkaseños were asked to name the top three expenses for which remittances were used, nearly nine out of ten mentioned household subsistence (see figure 2.13). This is consistent with a large body of research affirming that the majority of remittances are spent on "current consumption" (see, for example, Conway and Cohen 1998).

Figure 2.12. Principal Recipients of Remittances in Tunkás

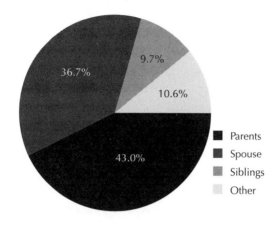

N = 207

Figure 2.13. Main Uses to Which Remittances are Directed in Tunkás

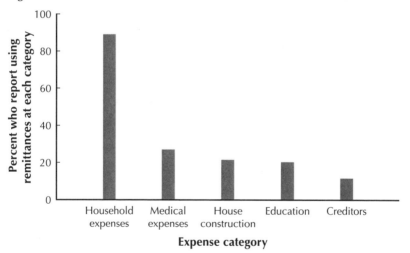

N = 184

Based on this profile, we divide Tunkaseño households that receive remittances into three categories: (1) remittance-dependent households, in which remittances are the primary source of income and are used mostly for recurring subsistence expenses; (2) remittance-complementary households, in which remittances are used in addition to other income streams to increase household consumption or for occasional voluntary or infrequent investment expenses; and (3) remittance-independent households, in which most remittances are directed to infrequent investment or occasional voluntary expenses. Figure 2.13 demonstrates that the vast majority of households receiving remittances can be classified as remittance-dependent. The current drop in remittances, therefore, has the potential to dramatically affect the economic well-being of many people in Tunkás.

While over half of Tunkaseño migrants reported sending less in remittances today than they did one year ago, only 37 percent of remittance recipients reported receiving less now than they did last year, and 52.5 percent said the remittance amounts they receive had not changed (see figure 2.14). This discrepancy is probably explained by the shifting exchange rate. As the dollar has gained strength vis-à-vis the peso, the more favorable exchange rate has meant that even though migrants are sending fewer dollars, the amount received might remain steady once it is changed to pesos. This does not mean, however, that the situation will not worsen. In its *Review of the Economic Situation in Mexico*, Banamex predicted that remittances will likely decrease another 2.5 percent in 2009 (Banamex 2009).

Figure 2.14. Change in Remittance Amounts Received by Tunkaseños in Tunkás

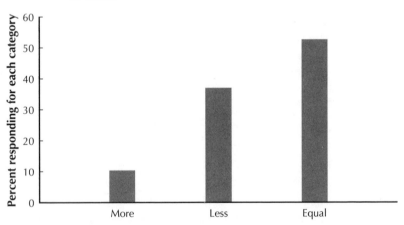

Amount of remittances sent compared to previous year

N = 162

Coping Strategies

When the income on which Tunkaseños in Tunkás depend shrinks—due to reduced remittances, crop losses, or both—they are forced to develop strategies to deal with the situation, such as reducing expenses, identifying alternative income sources such as the informal economy or informal credit systems, or all of the above. As with Tunkaseño migrants, individuals in Tunkás often rely on their social networks to get them through difficult times.

Food is a major expense for most Tunkaseños, and some are changing their diet in order to cut costs. Several families stated they were eating more beans and less meat. One woman who formerly raised pigs switched to turkeys because they require less food and thus cost less to keep. In one extreme case, a family reported that they had been eating only tortillas and habanero peppers for weeks because they could not afford anything else.

In addition to reducing expenses, many Tunkaseños are entering the informal economy in search of an alternate source of income. Some launch home-based businesses, such as selling prepared food to other town residents or engaging in traditional jobs that require low start-up investments, such as weaving hammocks. Identifying a profitable niche involves innovative thinking and a unique business strategy that enables someone to compete in the town's large informal sector. For example, one woman sells food and cold drinks to schoolchildren at lunchtime, while another gives haircuts when her U.S.-based husband is unable to send his usual remittance amount.

While some people enter the informal economy to replace lost income, others turn to informal credit systems. For instance, many Tunkaseños resort to one-time measures such as pawning jewelry. Both Doña Yolanda and Doña Margarita, for example, pawned jewelry in the neighboring town of Izamal. However, neither could cover the monthly interest payment, and both lost their jewelry to the pawnshop. At the time of the interview, Doña Margarita was trying to sell her mother's house to offset a loss in remittances but had not found a buyer, and Doña Yolanda was using her home's title as collateral for a loan.

Other informal credit systems use social relations as the basis for ensuring repayment. Being known as a trustworthy person, a recipient of regular remittances, and/or a beneficiary of government social programs such as Oportunidades often serves to guarantee a loan or line of credit. Lending systems like Compartamos exemplify this. Compartamos generally involves a group of women who take a relatively large loan from an outside source. The women pay off the loan collectively and take turns using the money as start-up capital for individual projects like hammock production, small livestock raising, or making food for sale. Systems like Compartamos use social pressure to ensure that their members fulfill their obligations. The social pressure to repay one's debts can be powerful. Former member Doña Margarita explained why she recently decided to leave the program:

> Tunkás is a really small town and everyone knows everything here. I was falling behind on my payments, and I heard various people talking about me, saying they weren't going to let me be involved because I wasn't paying my debts. That's why I decided to drop out.

Reputation, especially in a small town like Tunkás, can be an important asset. It is expected that people will repay their loans in order to avoid the kind of public shaming employed by a Tunkaseño debt collector, who places signs in the yards of delinquent debtors and posts debtors' names in public places until the debt is repaid.

Many businesses in Tunkás also operate informal credit systems. Small, family-owned businesses are fundamental to daily life in Tunkás, not only for the goods they sell but also for the informal credit they supply. From neighborhood shops to the local doctor, nearly every entrepreneur in Tunkás extends some kind of credit to clients and customers. Like many other practices in Tunkás, this credit system is based on social relations and the business owners' knowledge of the economic activities of their customers. Small grocery stores, for instance, will only extend lines of credit to customers from their neighborhood. Employees at a private clinic mentioned that forty-three of their patients together owed over 20,000 pesos, or approximately US$1,500. The clinic does not set deadlines for loan repayment, but it does require returning patients to pay part of their debt before being seen a second time. The clinic's doctor is not from Tunkás, but in keeping with the importance of social relationships in the town, he has hired a Tunkaseño to manage the clinic's accounts receivable. Throughout Tunkás, storeowners know the people to whom they are extending credit and have some way of holding them accountable.

Of course, these small businesses are far from immune to the economic crisis. Indeed, the drop in remittances to Tunkaseño families, coupled with the agricultural disaster, has shaped the way such informal credit systems operate in Tunkás. Before the economic crisis, owners of such businesses were especially willing to grant credit to women whose husbands were working in the United States, Cancún, or Playa del Carmen, because they knew their customers would use some of future remittances to repay the loan. But as the flow of remittances has ebbed, business owners are less willing to offer credit. Many former remittance recipients in Tunkás fear being excluded from the informal credit systems on which they have come to depend, but business owners are afraid of the consequences of extending credit to customers who may not be able to repay them. For example, Juan and Carolina, owners of a clothing store in Tunkás, stopped offering credit in early 2008 because of the trouble they had collecting on debts owed and began requiring on-the-spot payment for all purchases at their store. After seeing their sales drop by 40 percent between October 2008 and January 2009, Juan and Carolina now wonder if the drop in sales is the result of the economic crisis or of their decision to stop selling on credit. In either case, their fear that customers will not repay their debts is very real.

Some business owners, acutely aware that the economic crisis has hit their customers hard, are willing to wait a little longer for repayment. This decision, once again, is dependent on social relationships. For example, a furniture store manager explained her logic in relaxing her repayment demands:

> Well, sometimes somebody comes in and says her husband
> has a good job or something, and tells me, "I'm going to
> pay you more this time." But sometimes they don't have
> a lot, and I'm from here, I know them and I understand
> them, too.

While some business owners in Tunkás continue offering flexible payment terms, others have decreased their lines of credit or stopped offering credit altogether. All, however, see the economic difficulties of their neighbors reflected in their sales figures, and most are themselves affected by the economic downturn. Business owners must calculate how best to maintain good social relations with their customers while also remaining financially viable. Extending credit ensures that friends and neighbors can eat, but it increases the shop owner's risk of being left with unpaid loans. Conversely, refusing to provide credit can damage social relationships and leave customers with few resources for necessary purchases. In addition, extending credit lines to "privileged" consumers only, those deemed capable of repaying them, decreases the business's potential pool of customers in times of economic difficulty—and perhaps during future periods of prosperity as well. Some businesses try to mitigate their risks by offering different credit or loan terms to customers depending on their credit histories. Thus customers purchasing the same item may get different credit terms and ultimately pay different prices. This variation in the credit system allows Tunkaseños to share the costs of the crisis communally, in that purchases by individuals who are better able to pay for goods allow storeowners to offer credit to customers who may be less able to pay.

Nearly all Tunkaseños in Tunkás have been affected by the crisis, but the effects vary depending on the household's degree of dependence on remittances and/or agriculture. A decrease in remittances in remittance-dependent households forces these families to employ any number of compensatory strategies. These typically involve reducing expenditures and seeking alternate sources of income and access to credit. Continued access to credit, however, depends on one's reputation and ability to repay one's debts. In the midst of the current crisis, many individuals wonder how long it will be before they can repay their debts and be self-sufficient once again.

HOW THE CRISIS AFFECTS MIGRATION FLOWS

Having analyzed the effects of the crisis on Tunkaseño households on both sides of the border, we now examine the effects of the downturn on migration flows. Tunkaseños migrate both internationally, largely to Southern California, and domestically, either to Mérida or to tourist destinations in the Mayan Riviera.

Migrants' and potential migrants' migration and settlement decisions depend on a complex set of macro- and micro-level factors. Classical migration theories, which inform the media and shape the intellectual basis of much immigration policy, view migrants as rational actors motivated mostly by economic decisions (Borjas 1987; Borjas and Bratsberg 1996; Cornelius and Rosenblum 2005; Massey 1999; Massey et al. 1993). In particular, what most drives the migration decision is the wage differential between sending and receiving communities. In line with this argument, table 2.3 illustrates that the wage differential in two of the top job niches that Tunkaseños occupy has remained high.

Table 2.3. Wage Differentials in Employment Sectors Occupied by Tunkaseño Migrants

| | Average Weekly Wages, PPP 2001 U.S. Dollars | | | | | |
| | Services[a] | | | Food and Accommodation | | |
Year	Mexico[b]	U.S.[c]	Difference	Mexico	U.S.	Difference
2001	78	285	207	91	288	197
2002	81	292	212	93	292	200
2003	81	288	207	94	292	198
2004	81	285	204	93	297	204
2005	86	282	196	98	294	196
2006	87	285	198	99	294	195
2007	88	291	204	100	301	201
2008[d]	86	285	199	100	299	199

Sources: For United States, BLS and Econstats; for Mexico, Mexican Labor Ministry.

[a] In Mexico, "services" corresponds to "diverse personal services." In the United States, it refers to "car washes."

[b] Data in Mexico are reported daily, so the reported data were multiplied by seven and converted to PPP (purchasing power parity) U.S. dollars.

[c] U.S. data correspond to California.

[d] U.S. data are reported up to the third quarter of 2008, so the 2008 data are estimated using an average of the first three quarters and a correction factor.

Migrants are motivated by more than pure economics, however. Massey and colleagues propose to understand migration in dynamic terms as a cumulative process, what they call "cumulative causation" (Massey 1999; Massey et al. 1993). According to this argument, migrants may be "pushed" out of their sending community due to economic factors, but they may also be "pulled" by what has become an entrenched culture of migration (to be discussed further in chapter 7) or by the desire to reunite with family members in the receiving community. Moreover, many migrants leave with a specific objective, such as earning enough to build a house or cover health care costs, and plan to return after that objective is realized. However, as their circumstances change in the United States, so do the contexts for their life decisions. Regardless of legal status, many migrants bring their families from Mexico or start families in the United States and ultimately find themselves becoming part of a settled community north of the border.

The classical theories of migration predict that Mexican migrants who have lost their jobs in the United States would have a strong incentive to return to their hometowns in Mexico. Recent media coverage echoes this logic with headlines such as these: "Mexican laborers giving up, going home" (O'Boyle 2008) and "Reverse migration rocks Mexico" (Beith 2009), along with articles promoting the idea that job losses in the United States have produced substantial return migration to Mexico.

Although Hispanic immigrants have been hit hard by the economic crisis (Kochhar 2008, 2009; Lopez, Livingston, and Kochhar 2009; Camarota and Jensenius 2009), we did not find that Mexican migrants are returning home in large numbers. Indeed, those who did return did so not because they had lost their jobs, but for other reasons. When U.S.-based respondents were asked if they were thinking of going back to Tunkás in 2009, 13 percent responded affirmatively. The two main reasons respondents gave for planning to return to Mexico were family reunification and dislike of life in the United States. Only one out of sixteen respondents mentioned the loss of a job as his reason for leaving the United States. Indeed, many Tunkaseño migrants are keenly aware of the dire economic situation in Mexico. One migrant who has been in the United States for several years told us he did not want to return home, "because there aren't enough jobs in Mexico either. When I think about it, I want to go back, but I don't because of the situation that Mexico is in right now."

Our findings parallel those of Alarcón and colleagues (2008, 1), who conclude that despite worsening economic conditions in the United States, "there is no evidence of a massive return of migrants or of a migration pattern different from that observed in previous years." Numerous migrants in our sample have lived in the United States for many years, settling down, having families, and becoming a part of the Tunkseño/Yucatecan community on the U.S. side of the border. Among migrants in our survey, 73 percent have five or more years of U.S. experience, and many have families here. For many of these migrants, the question of returning "home" to Tunkás is a misnomer; the United States is now their home. In general, these difficult times are forcing migrants to tighten their budgets, seek secondary employment, and rely on their social networks, but very few are leaving due to the economic crisis.

Table 2.4 illustrates these points with a multivariate regression analysis. The table shows the results of a probit regression that estimates the probability of a person being a "recent returner" (that is, a migrant who returned from the United States in or after 2005 and is currently residing in Mexico). Consistent with the arguments made above, some of the main variables that explain recent return migration flows are: being married, with the spouse being in Mexico, and (2) having children living in Mexico. Other variables were negatively related to the probability of recently returning: (3) having a spouse in the United States, (5) having children in the United States, and (6) U.S. experience. These are all variables that have been shown in other studies to be associated with a higher likelihood of permanent settlement (see, for example, Appleby, Moreno, and Smith 2009). These results are significant and consistent throughout different specifications.

When comparing this regression with a regression that uses "ever migrated" as a dependent variable (as opposed to "recently returned migrant"), most results are similar. However, the magnitudes are usually higher in the "ever migrated" case. Some variables that did not seem to be important in the first model are significant in the second (age structure, in particular).[7] The only exception is U.S. experience, which is significant in the former but not in the latter regression.

---

7. The regression considers both the age and age-squared variables because we assume that the most common migration behavior is migration by young people of working age. The probability of returning decreases as a migrant accumulates experience, but the trend reverts as a migrant may become more likely to return upon reaching retirement age.

Table 2.4. Probit Regression Results

Independent Variables	Dependent Variables					
	(1) Returner	(2) Returner	(3) Returner	(4) Returner	(5) Returner	(6) Returner Ever
Age	.0112 (.0202)	.0015 (.0184)	.0085 (.0172)	.0121 (.0198)	−.0007 (.0177)	−.0303 (.0253)
Age-squared	−.0002 (.0003)	0.0000 (.0002)	−.0001 (.0002)	−.0002 (.0003)	.0001 (.0002)	**.0005*** (.0003)
Education	−.0001 (.0002)	−.0001 (.0002)	.0001 (.0002)	−.0001 (.0001)	.0001 (.0001)	.0001 (.0001)
Married	**.1304*** (.0567)	**.1395*** (.0541)	**.1022*** (.0544)	.0631 (.0730)	.0775 (.0728)	.0373 (.1327)
Spouse in U.S.	**−.3203*** (.0537)	**−.3060*** (.0534)	**−.2699*** (.0744)	**−.2125*** (.0800)	**−.1536*** (.0490)	**−.5157*** (.0423)
U.S. experience			**−.0052*** (.0024)		**−.0049*** (.0019)	.0001 (.0001)
Children				**.1551*** (.0738)	.0612 (.0468)	**.3474*** (.0957)
Children in U.S.				**−.2339*** (.0943)	**−.1950*** (.0473)	**−.3728*** (.0201)
Controlling for undocumented	No	Yes	No	No	Yes	Yes
Clustered SE by occupation	No	No	No	No	Yes	Yes
No. of observations	186	186	166	186	150	220

Robust standard errors in parentheses.

Coefficients represent the marginal changes in probability for a change in the independent variables.

*** $p < .01$; ** $p < .05$; * $p < .1$.

Note: Dependent variables (1)–(5): Returners = 1 if migrant returned to Tunkás after 2005; 0 if migrant still living in United States.

Dependent variable (6): Returner ever = 1 if migrant returned any time; 0 if migrant still living in United States.

Finally, we analyze the migration decisions of Tunkás-based respondents. When comparing the results from the 2006 and 2009 surveys, we find that the percentage of respondents thinking of migrating to the United States declined considerably, from 24 to 8 percent, and from 34 to 8 percent if we only consider the migration-prone respondents (see figure 2.15).[8] This may be due to widespread awareness of the economic downturn in the United States. When Tunkás-based respondents were asked how difficult it is to find a job currently compared to one year ago, 90 percent answered that it was now more difficult.

Figure 2.15. Migration Plans of Tunkás-Based Tunkaseños, 2006 and 2009

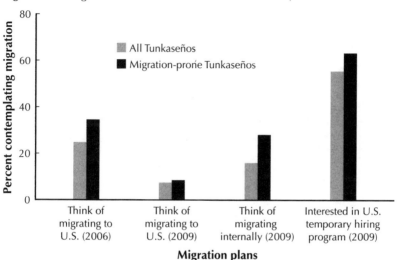

It is also interesting to note in figure 2.15 that the declining likelihood of migrating to the United States does not reflect a lack of motivation. When asked if they would be interested in participating in a temporary jobs program like the former Bracero program, 55 percent of the overall population and 63 percent of migration-prone Tunkaseños said they would be interested in such a program. Thus it is clear that their awareness of economic conditions in the United States is leading many Tunkaseños to stay in Mexico until the situation improves.

The information in figure 2.15 also indicates that Tunkaseños who are not considering international migration may be looking at domestic migration as a viable option. Internal migration offers numerous advantages: lower migration costs, lower risks, closeness to the hometown and

8. Migration-prone respondents are those between sixteen and thirty-four years of age at the time of the survey.

family, and better job availability in the Mayan Riviera region. Roberto, for example, who has worked as a private security guard for three years at a theme park on the Mayan Riviera, told us: "I don't even think about going to the United States now. Governor Schwarzenegger said there would be a massive layoff of *paisanos* [Mexican countrymen]." Roberto had read an article in a local newspaper that discussed the recent firing of large numbers of Yucatecans in California.[9] He also mentioned that he has not felt the effects of the crisis particularly strongly, since tourism has been less affected than other sectors in Mexico.

Like Roberto, many Tunkaseños seem to be looking for safer and more affordable migration alternatives, such as jobs in nearby areas. This does not mean, however, that they are swearing off international migration forever. When the U.S. economy recovers, the number of Tunkaseños heading north will likely return to levels seen before the current crisis.

CONCLUSION

At the time of writing, the economic outlook in the United States is unclear. While some observers see signs of improvement, others remain pessimistic, suggesting that the economy will continue to limp along for the foreseeable future. What is clear, however, is that the recession declared in December 2007 has been painful for everyone, including immigrants. Tunkaseños in the United States have lost work hours and sometimes their jobs outright. Though Tunkaseño migrants, who are concentrated in the service sector, have been shielded from the direct impacts of the burst housing bubble that heavily affected Hispanic construction workers, the indirect consequences of the economic downturn are clearly evident in their daily lives.

Tunkaseño migrants are coping with the crisis largely by relying on their social networks. Marginalized by their undocumented status, many Tunkaseños are unable to draw on government assistance programs to get them through the difficult times, and rates of participation in these programs remain low. It is logical, then, that many would fall back on the social safety net that is available to them: fellow Tunkaseños. People are relying on each other for job leads, moving in together to save on rent, sharing meals to save on food, and sometimes even accepting the charity

---

9. *Por Esto,* January 30, 2009.

of other Tunkaseños to get them through. With less income, migrants are, understandably, sending less in remittances, a change that is having ripple effects in Tunkás itself.

The drop-off in remittances has hit Tunkaseños in Tunkás hard, but it is only one of many crises they face. The Mexican economy as a whole has been hard-hit by the global economic crisis, job prospects in domestic destinations like Cancún and Playa del Carmen are less than ideal, and a combination of drought and freezes claimed part or all of many local farmers' 2008 harvest. Tunkaseños in Tunkás are dealing with *la crisis* in various ways. Many are reducing their expenditures, including by changing their diets, substituting inexpensive staples like corn and beans for more expensive meat. Tunkaseños have also sought out new income sources to compensate for what they have lost. This can involve entering the informal sector by, for example, selling food and drinks from home or doing piecework. Tunkaseños also rely on access to credit for daily survival, and their reliance on loans has increased with the crisis. Access to credit in Tunkás depends largely on one's reputation and the deterrence effect of the social stigma that marks someone in this small town who defaults on his or her debts. Through their participation in informal credit systems, Tunkaseños in Tunkás, like those in the United States, are falling back on their social networks to help them through the crisis. But the safety net these networks provide has been strained by the magnitude of the current crisis. Business owners feel trapped, wanting to continue to offer credit to customers who are also their neighbors but fearing that, without remittances from family members in the United States and income from crops, many will be unable to repay their debts. In fact, some Tunkaseños reported selling assets (pigs, vehicles, and other "buffer stocks"), pawning jewelry, and even incurring further debt to satisfy their debt obligations.

How has the crisis affected migration between the two countries? Our research indicates that there has been a decline in the international movement of migrants, with lower numbers of Tunkaseños heading north and fewer Tunkaseño migrants in the United States returning to Mexico. Tunkaseños in Tunkás are keenly aware of the economic troubles in the United States. As a result, many are postponing trips north until things improve, not wanting to pay a people-smuggler thousands of dollars only to arrive in the United States and not find work. Tunkaseños already in the United States, contrary to numerous anecdotal reports in the media, are not returning home in significant numbers. This is especially true for those who have spouses, children, and established lives in the United States. In addition, the social networks that migrants have built in California enable financially stressed Tunkaseños to survive these difficult times without returning to Mexico.

As a result of all these factors, the international migration circuit that had seen a steady stream of Tunkaseños head north and then back south has come to a virtual standstill. What is happening is that Tunkaseños in Tunkás are considering domestic migration to be a less costly and less risky alternative. Over three times more migration-prone Tunkaseños are considering domestic migration in 2009 instead of envisioning the United States as their migration destination. Although the employment situation in cities like Cancún and Playa del Carmen is not ideal, many Tunkaseños are willing to take their chances there rather than risk crossing the border.

One would be hard-pressed to find a Tunkaseño anywhere—in Los Angeles, Anaheim, Cancún, Playa del Carmen, Mérida, or Tunkás itself— who has not been deeply affected by the crisis. Like people all around the world, Tunkaseños are wondering how long the crisis will last. What will be the ultimate effects of *la crisis* on Tunkaseños on both sides of the border? Only time will tell.

REFERENCES

Alarcón, Rafael, Rodolfo Cruz, Alejandro Díaz-Bautista, Gabriel González-König, Antonio Izquierdo, Guillermo Yrizar, and René Zenteno. 2008. "La crisis financiera en Estados Unidos y su impacto en la migración mexicana." Tijuana, Mexico: El Colegio de la Frontera Norte. December.

Appleby, Clare, Nancy Moreno, and Arielle Smith. 2009. "Setting Down Roots: Tlacotepense Settlement in the United States." In *Migration from the Mexican Mixteca: A Transnational Community in Oaxaca and California.* La Jolla, CA: Center for Comparative Immigration Studies, University of California, San Diego.

Banamex. 2009. *Review of the Economic Situation of Mexico* 84 (December 2008–January 2009).

Beith, Malcolm. 2009. "Reverse Migration Rocks Mexico," *Foreign Policy,* February.

Borjas, George J. 1987. "Self-Selection and the Earnings of Immigrants," *American Economic Review* 77, no. 4: 531–53.

Borjas, George J., and Bernt Bratsberg. 1996. "Who Leaves? The Outmigration of the Foreign-Born," *Review of Economics and Statistics* 78, no. 1: 165–76.

Camarota, Steven A., and Karen Jensenius. 2009. "Trends in Immigrant and Native Employment." Washington, DC: Center for Immigration Studies, May.

Conway, Dennis, and Jeffrey H. Cohen. 1998. "Consequences of Migration and Remittances for Mexican Transnational Communities," *Economic Geography* 74, no. 1: 26–44.

Cornelius, Wayne A., and Marc R. Rosenblum. 2005. "Immigration and Politics," *Annual Review of Political Science* 8 (June): 99–119.

Kochhar, Rakesh. 2008. "Latino Labor Report, 2008: Construction Reverses Growth for Latinos." Washington, DC: Pew Hispanic Center. June 4.

———. 2009. "Unemployment Rises Sharply among Latino Immigrants in 2008." Washington, DC: Pew Hispanic Center. February12.

Lopez, Mark Hugo, Gretchen Livingston, and Rakesh Kochhar. 2009. "Hispanics and the Economic Downturn: Housing Woes and Remittance Cuts." Washington, DC: Pew Hispanic Center. January 8.

Massey, Douglas S. 1999. "Why Does Immigration Occur? A Theoretical Synthesis." In *The Handbook of International Migration: The American Experience,* ed. Charles Hirschman, Philip Kasinitz, and Josh DeWind. New York: Russell Sage Foundation.

Massey, Douglas S., Rafael Alarcón, Jorge Durand, and Humberto González. 1987. *Return to Aztlan: The Social Process of International Migration from Western Mexico.* Berkeley, CA: University of California Press.

Massey, Douglas S., Joaquín Arango, Graeme Hugo, Ali Kouaouci, Adela Pellegrino, and J. Edward Taylor. 1993. "Theories of International Migration: A Review and Appraisal," *Population and Development Review* 19, no. 3: 431–66.

National Bureau of Economic Research. 2008. "Determination of the December 2007 Peak in Economic Activity," *NBER,* December 11, http://www.nber.org/cycles/dec2008.html.

O'Boyle, Michael. 2008. "Mexican Laborers Giving Up, Going Home," *Reuters,* October 15.

Silverman, Bernard W. 1984. "Density Estimation for Statistics and Data Analysis." Monographs on Statistics and Applied Probability. London: Chapman and Hall.

Gravesite of María de los Ángeles Manzanero, a 46-year-old Tunkaseña who died of hypothermia in the mountains of east San Diego County on President's Day 2007, attempting to enter the United States clandestinely.

3 Double Jeopardy: How U.S. Enforcement Policies Shape Tunkaseño Migration

JONATHAN HICKEN, MOLLIE COHEN, AND JORGE NARVAEZ

> *It's impossible to stop immigrants. I hope that one of these days there's an amnesty so people can stop crossing with coyotes. I hope they give us this amnesty so people can stop risking their lives at the border.*—Alejandro, an experienced Tunkaseño migrant

> *If the American people don't feel like you can secure the borders, then it's hard to strike a deal that would get people out of the shadows and on a pathway to citizenship who are already here, because the attitude of the average American is going to be, "Well, you're just going to have hundreds of thousands of more coming in each year."*—President Barack Obama, April 29, 2009

After years of steady dedication to physical and virtual fortifications on the United States' southern border, former Homeland Security Secretary Michael Chertoff announced in October 2008 that as a result of his department's "multi-year strategy for dealing with the issue . . . we have reversed the trend of increasing illegal immigration into our country" (Barry 2008). Chertoff claimed that "border enforcement is working," and he pointed to a 17 percent decrease in border apprehensions from fiscal year 2007 to fiscal year 2008, and a 40 percent decrease in apprehensions since 2005. We found that Tunkaseños continue to cross the border each year but in fewer numbers than in the recent past. In the MMFRP's 2006 survey of Tunkás residents, 34 percent of economically active Tunkaseños of prime migration age (sixteen to thirty-four years old) reported that they were planning to migrate to the United States that year. In our 2009 survey, only 8 percent of the same demographic group intended to go north in the next twelve months. But to what can we attribute the reduced propensity of Tunkaseños to go north, as well as the decline in Border Patrol apprehensions of undocumented migrants since the 2007 fiscal year?

The claim that tougher border enforcement has been responsible for reducing unauthorized immigration begs the question of whether fewer migrants are, in fact, entering the United States. There are at least two reasons why apprehensions may decline even if the number of illegal entries remains unchanged, because the success rate has risen. First, as the border becomes more dangerous and difficult to cross, migrants increasingly rely on professional people-smugglers (known as *coyotes* or *polleros*) to evade the Border Patrol and reduce their physical risks. The *polleros* (literally, "chicken farmers") track the Border Patrol's changing tactics and deployment and are usually able to stay one step ahead of the latest enforcement strategies. Second, there is some indication that migrants are turning to unconventional modes of entry that offer a high probability of success, such as crossing through legal ports of entry concealed in vehicles or using false or borrowed documents.

Even if we assume that the number of clandestine entries has, in fact, declined, there are plausible alternatives to the border enforcement explanation. First, in recent years there has been a drastic reduction in circular migration between Mexico and the United States. The traditional pattern of short-term migration (averaging about six months of employment in the United States) that prevailed from the 1940s through the 1980s has been replaced by a largely one-way flow, with migrants staying in the United States longer or settling permanently. If there are fewer trips back to Mexico, and consequently fewer return trips to the United States to resume employment, there will be fewer apprehensions. Finally, since 2006 the U.S. demand for migrant labor has weakened significantly, particularly in the construction industry, which was hard-hit by the collapse of the long-running housing boom (see chapters 2 and 4, this volume).

In addition to continuing the border enforcement buildup begun by President Clinton in 1993, the George W. Bush administration ordered the U.S. Immigration and Customs Enforcement agency (ICE) to carry out hundreds of worksite raids at businesses suspected of employing undocumented workers. Worksite raids were particularly frequent in Bush's last two years in office (Centro Legal 2008). The intent of these policies was to reduce the stock of unauthorized foreign workers and to deter new unauthorized migration to the United States. In this chapter we use data from our interviews with Tunkaseños on both sides of the border to assess the extent to which U.S. policies have, in fact, created an effective deterrent to unauthorized migration and how immigration enforcement at the border and in the interior of the country has affected the conditions under which undocumented immigrants live in the United States.

The schema presented in figure 3.1 illustrates, in highly simplified fashion, how contemporary U.S. immigration control policies are structured; our chapter is organized to follow this policy structure. U.S. immigration law is a complex system of behind-the-scenes legislative activity combined with a massive network of on-the-ground enforcement. The schema should serve as a guide to the discussion of historical and contemporary policies and where they fit into the larger immigration debate.

We begin with a brief review of recent developments in border enforcement, followed by a detailed analysis of their impacts on Tunkaseños living on both sides of the border. The MMFRP's previous study of U.S.-bound migration from Tunkás, conducted in 2006, concluded that tighter border control measures had been "ineffective in reducing unauthorized migration to the United States" (Kimball, Acosta, and Dames 2007, 111). Our data, gathered in 2009, support a similar conclusion with respect to border enforcement, and we also find that interior enforcement (workplace raids, random traffic stops, and so on) has no deterrent effect on would-be unauthorized migrants. However, U.S. border enforcement measures have had several major unintended consequences: they have bottled up undocumented migrants within the United States, they have fueled the people-smuggling industry, and they have contributed directly to the deaths of thousands of migrants attempting to enter the United States clandestinely. The second half of our chapter will examine the effects of interior (non-border) enforcement policies on Tunkaseños living on both sides of the border, paying particular attention to the occurrence and effects of random traffic stops, local police collaboration with ICE, and worksite enforcement operations in Tunkaseño receiving communities.

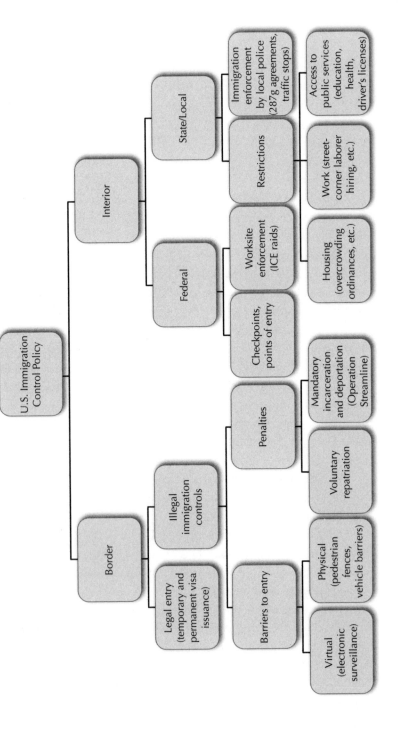

Figure 3.1. A Schema of U.S. Immigration Control Policy, 2009

BORDER ENFORCEMENT

Contemporary Policy Environment

In April 2009, President Barack Obama declared that promoting comprehensive immigration reform would be on the list of priorities for his first year in office (Preston 2009). The president and his homeland security secretary, former Arizona Governor Janet Napolitano, pledged to continue fortifying the border, but they also advocated legalizing most undocumented immigrants already living in the United States, as well as shifting the target of worksite enforcement from undocumented workers to the employers who hire them (although workers would still be vulnerable to arrest in conjunction with employer investigations) (Thompson 2009).

The Obama administration began to grapple with the challenges of immigration in the aftermath of the U.S. Congress's failure to pass major immigration reform legislation in 2006 and 2007. The Kennedy-McCain bill, named for Senators Edward M. Kennedy and John McCain, its principal Democratic and Republican sponsors, respectively, in the Senate, was a truly comprehensive attempt at immigration reform. Its legalization and guestworker programs, among other provisions, provoked fierce opposition, and the bill died in the Senate in June 2006. The bill's "path to citizenship" provision to regularize undocumented immigrants already living in the United States was criticized from the political right for rewarding people who had broken federal immigration law. The political left criticized the bill's "point system" (a system for granting visas and green cards based on an individual's human capital and professional qualifications) because it moved away from the traditional system of immigrant admissions based on family ties to the United States. Its proposed guestworker program was criticized by labor unions and human rights organizations for undermining the labor rights of the workers who participated in the program. An attempt in 2007 to revive and modify the Kennedy-McCain bill also failed. The de facto consequence of Congress's failure to legislate was a continuation—indeed, an intensification—of the border enforcement buildup that had begun in 1993, as well as more frequent, high-profile workplace raids.

Border Enforcement: Implementation History

Since the early 1990s, U.S. border enforcement has focused on discouraging the migration of undocumented Mexicans and preventing those who do leave their hometowns for the borderlands from entering the United States. In 1993 the Clinton administration implemented the first of four "concentrated border enforcement operations"—Operations Hold the Line (El Paso, Texas), Gatekeeper (San Diego, California), Safeguard (central Arizona), and Rio Grande (south Texas)—which introduced more substantial physical fencing, high-intensity lighting, video surveillance cameras, and larger numbers of Border Patrol agents in strategic urban crossing corridors along the U.S.-Mexico border (Cornelius 2005). Prior to these developments, migrants were able to enter the United States with relative ease, as Tunkaseño interviewee Rafael recalled: "I came with a brother of mine; there were four or five of us. The smuggler charged us about $300 each. He crossed us in the trunk of a car. It was very easy at that time; I even went once in an airplane." However, the border-crossing experience began to change dramatically in the early 1990s.

Implementation of the concentrated border enforcement strategy mainly had the effect of redistributing illegal entries to less heavily fortified segments of the border. It simultaneously increased the rate of migrant fatalities because more crossings were occurring in remote desert and mountainous areas, where migrants had to walk for up to six days under extreme climatic conditions in order to reach a pickup point (Cornelius 2005; Reyes, Johnson, and Van Swearingen 2002). Elí, an experienced Tunkaseño migrant, described his crossing of the border with his wife and five-year-old daughter in 1997, four years after the U.S. border enforcement buildup had begun:

> We arrived in Tijuana, and on Friday we went to the smuggler's house. He charged $2,500 for all three of us. On Saturday we left for the border. It took one hour to get to where we needed to arrive. The Border Patrol were on the hills. We got in a car and drove up another hill. I was in the trunk. There were eleven people in the car, a Honda. . . . They never caught us.

Following the terrorist attacks of September 11, 2001, U.S. policy shifted toward a "risk management approach" to border security, which focused on identifying and mitigating potential threats along the border (Heyman and Ackleson 2009). The policy of increasing the Border Patrol's presence and erecting more formidable fencing along the United States' southwestern border continued, along with an increase in technology-based security measures, including the US-VISIT program (which uses biometrics—fingerprints and digital photos—to confirm entrants' identity) and the Western Hemisphere Travel Initiative (WHTI), which requires U.S., Mexican, and Canadian citizens to present passports when crossing the borders (Andreas 2009).

Alejandro, a Tunkaseño migrant with four successful illegal entries into the United States between 1977 and 1995, noted how much the border-crossing experience had changed during his quarter-century of migration to the United States. In 2002 he encountered things that he had not experienced in his previous crossings. On that journey to Oregon, passing the border through a rugged area east of San Diego, he was chased by the Border Patrol and bribed a Border Patrol agent to not detain him:

> From Tecate [California] we walked for about four hours. We came upon a port of entry, where there were Border Patrol agents. They started chasing us, but they didn't catch us. We arrived in San Diego and then Los Angeles. Then the *pollero* passed us on to another *pollero* [who took him to Oregon].

In 2005 the Bush administration augmented the strategy of fence building and increased manpower on the border by introducing tougher legal penalties to discourage undocumented migrants. Under Operation Streamline, begun in the Yuma sector, all undocumented migrants apprehended in "streamlined" areas were subject to mandatory incarceration for between two weeks and six months and placed in formal deportation proceedings. Such treatment was in sharp contrast to the usual "voluntary repatriation" of apprehended migrants, who typically were kept in custody for only a few hours, waived their right to contest their arrest, and then were transported to border gates, where they were received by Mexican authorities. By early 2009 Operation Streamline had been implemented in four Border Patrol sectors—Yuma, Tucson, Del Rio, and Laredo. But within these sectors the new mandatory incarceration and formal deportation penalties have been applied to only a small minority of apprehended migrants. For example, in 2008, five out of six migrants caught in the Tucson sector were still being "voluntarily repatriated"[1] rather than "streamlined" (Rotstein 2009). Implementation of Operation Streamline has been constrained by a lack of capacity in the federal court system as well as inadequate bed space in the immigrant detention system.[2]

A new chapter in the border enforcement buildup opened with passage of the Secure Fence Act by Congress in October 2006. This legislation mandated construction of 670 miles of new physical fencing and vehicle barriers along the U.S.-Mexico border.[3] It also provided funds to hire more Border Patrol agents and for the planning of a new electronic fence along the southwestern border of the United States. This "virtual fence" was part of the Bush administration's Secure Border Initiative, a program focused on "transforming border control through technology and infrastructure" (Boeing Company 2009). At the heart of this $6.7 billion project are 1,800 high-tech towers packed with advanced radar and video surveillance systems, state-of-the-art communications equipment, and motion-detecting sensors. The program has had substantial setbacks: the U.S. Government Accountability Office declared that Project 28, a pilot project built along a 28-mile stretch of the Arizona border, "encountered performance shortfalls" (GAO 2008). Its performance was compromised by both hardware and software glitches.

Nevertheless, the Bush administration requested $775 million in fiscal year 2009 for the further development of the virtual fence, in addition to funds for construction of more vehicle barriers and better access roads for the Border Patrol. In his initial $27 billion request for border and transportation security, submitted to Congress in May 2009, President Obama completely omitted funds to continue construction of physical fencing

---

1. Entering the United States without proper inspection is a misdemeanor. Voluntary repatriation is the process by which the vast majority of apprehended undocumented migrants return to Mexico. They are asked a series of questions and then given the option to voluntarily return to Mexico, with no fine or prison sentence imposed. Because they have not been formally deported, they are not barred from a legal reentry.

2. Only about 32,000 beds were available for immigration detainees on a given night in fiscal year 2008. Most immigration detention is outsourced by the federal government to private companies like the Corrections Corporation of America, which build and operate the detention facilities. In 2009 it cost between $90 and $119 per day to keep an apprehended migrant in federal custody.

3. The cost proved to be between $3.9 and $7.5 million per mile, depending on the time and place of construction.

and vehicle barriers on the southwestern border, beyond the 670 miles of fortifications already completed or planned. But the Obama administration did seek major new funding for the virtual fence project, promising to extend it all along the U.S.-Mexico border within five years.

Overall, federal spending on immigration enforcement, including interior enforcement, is now thirteen times greater than in 1990 (figure 3.2). Border enforcement funding alone has increased tenfold, and the number of Border Patrol agents has tripled in the same period.

Figure 3.2. Federal Immigration Enforcement Spending, 1990–2009

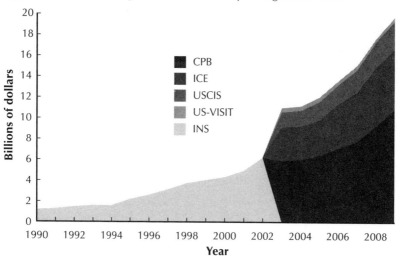

Source: Tabulations by the Migration Policy Institute, Washington, DC, February 2009.

From 1990 to 2003, all immigration enforcement spending was done by a single agency, the U.S. Immigration and Naturalization Service (INS). In 2003 the INS was abolished and replaced by three separate agencies: U.S. Immigration and Customs Enforcement (ICE), U.S. Citizen and Immigration Services (USCIS), and Customs and Border Patrol (CBP). In addition, the US-VISIT program was created to more efficiently and accurately record visitors with non-U.S. visas or passports who enter the United States.

How cost effective have these massive investments in immigration enforcement proven to be? As noted above, Homeland Security officials have already attributed the post-2006 decline in migrant apprehensions to greater investment in Border Patrol manpower, fencing, and border surveillance technologies. In the sections that follow we scrutinize this claim and examine several alternative explanations for what is happening at the U.S.-Mexico border.

ALTERNATIVE EXPLANATIONS FOR THE DECREASE IN APPREHENSIONS AT THE BORDER

Alternative Explanation #1: Reduced Circularity of Migration

Before serious attempts to fortify the border began in the late 1990s, Mexican migrants were able to cross in both directions with relative ease and at relatively modest cost. In early 2009, Tunkaseños expressed the view that migration to the United States now requires serious deliberation, coordination, planning, and a substantial investment of cash. We found that Tunkaseños were still deciding to go north (though in smaller numbers than we found in 2006), but return migration from the United States had dwindled to a trickle. Tunkaseño migrants are remaining in the United States longer than they used to and longer than they intended upon arrival. In our 2009 survey, 45 percent of respondents with U.S. migration experience had stayed in the United States longer than they had originally planned to do on their most recent trip (figure 3.3). The calculation is simple: if migrants make fewer trips to the United States, there are fewer opportunities to be apprehended, which may partly explain the decrease in apprehensions statistics reported by the Department of Homeland Security.

Regardless of how long Tunkaseños *expect* to stay in the United States, they actually remain for more than two years, on average, before returning to Tunkás. Staying in the United States for increasingly extended periods is not unique to Tunkaseño migrants. The data from the past three MMFRP studies reveal the same pattern. Figure 3.4 demonstrates that the median length of stay in the United States has risen steadily, with a sharp increase after the advent of heavy border fortifications.

Indeed, during the five years preceding the 2009 survey, the average Tunkaseño migrant living in the United States had returned to Tunkás only once. Because Tunkaseños are returning to Mexico less frequently, they present the Border Patrol with fewer opportunities for apprehension, which may contribute to the decline in apprehensions data.

Figure 3.3. Length of Migrants' Stay on Most Recent Trip to United States

N = 243

Figure 3.4. Median Length of Migrants' Stay in the United States

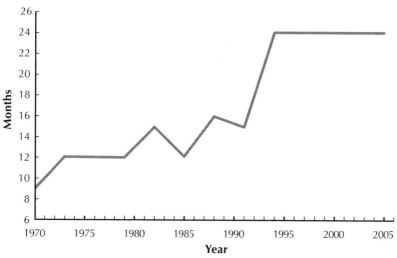

Sources: MMFRP surveys in 2007, 2008, and 2009.

Another indicator of reduced circularity is that half of the interviewees with at least one close family member[4] living in the United States

---

4. Defined as a spouse, sibling, parent, child, or grandparent.

reported that, in the preceding twelve months, at least one family member had stayed in the United States because they feared not being able to reenter the United States after a return visit to Mexico. Some reasons for their concern were the inability to pay the people-smuggler's fee and fear of interdiction and incarceration, and even death (to be discussed below). Other interviewees said they were afraid of losing their job in the United States if they returned to Tunkás, even for a short visit, because their employer would replace them. Gerardo is a U.S.-based migrant who had not returned to Tunkás since 2004. When asked if he would be able to return to his restaurant job if he visited Tunkás, he responded: "No, I don't think so, because they really need people at the restaurant. If I leave, they would look for someone else. I had plans to go, but I would lose years of seniority [at the restaurant]." Had he left his job, he would have forfeited a position he had worked years to attain. Gerardo cancelled his plans to return to Tunkás in 2009, and he is not alone in this: nearly nine out of ten Tunkaseños currently living in the United States did not plan to return to Tunkás in 2009.

While migrants and their families remain in the United States, their homes in Tunkás stand vacant. Tunkás had 1,109 dwelling units during our 2009 fieldwork. We found that nearly 8 percent of them, or 85 houses, were uninhabited, many with tropical vegetation creeping in. This incidence of abandoned homes is surprisingly high since Tunkás is still a community of recent emigration to the United States; only one-quarter of the population has any international migration experience. The proliferation of abandoned homes suggests that whole families are migrating to the United States and staying there.

Another explanation for migrants extending their stays in the United States lies in the steady uptick in the financial investment that clandestine entrants put at risk. As discussed in following sections, migrants now pay thousands of dollars to people-smugglers to facilitate their journeys. Figure 3.5 represents the number of hours an undocumented migrant would need to work in the United States in order to repay the debt (usually to a kinsman or friend) accrued to cover the smuggler's fee. According to this calculation, between 2006 and 2009, a Tunkaseño would need to work 382 hours and use all of his income to satisfy this debt. Tunkaseños reported a median workweek of 40 hours, which means that the 382 hours translate to nine and a half weeks of work. Interestingly, when asked out-right, Tunkaseños reported that it took them a median of three months to pay back their people-smugglers' debts.

Figure 3.5. Average Number of Hours an Undocumented Migrant Must Work to Repay His/Her *Pollero* Fee, by Year

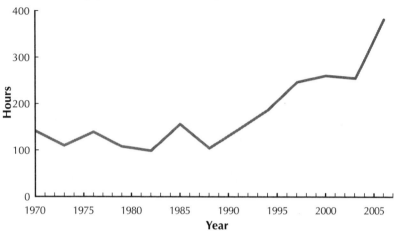

Border enforcement has had an adverse effect on the circularity of Tunkaseños' migration patterns; Tunkaseños are remaining longer in or-der to avoid paying exorbitant people-smugglers' fees, losing their jobs in the United States, and risking their lives in a dangerous border crossing (to be discussed below). This shrinking of circular migration may have contributed to the decrease in apprehensions reported by the Border Pa-trol. However, *how* migrants enter the United States is equally important as how long they stay.

Alternative Explanation #2: Use of Unconventional Modes of Entry

Because of tighter border enforcement, many U.S.-bound migrants from Tunkás seek out new ways and locations through which to enter the United States clandestinely. The Tunkaseños in our 2009 survey who had entered the United States most recently without authorization had utilized six different modes of entry on their most recent trip. Seventy-six percent of unauthorized Tunkaseño migrants crossed most recently by foot through the mountains and deserts of the U.S.-Mexico borderlands, the so-called traditional entry method. Beyond the traditional entry, we also encountered Tunkaseños who had swum across the Rio Grande, passed through a legal port of entry using fake/borrowed papers, crossed through a legal port hidden in a vehicle, crawled through tunnels dug by people-smugglers, and trudged through sewage pipes that traverse the border.

While undocumented Tunkaseños, like most migrants from Yucatán, cross at a variety of locations along the border, they have consistently favored the California-Mexico border (figure 3.6); 87 percent of our respondents in 2009 had crossed through California. Using the ENFORCE database (an official digital archive of detailed information on all undocumented migrants apprehended by the Border Patrol between 1999 and 2006), John Weeks (2009) found that most migrants originating in Yucatán are apprehended in places to the east of San Diego (Calexico/Mexicali and Tecate); only 20 percent had been apprehended in San Diego/Tijuana. While the ENFORCE data only contain information on apprehended migrants, our study captured information about all border crossings, including those made by entrants who were never apprehended. In contrast to the ENFORCE data, our data reveal that three-quarters of Tunkaseño migrants who crossed through California did so via San Diego/Tijuana, with the remainder crossing near urban areas east of San Diego.

Figure 3.6. Border-Crossing Locations, by Year of Most Recent Trip to United States

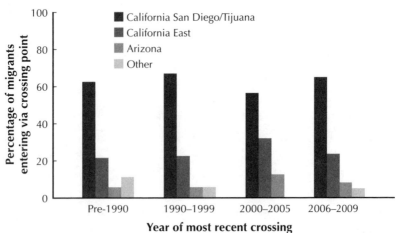

Thus, in choosing a border-crossing site, Tunkaseño migrants appear to behave differently from the majority of (apprehended) Yucatecan migrants. One explanation for this difference could be that most migrants from Tunkás are using the same set of people-smugglers, who prefer to pass their clients through the San Diego/Tijuana metropolitan area. Another possible explanation is that apprehended migrants (represented in the ENFORCE data) and un-apprehended migrants (included in our study) behave differently.

The principal U.S. receiving communities for Tunkaseños are both located in Southern California, which explains why most Tunkaseños choose to cross along the California-Mexico line. That segment of the border offers an array of crossing environments: mountains, deserts, valleys, and urban and rural areas. There are also several major ports of entry (POEs) on the California-Mexico border. To avoid the perils of the mountains and deserts, many Tunkaseño migrants are attempting to cross through these entry ports. Over 73 million crossings were made in fiscal year 2008 through California's six land ports of entry that connect the United States to Mexico,[5] which translates to more than 200,000 entries per *day*.[6] The San Diego/Tijuana port of entry is the busiest land-border crossing in the world, and it is virtually impossible to conduct a close scrutiny of the torrent of vehicles and pedestrians passing through it.

More than one out of four (28 percent) Tunkaseño migrants whom we interviewed reported entering through a legal POE on their most recent trip to the United States. Of those who crossed through a legal entry port, 94 percent had done so at San Ysidro or Otay Mesa, both in Tijuana (figure 3.7). The ports in San Diego/Tijuana are much more heavily trafficked than those in eastern California, which may provide more cover for undocumented Tunkaseño migrants. Of those who crossed through the legal ports of entry, 54 percent crossed hidden in a vehicle, and 44 percent showed inspectors fake or borrowed papers.

---

5. Interview conducted by Jonathan A. Hicken with J. Dizdul, of the U.S. Customs and Border Protection, San Diego, May 10, 2009.
6. Crossings include those made by truck, bus, train, passenger vehicle, private aircraft, and on foot.

Figure 3.7. Migrants Entering through a Legal Port of Entry on Most Recent Trip to United States, by Location of Crossing

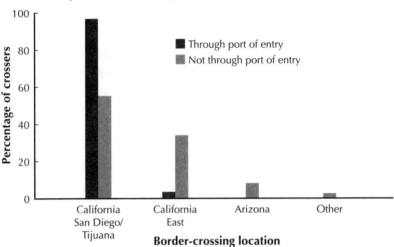

Unauthorized Tunkaseños are having great success in entering the United States through the POEs; in our survey, the mean number of apprehensions per trip per migrant when crossing the border somewhere between official POEs (0.73 apprehensions per trip) was double that for crossings through POEs (0.36 apprehensions per trip). Though crossing the border through a POE costs significantly more than crossing in remote areas (people-smugglers charge up to $5,000 for POE crossings), that mode of entry is much more likely to yield success. Migrants are increasingly electing to cross through POEs and are less likely to be apprehended in this manner, which may also contribute to the decline in apprehensions reported by the Department of Homeland Security. Whether crossing through ports of entry or not, Tunkaseños rely heavily on the assistance of professional people-smugglers.

Alternative Explanation #3: High Reliance on People-Smugglers

The vast majority of undocumented Mexican migrants hire a professional people-smuggler to assist them in crossing the U.S.-Mexico border. As the border has become more heavily patrolled than at any previous time in U.S. history, *polleros* have become essential to a successful and relatively safe crossing (Fuentes and García 2009, 79–102). Given the growing demand for their services, *polleros* have increased the fees they charge Tunkaseños fourfold since 1990 (figure 3.8). Despite the high cost of hiring a people-smuggler, nine out of ten Tunkaseño migrants do so. In fact, only seven individuals interviewed in 2009 had crossed the border without a people-smuggler since 2000; these individuals were likely to have been highly experienced migrants who were familiar with the border-crossing experience and felt comfortable guiding themselves. The most successful people-smugglers are highly sought after by migrants because of their superior knowledge and expertise in evading the Border Patrol.

Figure 3.8. People-Smugglers' Fees Paid by Tunkaseño Migrants, 1978–2009

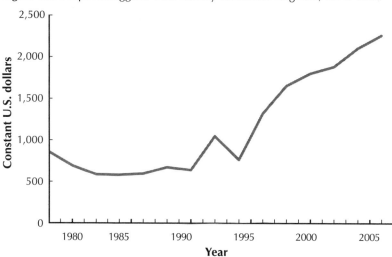

The importance of knowing a trustworthy *pollero* with an established record of successful border crossings emerged very clearly in our interviews with Tunkaseños. The consequences of choosing an untrustworthy *pollero* can be serious, as Nicolás, a recent Tunkaseño migrant, explained:

> The three women who crossed with us, they were around twenty years old, were raped by the smugglers in front of everyone. They cried. . . . The smugglers were armed and threatened to kill them. It was very sad and difficult at the

same time, because we couldn't do anything. I talked to one of the women after we crossed; she said she would do anything as long as she could get to her family. This I will never forget.

Nicolás's experience was an extreme case, but it demonstrates the importance of trusting the professional who assists a migrant through a dangerous journey. Since 1990, the relative importance of word-of-mouth recommendations in hiring a *pollero* has grown. Among our undocumented interviewees who crossed most recently between 2006 and 2009, 66 percent got their *pollero* through a referral from a family member or friend; the remainder found their most recent *pollero* on their own (figure 3.9).

Figure 3.9. *Question:* "How did you meet the *pollero* who helped you cross the border?"

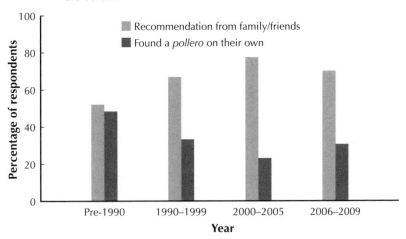

Interestingly, 88 percent of our respondents met up with their *pollero* at the border, which suggests that there was tight coordination between the smuggler, the migrant, and the migrant's family to ensure a successful linkup. This is consistent with the findings of previous MMFRP surveys in other migrant-sending communities (Fuentes and García 2009, 79–102). Family members and friends are also the most important source of funds with which to hire a *pollero*. Among our respondents who used a *pollero* on their most recent trip, 71 percent reported that a family member or friend lent them money to pay the smuggler.[7]

Given the tighter enforcement of the border in areas between legal POEs, *polleros* have begun offering a wider range of services. Jaime, a Tunkaseño migrant who crossed in 2008, experienced several different modes of entry on the same trip to the United States:

> The 2008 crossing was the hardest I have ever experienced. My wife and I traveled with forty-five people and attempted to cross in many ways. . . . We tried four times to cross through Tijuana, but we were caught every time. The *pollero* offered to cross us in a small boat [from a fishing village in Baja California to a beach in San Diego County], but it was too expensive. We drove to Mexicali and tried through there in a truck with twenty other people, but we were detained by the Border Patrol. Then we used another *pollero*, who offered to cross us through sewage pipes full of mud and fecal matter, where immigration agents never go. We walked for two hours in those pipes and got through.

Even with the aid of people-smugglers, the Border Patrol indeed may have become more adept at intercepting undocumented migrants: the average number of apprehensions per Tunkaseño migrant per trip has increased from 0.35 before 1990 to 2 between 2006 and 2009 (figure 3.10). Before 1990, only 29 percent of border crossers were apprehended even once. In the 2007–2009 period, however, 44 percent of undocumented migrants were apprehended at least once.

However, the rising probability of apprehension made little difference in terms of actually keeping undocumented Tunkaseños out of the United States. As shown in figure 3.11, the eventual success rate[8] among undocumented entrants has remained extremely high. Overall, 97 percent who

---

7. The current U.S. economic crisis undoubtedly has reduced the disposable income of U.S.-based Tunkaseños, thereby potentially restricting the ability of their Tunkás-based relatives to migrate to the United States. For further discussion, see chapter 2, this volume.

8. Eventual success is defined as entering the United States on the same trip (without returning to one's hometown), regardless of the number of apprehensions or deportations (whether forced or voluntary).

had attempted to cross the border without authorization on their most recent trip to the United States had succeeded, usually on the second or third try, without returning home. Among Tunkaseños who had entered illegally since 2007, 100 percent eventually succeeded.

Figure 3.10. Average Number of Apprehensions per Migrant per Trip, Using a *Pollero*

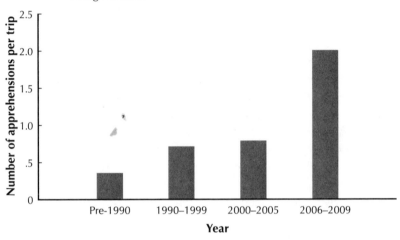

These findings are consistent with four previous MMFRP surveys conducted since 2005. In none of these studies did migrants' eventual success rate fall below 92 percent. These data indicate that fewer than half of undocumented migrants are being apprehended even once on a given trip to the border, and all but a tiny fraction are able to enter successfully. If keeping undocumented migrants out of the U.S. labor market is the indicator of efficacy, it is clear that the current U.S. border enforcement strategy is failing.

PERCEPTIONS OF BORDER-CROSSING DANGERS AND DIFFICULTIES

In our 2009 fieldwork we found that most Tunkaseños are aware of the dangers and obstacles they may confront during a clandestine border crossing. Interviewees were asked a series of questions to elicit their knowledge and perceptions of the border-crossing experience. When asked how difficult it was to evade the Border Patrol during an unauthorized border crossing, 85 percent of our respondents believed it was either "very difficult" or "somewhat difficult." A similar proportion of respondents, 87 percent, believed it was "very dangerous" to cross the border illegally.

Figure 3.11. Apprehension Rates and Eventual Success Rates among Undocumented Tunkaseño Migrants, by Year of Most Recent Border Crossing

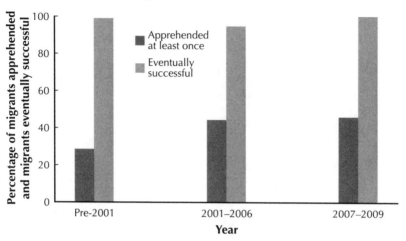

The survey probed deeper to determine exactly what factors worried migrants when they considered making a clandestine entry into the United States. We showed respondents a set of images depicting several potential sources of concern for a person considering making the journey north without authorization. The images depicted border bandits, extreme climatic conditions, the Border Patrol, incarceration upon apprehension (Operation Streamline), Mexican police, inability to find work in the United States, and border fencing (see figure 3.12).

In figure 3.13 we report the interviewees' first responses to the question presented in figure 3.12 and also a weighted calculation of their three responses. Consistent with previous MMFRP studies, an overwhelming fraction of respondents were concerned about the extreme climatic hazards they might encounter. Most of the U.S.-Mexico border is desert or mountainous terrain. During summer months, triple-digit heat can cause dehydration and heat stroke. In winter, sub-zero temperatures, cold rains, and snow can cause hypothermia. Tunkaseños also mentioned dangerous wildlife, including poisonous snakes and scorpions, as a cause of concern when contemplating a clandestine border crossing.

Figure 3.12. Potential Sources of Concern to Persons Crossing the Border Clandestinely

Figure 3.13. Sources of Concern about Clandestine Entry: First Response and All Responses, Weighted

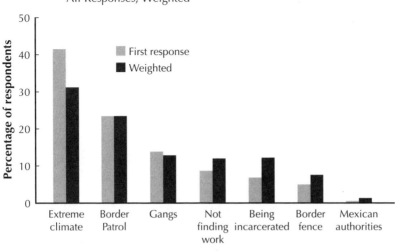

Note: The weighted scale was calculated by assigning three points to the first response, two points to the second, and one point to the third.

Perceptions of the level of danger and difficulty associated with illegal entry, as well as specific sources of concern about clandestine border crossings, varied little by age, gender, migration experience, or the respondent's principal residence (Tunkás or the United States). This suggests that the grueling realities of the current border-crossing environment are well known among Tunkaseños. Simón, a Tunkaseño migrant, described the difficulties he and others endured to get to the United States: "We crossed through the desert hidden in a truck with fifteen other people. We were all lying down; people were crying, vomiting, our legs and arms would go numb. . . . It was really hot; one woman burned her leg because she was next to the truck's hot metal door."

The mass media undoubtedly play a role in creating such perceptions of danger. Among our interviewees who lived in Mexico at the time of our survey, 75 percent reported that migration was discussed frequently on television and radio.[9] In open-ended interviews, many respondents

_____

9. See chapter 8 for a more detailed analysis of information flows regarding migration in Tunkás.

told us that the media described the border as a very dangerous place. Migrants' and potential migrants' concerns about the dangers and difficulties of clandestine entry are well-founded: tougher U.S. border enforcement clearly has changed the experience of an undocumented migrant, and Tunkaseños are aware of this fact.

UNINTENDED CONSEQUENCE OF BORDER ENFORCEMENT: RISING MIGRANT FATALITIES

The physical danger involved in entering the United States illegally has risen dramatically since the U.S. border fortification project began in the mid-1990s. According to official statistics compiled by Mexico's consulates in U.S. border cities, since 1995 there have been more than five thousand migrant fatalities, with bodies found in the desert, mountains, and irrigation canals, or washed ashore on the banks of the Rio Grande. Since 2000 the annual death toll has exceeded four hundred in most years (see figure 3.14).[10]

Figure 3.14. Migrant Fatalities in the U.S.-Mexico Borderlands, 1995–2008

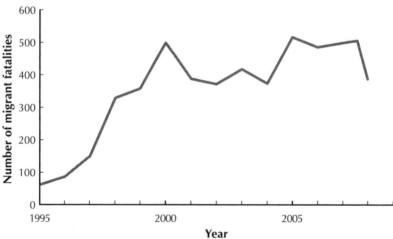

Source: Unpublished information from Mexican consulates in U.S. border cities, 2009.

---

10. The actual number of deaths on the border may be higher than the official count, since many migrants' bodies go unfound. In addition, there are rigid standards for categorizing a body found in the desert as an "undocumented border-crosser" death (Sisco and Hicken 2009). Reverend Robin Hoover, leader of an organization that

Alejandro, a Tunkaseño migrant who crossed the border in 2002, came across a pregnant woman who had collapsed along the way; Alejandro believed she would not survive the trip. "We couldn't stop for a pregnant woman because [the Border Patrol] might have caught us. The woman stayed behind. We felt awful, but what could we have done?" Alejandro is not the only Tunkaseño familiar with death at the border: 44 percent of our respondents reported that they personally knew someone who had died during a border-crossing attempt.

Many of these respondents were probably thinking of María de los Ángeles Manzanero, a 46-year-old wife and mother from Tunkás who died on President's Day, 2007, while braving the mountains of eastern San Diego County during a winter storm. What follows is María's story as told to us by her daughter Alejandra, who was at the family home in Tunkás at the time of our interviews:

After spending a decade in Southern California with no visits home to Tunkás, María decided to return for the town's annual fiesta. She visited with her brothers and other family members there and then was ready to return home to Anaheim. She was determined to go back to the United States, where her home, family, and life awaited. She tried crossing through a legal port of entry but her visible nervousness gave her away and she was apprehended. When she was released and returned to Mexico, she decided it was better to cross with other Tunkaseños through the mountains east of San Diego. Before María left, Alejandra said she tried to stop her mother from crossing through such dangerous terrain:

> I told her, "don't cross; don't cross." But she said, "I'm going to cross. I already talked with the other Tunkaseños; we'll all cross together." Then I spoke to a Tunkaseño who was part of the group. "I beg you, do not leave my mom behind."
>
> "Don't worry," he said; "we'll all cross together."
>
> On the third day, family members in Anaheim called us from a pay phone—nothing. "Your mom's not here. We don't know what happened, but she's not here." We called

_____

documents migrant deaths in Arizona, explains: "In Arizona, there have only been 1,500 deaths recorded by the office of the Pima County medical examiner in the last ten years. Each one has to be treated as a homicide investigation. . . . The higher figures [reported by other sources] may include missing persons, people that died on the Mexican side of the border while trying to cross, etc."

the *pollero*: "Don't worry; she got tired on the road and we left her in a safe place." I went to her room and prayed to the Virgin Mary.

Shrine dedicated to María de los Ángeles Manzanero, victim of a failed border-crossing attempt, located in the Tunkás home of her daughter Alejandra.

They told me that she got tired; she died just about fifteen minutes before a volunteer group found her, with a jacket pulled over her head, lying beside a paved highway. On that Monday [President's Day, 2007] the Border Patrol was off work. We went to San Diego and had to identify her. I saw her clothes; we knew it was her. My mother was young and smart, but she didn't make it. The autopsy showed she died of hypothermia—first her legs, then her hands, then her heart. I never imagined I would lose my mother.

Supposedly, Alejandra's mother was abandoned in a remote area because the group was unable to continue helping her, something that Alejandra finds difficult to believe. María's body was returned to Tunkás, where she now lies in the municipal cemetery. Alejandra was in Tunkás at the time of our fieldwork while trying to legalize her status in the United States. She hopes someday to reunite with family members in Anaheim, where she was living when her mother died. She remains devastated by the death. To all Tunkaseños, María's tragic end is a potent reminder that clandestine border crossings are very dangerous journeys.

INTERIOR ENFORCEMENT

Policy Overview

In 1986 the U.S. Congress passed the Immigration Reform and Control Act (IRCA), which addressed interior immigration enforcement in two major ways. First, IRCA attempted to decrease the stock of undocumented migrants in the United States by offering "amnesty" (the opportunity to receive legal status) to some three million undocumented migrants already living and working in the United States. Second, IRCA sought to limit the number of undocumented immigrants working in the United States by introducing employer sanctions and making it unlawful to knowingly hire or refer undocumented immigrants for work (Meissner and Kerwin 2009).

This bill resulted in a shift in the interior enforcement of U.S. immigration law. First, by providing an amnesty provision, IRCA encouraged the permanent settlement and integration of a subset of migrants who were already living in the United States. Second, IRCA discouraged the settlement and integration of new immigrants by creating criminal penalties for them. Third, IRCA illegalized the hiring of undocumented migrants and introduced enforcement mechanisms to reduce the employment of migrants who lacked legitimate work permits.

Since IRCA's passage, interior enforcement legislation has focused on these same three areas. The following sections provide a brief overview of post-IRCA interior enforcement legislation related to the settlement, criminalization, and employment of undocumented immigrants in the United States, and explore the impacts of various types of interior enforcement on Tunkaseño immigrants in the United States.

Settlement-Related Interior Enforcement

By legalizing the status of formerly undocumented migrants, IRCA offered three million of them the opportunity to settle in the United States as lawful permanent residents and ultimately to naturalize as citizens. What IRCA did not provide was the opportunity for those migrants to bring their families across the border to join them. Many migrants who qualified for legalization had to choose between long-term settlement in the United States or returning to Mexico to be with their families. Of those who stayed in the United States, many identified a third choice: bringing their wives and children to the United States without benefit of documentation, valuing family unification above legality. As a result, there was a sharp but transient increase in the clandestine entry of women and children in the years immediately following IRCA's passage (Cornelius 1989).

In normaling the status of much of the undocumented population circa 1986, IRCA intensified a long-term trend toward Mexican immigrants' permanent settlement in the United States. However, erratic enforcement of IRCA's interior enforcement policies meant that the underlying incentive structure that encouraged undocumented migration in the first place did not change (Tichenor 1994). This failure to address the incentives for businesses to hire undocumented labor (and for immigrants to migrate clandestinely) resulted in a continued heavy flow of undocumented migrants from Mexico in the post-IRCA period (see figure 3.15).

Local communities have responded to the influx of undocumented migrants with a variety of policies, which can be broadly categorized as "pro-settlement" and "anti-settlement." Pro-settlement policies aim to integrate undocumented immigrants into the larger community. One such policy is the local decision to accept *matrículas consulares* (identification cards issued by the Mexican government through Mexican consulates) as a valid form of personal identification from immigrants who are ineligible for state-issued IDs. In 2009 these personal identification cards were being accepted by 1,204 police departments and 393 city and 168 county governments (Varsanyi 2010). Another pro-settlement policy is the passage of "sanctuary" ordinances. A city that passes such an ordinance declares its refusal to provide monetary and personnel assistance to federal immigration authorities except in cases involving felony crimes (National Immigration Law Center 2008). Both of these policies aim to bring undocumented migrants out of the shadows and encourage their participation in and cooperation with the local community and local law enforcement.

Figure 3.15. Mexican-Born Population in the United States, Pre- and Post-IRCA

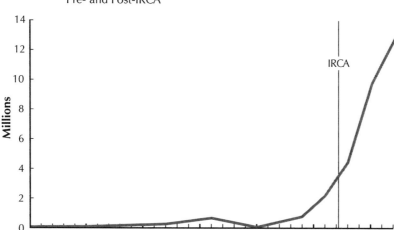

Source: Pew Hispanic Center 2009.

Anti-settlement policies aim to separate undocumented immigrants from the greater community. These include Illegal Immigration Relief Acts (IIRAs) and other local ordinances that penalize local employers who hire undocumented workers and local landlords who rent to undocumented residents (Varsanyi 2010). The most famous IIRAs are ordinances approved in 2006 by the cities of Hazleton, Pennsylvania, and Escondido, California, which required landlords to evict and refuse to rent to tenants who could not provide proof of U.S. citizenship. Both the Hazleton and Escondido ordinances were struck down as unconstitutional in 2007 (Preston 2007).

Another anti-settlement policy is the use of traffic stops and license checkpoints by local police, as done in Escondido. If a driver is unable to produce a valid driver's license, his or her immigration status may be questioned. If a driver is found to be undocumented, he or she will be held by the police or referred to federal authorities for investigation (Gorman 2008). Local cooperation with federal immigration authorities via the signing of 287(g) agreements, discussed in the following section, is another anti-settlement policy.

Settlement-related interior enforcement does not only affect the undocumented community. In recent years, the stock of mixed-status families (in which at least one member is undocumented or, in a primarily undocumented family, at least one member is legal) in the United States has increased. The enforcement of local immigration policy sometimes leads to the removal of undocumented parents—and their forced abandonment of their citizen children. U.S.-based Tunkaseños, most of whom live in Orange and Los Angeles counties in California, experience pro- and anti-settlement enforcement actions daily. The following section details their perceptions of and responses to some of these policies.

Tunkaseños and Settlement-Related Enforcement

In order to better understand the impacts that settlement-related enforcement policies have on Tunkaseños' daily lives, we showed respondents a set of images depicting several potential sources of concern for a person who resides in the United States without legal documents. Options (shown in figure 3.16) included the following: going to the hospital, going shopping, going to school, going to work, driving a car, using public transit, and walking in the street.

Tunkaseños living in the United States reported fear of driving a car, going to work, and even walking in the street. Interestingly, perceptions of life in the United States are similar among Mexico-based Tunkaseños and those living in the United States. Both groups consistently rank driving a car, walking in public, seeking medical attention, and going to work as the most frightening aspects of daily life in the United States. U.S.-based Tunkaseños are significantly more concerned about the risks of driving a car without papers, no doubt fearing that their vehicle might be confiscated at a traffic stop (see figure 3.17). Gerardo, an undocumented Tunkaseño who lives in Anaheim, explained:

> I don't drive because I'm afraid of the police. When I see them, I get nervous. Why risk it? I'm afraid of getting detained and deported by the police. . . . I know how to drive, but it's dangerous. It's also a pain to have a car. With the insurance, and the payments . . . it's expensive. On what I make, I can't afford it.

Figure 3.16. *Question:* "Of the things shown in these pictures, which three are the most worrisome to a person who lives in the United States without papers?"

Of the things shown in these pictures, which ones are most worrisome to a person who lives in the United States without papers?

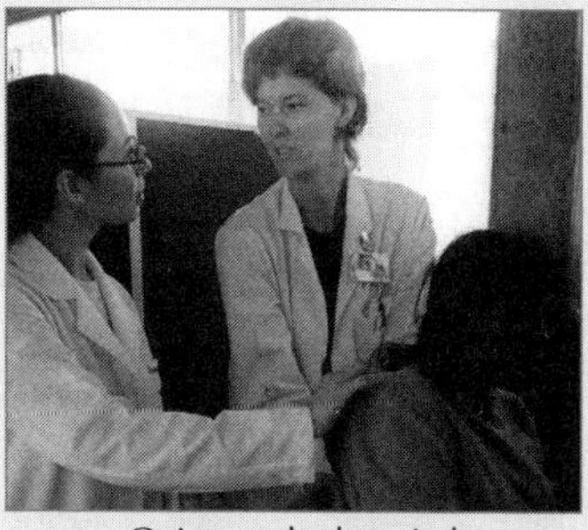

Going to the hospital    Going shopping

Going to school    Driving a car

Walking in the street    Using public transportation

Going to work

Figure 3.17. Sources of Concern among U.S.-based and Mexico-based
Respondents regarding Living in the United States without
Documents

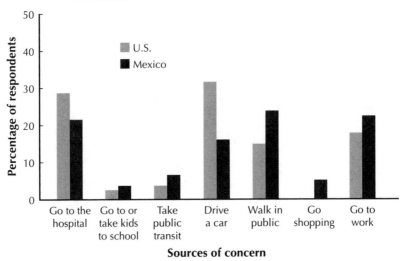

Perceptions are remarkably similar among male and female migrants
living without papers in the United States (see figure 3.18). Although men
reported greater fear of driving and women reported greater fear of walking in public, men and women alike ranked going to the hospital and
going to work as chief concerns to undocumented migrants living in the
United States.

Although the number of cases was limited, we found some variation
in responses from U.S.-based Tunkaseños by place of residence (figure
3.19). Thirty-six percent of Tunkaseños living in Anaheim feared driving
a car, versus 28 percent of those based in Inglewood. Nearly 7 percent of
Anaheim-based Tunkaseños reported fear of taking public transit, compared to a mere 1.5 percent of Inglewood-based Tunkaseños. These numbers probably reflect the use of random traffic stops in Orange County
as an immigration enforcement mechanism. One-quarter of Tunkaseños
living in Inglewood feared going to work, compared with 13.6 percent
of those in Anaheim. This difference may reflect the higher incidence of
workplace raids in Los Angeles County, particularly the highly publi-
cized series of raids occurring between 2006 and 2008.

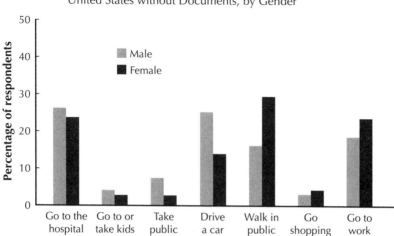

Figure 3.18. Sources of Concern among U.S.-based Tunkaseños Living in the United States without Documents, by Gender

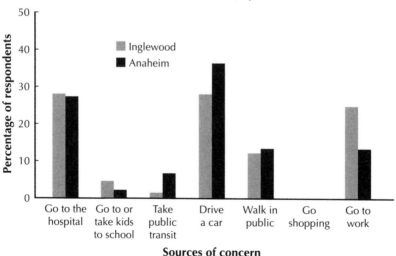

Figure 3.19. Sources of Concern among U.S.-based Tunkaseños Living in the United States without Documents, by U.S. Place of Residence

Our interviewees often mentioned the low-level fear that pervades their daily lives in the United States. Gerardo elaborated: "I'm afraid all the time. I'm afraid of getting caught by the police, and of getting deported. . . . But it's just a little fear. It doesn't stop me from going to baseball games or to the park. You can't live like that, being afraid of everything."

This constant state of worry—a "culture of fear"—among the undocumented population in the United States is attributable not only to the introduction of local legislation with pro- or anti-settlement aims, but also to the introduction of criminal penalties, such as incarceration and deportation, for migration violations. The following section discusses the creation and enforcement of such legislation.

Criminal Enforcement

Under legislation passed post-IRCA, the act of migrating without documents became a civil offense, enforceable by both federal and local officials. The introduction of criminal penalties for being an undocumented resident in the United States turned otherwise law-abiding immigrants into criminals. The prescribed punishment for immigrating without the correct documentation was the same as the punishment for an undocumented individual who commits a felony: deportation.

In 1996 Congress passed the Illegal Immigration Reform and Immigrant Responsibility Act (IIRIRA), which included an amendment to the Immigration and Nationality Act (INA). This amendment, INA Section 287(g), allowed local police officers to be deputized as agents of the Immigration and Naturalization Service (INS, now part of Immigration and Customs Enforcement, or ICE) and enforce federal immigration law at the local level. Two kinds of officers can be deputized under Section 287(g): jail enforcement officers (JEOs) and task force officers (TFOs). A deputized JEO can only enforce immigration law within jails or prisons, while TFOs have broader jurisdiction and may enforce immigration law on the street (U.S. Immigration and Customs Enforcement 2008).

The Homeland Security Act of 2002 (HSA) established the Department of Homeland Security (DHS) in November of that year in response to the terrorist attacks of September 11, 2001. The DHS functions as an umbrella, consolidating some twenty-two "security-related" government agencies under its aegis (Department of Homeland Security 2008). The Homeland Security Act also established Immigration and Customs Enforcement, which assumed the investigatory and enforcement duties of the Immigration and Naturalization Service when that agency was incorporated into the DHS in 2003.

The incorporation of the INS into the new Department of Homeland Security reframed the immigration issue as a matter of national security. The 287(g) designation was created in 1996; however, the first Memorandum of Agreement (MOA) between the federal government and a locality was not signed until 2002. This is attributable in part to the changing political climate in the United States: Attorney General Janet Reno had denied state and local law enforcement's authority to enforce civil immigration law during the Clinton administration, while Attorney General John Ashcroft issued a classified memo in 2002 that affirmed this authority (Varsanyi 2010). It is also partly attributable to the new national security climate: following the September 11 attacks, locales were anxious to avert any potential terrorist threats. Tightening local immigration enforcement seemed like a rational means to achieve this goal (Pham 2004). As of this chapter's writing, there were sixty-three active 287(g) MOAs, and more than 840 officers had been trained and certified through the 287(g) program (U.S. Immigration and Customs Enforcement 2008).

Academics and policy makers have questioned the efficacy of Section 287(g) as a law enforcement mechanism, citing its negative impact on relations between undocumented communities and the police as counterproductive to law enforcement's primary goal of community safety. Legal experts question the constitutionality of 287(g) agreements, referring to the constitutional mandate for uniform enforcement of immigration law, and they also question what Ashcroft called the "inherent authority" of state authorities to enforce immigration law (Pham 2004).

Tunkaseños and Criminal Enforcement

Tunkaseños experience criminal enforcement policies through their interactions with local police. The Pew Hispanic Center reported that 17 percent of a national sample of Latino immigrants interviewed in 2009 said they or a family member had been stopped and questioned by the police within the preceding five years (Lopez 2009). Twenty-three percent of Tunkaseños interviewed in 2009 reported being personally stopped and questioned by police in the preceding twelve months, reflecting in part the higher incidence of "random" traffic stops of suspected undocumented immigrants in Southern California. Of those stopped by the police, 48 percent were first asked for their driver's license, 39 percent were first asked for an ID from the Department of Motor Vehicles, and 13 percent were asked to produce their *matrícula consular*, signaling a growing acceptance of the *matrícula* as a standard form of identification.

Among Tunkaseños who had been stopped by the police, 56 percent were fined and 35 percent had been incarcerated. Nine percent had their cars impounded, but only one individual was turned over to Immigration and Customs Enforcement and eventually deported. ICE officials are authorized to stop and question individuals if they have reason to believe those individuals are undocumented. This happened to Nicolás, a Tunkaseño migrant who was detained on his way to work and deported:

> A friend gave me a ride to work. I went into Burger King to buy something and because I don't know any English, [some police officers] became suspicious. There was a police officer there; her shirt said "immigration." She asked if I had a passport. I said I didn't. She then called in [for backup] and the other police arrived. They told me to get in the car and they asked me how I got [into the United States]; I said I was undocumented. The officers took me with them and kept me somewhere for two days. Then they released me in Ciudad Juárez. They told me that if I returned and got caught again, I would go to jail for several years.

Academics and policy makers have questioned the impact of interior enforcement on the rule of law, asking whether, if immigrants fear detection and deportation, they are less likely to report crimes. Anaheim and Inglewood, where most U.S.-based Tunkaseños live, both have JEO 287(g) agreements, meaning that neither city's police officers can enforce immigration law on the street. Yet Tunkaseños living in Anaheim and Inglewood differed in their responses to questions about the rule of law. When asked if they would report a crime to the police even though they were undocumented, 86 percent of migrants in Anaheim responded in the affirmative, compared to only 53 percent of those living in Inglewood.

There are two possible explanations for this difference: fear of police brutality and fear of gang violence. The Inglewood police department has a history of violence; in 2009 the department was under federal investigation for the fatal shootings of four men—three of them unarmed—over a four-month period (Leonard 2009). It is possible that this violence reduces overall compliance with the Inglewood police, and Tunkaseños' responses may reflect that generalized distrust. A second explanation is the notable gang presence that exists in Inglewood but not in Anaheim. Gangs clearly affect the lives of Tunkaseños in Inglewood. When asked if she would report a crime, Yolanda, an Inglewood resident, answered, "Of course, if it wasn't committed by a black man."[11] Xavier, another Inglewood resident, elaborated on the racial tensions that exist in Inglewood and are exacerbated by the gang presence. When asked if he would report a gang-related crime, Xavier said he would, but only anonymously. He went on to explain that he understands why someone would not report a crime: "It could create problems [for whoever is reporting], with both the police and the gangsters. The less trouble we cause, the better we live."

Although we did not collect quantitative data on gang activity and deaths, several Tunkaseños interviewed in Inglewood mentioned recent gang-related killings of Yucatecans sporting the wrong colors in the wrong neighborhood. Fear of violent backlash from local gangs may explain why Tunkaseños in Inglewood show lower levels of cooperation with local law enforcement than their compatriots in Anaheim.

Employment-Related Interior Enforcement

In 1986, IRCA made the hiring of undocumented immigrants illegal for the first time in U.S. history. To enforce this provision, IRCA introduced the I-9 form, on which employers must state that they have reviewed government-approved identification documents presented by a job applicant and attest that they appear valid "on their face." If an employer makes a "good-faith" effort to complete I-9 forms for all new hires, that employer is deemed to have complied with the law (GAO 2008).

The Illegal Immigration Reform and Immigrant Responsibility Act, enacted in 1996, introduced measures to bolster the effectiveness of I-9 screening by creating a voluntary electronic employee verification system,

---

11. According to the 2000 U.S. population census, of Inglewood's 114,914 residents, 47.1 percent were black, 19.1 percent were white, and 46 percent were Hispanic (white and non-white). http://quickfacts.census.gov/qfd/states/06/0636546.html.

later known as E-Verify. E-Verify uses information from the Department of Homeland Security and the Social Security Administration (SSA) to match information on employees' I-9 forms. As of early 2009, over 100,000 businesses were enrolled in E-Verify. Federal legislation passed in 2008 requires that federal contractors receiving $100,000 or more in exchange for their services enroll in the program; however, as of this writing, implementation of this legislation had been postponed pending further review of the E-Verify system's performance (U.S. Citizenship and Immigration Services 2009).

E-Verify is not 100 percent effective. Though it "excels in detecting fake identity cards because they are not in the databases . . . it fails to detect the fraudulent use of borrowed or stolen documents that are in the databases" (Meissner 2006). The problem of "false positives"—individuals who appear legal to work but really are not—persists, as does the problem of "false negatives"—individuals who appear unauthorized to work but are in fact eligible. In order to solve this problem, an independent task force in 2006 recommended the creation of a "secure, biometric, machine-readable Social Security card." As of yet, no such card has been designed.

Since 1994 the SSA has been sending "no-match" letters to individuals whose name and social security number do not match information on individuals who have paid into the system. Further, the SSA sends letters to all employers who have ten or more mismatches in their employee base. Beginning in 2007, the DHS changed its "no-match" policy so that employers who receive no-match letters must take a series of actions, ending in the termination of ineligible employees. Otherwise, the employer risks being accused of "constructive knowledge" of an immigration violation (Federal Register 2008).

Immigration and Customs Enforcement has three ways to police employer compliance: auditing an employer's I-9 forms and fining the owners and/or managers who are found in violation; investigating and referring an employer for criminal prosecution; and conducting a "worksite enforcement operation"—a raid—against employers who are suspected of violating immigration law (Meissner and Kerwin 2009). From 2006 to 2008, ICE conducted a series of high-profile raids that focused on employers whose business models were built upon illegal migrant labor and on those who "engage(d) in identity theft, document fraud, and/or human smuggling" (Chertoff 2008).

These ICE enforcement actions, often driven by complaints from current or former employees of the raided firm, focused on the arrest and removal of unauthorized immigrant workers. The efficacy of these raids has been questioned by both humanitarian groups and academics, who point to the breakup of mixed-legal-status families via deportation[12] and to the raids' negligible impact on the fundamental systemic problems that lead to the hire of undocumented migrants in the first place.

Tunkaseños and Worksite Enforcement

Many Tunkaseños have been affected by the U.S. government's interior enforcement activities, both in the workplace and in their immediate residential areas. Given the overall low level of worksite enforcement in the United States, a surprising 8 percent of Tunkaseños with migration experience said there had been a raid at their most recent place of employment, and 18 percent reported having family or friends who were apprehended by ICE in worksite enforcement operations. Of those whose most recent place of employment had been raided, 46 percent were present during the raid; only 6 percent of those present were detained, and only one person was deported.

Pedro experienced such a raid. He was working at a car wash in 2006 when ICE agents arrived. To avoid apprehension, he jumped onto the roof of the building and lay flat, unable to see or hear what was happening below him. After a few hours, when he was sure that the ICE agents were gone, Pedro left work and went home. The following morning he returned to the car wash, where his employer put him right back to work.

Pedro's story points to major flaws in the current U.S. worksite enforcement regime. First, raids do not necessarily result in the apprehension and expulsion of unauthorized workers; migrants have escaped by jumping on roofs, hiding under cars, and simply running away. Second, raids do not discourage the hiring of undocumented workers. Pedro was rehired by his employer the day after the raid, no questions asked. Clearly, raids do not deter the hiring of undocumented workers by some

---

12. House Speaker Nancy Pelosi called the raids "un-American" in their consequences (Zito 2009).

employers. Nor, as shown below, do worksite raids reduce the propensity of Mexicans to migrate to the United States.

EFFECTS OF BORDER AND INTERIOR ENFORCEMENT ON MIGRATION BEHAVIOR: A MULTIVARIATE ANALYSIS

In order to better understand how U.S. immigration enforcement at the border and in the workplace affects an individual's propensity to migrate, we constructed a multivariate regression model of respondents in the prime migrant-age population (between the ages of sixteen and thirty-four). The dependent variable is whether the respondent reported that he or she intended to migrate to the United States in the next twelve months. Our independent variables are: (1) respondent believes it is difficult to evade the Border Patrol upon crossing; (2) respondent believes it is dangerous to cross the border without documentation; (3) respondent knows someone who died while crossing the border; and (4) respondent has been a victim of a workplace raid in the United States or has a family member or friend who has. We also chose seven standard demographic variables to act as controls: age, gender, marital status, education level, number of close family members living in the United States, wealth, and legal status in the United States.

Model 1 (table 3.1) estimates the likelihood that demographic attributes contribute to a potential migrant's intention to go north. We find that respondents planning to migrate were more likely to be younger, male, married, documented, and to have a stronger social network in the United States. These findings are consistent with our expectations about who migrates to the United States. Models 2 through 5 estimate the effects of believing that it is "very difficult" to cross the border clandestinely, "very dangerous" to do so, knowing someone who died while crossing the border, and personal or indirect (via relatives and friends) experience with a U.S. workplace raid. Model 6 incorporates all of the U.S. policy–related variables examined in our study.

Similar to analyses in previous MMFRP surveys, we find that knowledge of the border does not discourage potential migrants who intend to migrate. Moreover, knowing someone who died while crossing the border is *positively* correlated with an individual's intent to migrate (controlling for the effects of social network contacts in the United States). This could be due to the fact that individuals who knew about a death at the border are more deeply connected to the migratory community in Tunkás; the case of María de los Ángeles, discussed above, is well known, but it does not appear to have discouraged would-be migrants from trying their luck at the border.

Table 3.1. Effects of U.S. Immigration Enforcement on Propensity to Migrate

	Model 1	Model 2	Model 3	Model 4	Model 5	Model 6
Danger in crossing		−.728 (.572)				−.688 (.610)
Difficulty crossing			−.301 (.415)			−.164 (.478)
Knowing someone who died attempting to cross border				1.069* (.435)		1.092* (.477)
Experience with workplace raid					.201 (.452)	−.039 (.472)
Age	−.189*** (.041)	−.195*** (.044)	−.182*** (.040)	−.203*** (.041)	−.187*** (.041)	−.206*** (.042)
Male	1.219* (.491)	1.292** (.480)	1.142* (.496)	1.427* (.498)	1.195* (.491)	1.424** (.500)
Married	.817 (.503)	.952 (.514)	.833 (.507)	.862 (.506)	.791 (.503)	.993 (.501)
Education	.057 (.063)	.061 (.068)	.058 (.063)	.046 (.063)	.055 (.063)	.037 (.067)
Network in US	.390** (.146)	.413** (.148)	.408** (.157)	.339** (.127)	.390** (.145)	.377** (.144)
Wealth	.002 (.013)	−.004 (.013)	.003 (.013)	−.002 (.013)	.003 (.013)	0.000 (.013)
Documented	1.673** (.523)	1.666** (.542)	1.630** (.526)	1.455** (.539)	1.605** (.524)	1.391* (.538)
Constant	−.462 (.985)	.034 (1.092)	−0.421 (1.000)	−0.217 (.987)	−.489 (.983)	.395 (1.091)
Chi-squared	0.000	0.000	0.000	0.000	0.000	0.000
N	379	372	369	378	373	358

*$p < .05$; **$p < .01$; ***$p < .001$.
Robust standard errors in parentheses.

CONCLUSION

The Department of Homeland Security has attributed the decline in apprehensions of undocumented immigrants to the success of its border-policing efforts. The introduction of the border fence in 1993, along with a sustained increase in Border Patrol recruits over the past decade, has transformed the border into a heavily fortified zone and made the crossing significantly more difficult for would-be migrants. Our research suggests, however, that border enforcement has a limited effect on migration flows: once an individual makes the decision to migrate and amasses the necessary capital, success is virtually guaranteed.

In this chapter, we have suggested several alternative explanations for the recent decline in apprehensions:

- Border enforcement has reduced circularity of migration flows. Because of the increased physical and financial risks associated with a border crossing, migrants are being "bottled up" in the United States. The number of cumulative northbound crossings made by any given individual has fallen, shrinking the number of migrants available to be apprehended.

- The shift away from traditional modes of entry—on foot through the mountains and desert—in favor of newer, "unconventional" modes of entry—particularly through legal points of entry—decreases the likelihood of apprehension. These new crossing strategies are increasingly creative, and the Border Patrol has not yet found effective means to anticipate and intercept such crossings.

- High reliance on professional people-smugglers, who understand and track the activities of the Border Patrol, makes a successful crossing more likely. Although the Border Patrol apprehends Tunkaseños more times per trip today than they did twenty years ago, Tunkaseños are equally or more likely to ultimately enter the United States successfully.

- The falling demand for migrant labor in the United States has depressed the number of potential migrants. Because would-be migrants fear they will not find work after risking the trek across the border, many are staying where they are and waiting for the U.S. economy to rebound. Chapters 2 and 4 of this volume explore this topic in greater depth.

The border buildup has not eliminated clandestine entries to the United States, but it has led to increasing numbers of migrant fatalities along the U.S.-Mexico border. The story of María de los Ángeles serves as a potent reminder of the potential dangers of attempting to cross the border. Yet, as our results have revealed, knowledge of the dangers and difficulties of a border crossing is not statistically significant in predicting whether an individual will migrate.

Interior enforcement efforts have also had a limited impact on Tunkaseño migration and settlement in the United States. The series of ICE workplace raids between 2006 and 2008 and the increasing frequency of random police stops have made life more difficult for Tunkaseños living in the United States. However, U.S.-based respondents indicated that, although they live in a constant state of fear of arrest and deportation, they prefer to remain in the United States, where wages are higher, rather than return to Mexico.

Heightened interior enforcement efforts raise serious questions about maintaining the rule of law in the United States. If migrants live in constant fear of deportation, are they less likely to report crimes? Our data suggest that relations between immigrants and local police play an important role in maintaining the rule of law: if Tunkaseños trust that their reports will be anonymous, they are more willing to report crimes. However, more work must be done to clarify the relationship between community groups (particularly gangs), police officers, and the rule of law. Are immigrants willing to report gang-related crimes to the police? How active are gangs in migrant-receiving communities? What is the relationship between law enforcement officers and the community? Do local police have a reputation for violence? Do local police have an "anti-immigrant" reputation? All of these questions must be addressed in future studies if we are to better understand the relationship between interior enforcement mechanisms and the rule of law in the U.S. communities where migrants live.

Finally, workplace enforcement appears to have a negligible impact on migration and settlement decisions. Although more than 17 percent of Tunkaseños either experienced or had a close friend or family member who experienced a worksite raid at their most recent workplace, only one Tunkaseño reported being deported as the result of a workplace raid. Knowledge of or experience with raids is insignificant in predicting whether a Tunkaseño will migrate to the United States. Further, although 78 percent of Tunkaseños who live in the United States are undocumented, only 2 percent reported being unemployed at the time of our fieldwork, indicating that federal measures intended to prevent employment of unauthorized immigrants have not kept them out of the labor force.

In sum, our data suggest that immigration enforcement—at the border and in the interior—has little deterrent effect on Tunkaseños' migration decisions and on their employability in the United States. As Alejandro, an experienced Tunkaseño migrant, said, "It's impossible to stop immigrants. . . . No matter what, we will still come."

REFERENCES

Andreas, Peter. 2009. *Border Games*. 2d ed. Ithaca, NY: Cornell University Press.

Barry, Tom. 2008. "Chertoff's Challenge to Obama," *America's Program*, November 4, Center for International Policy, http://americas.irc-online.org/am/5647.

Boeing Company. 2009. "Boeing: Integrated Defense Systems—Secure Border Initiative (SBI) and SBInet," http://www.boeing.com/defense-space/sbinet/index.html.

Centro Legal. 2008. "Comprehensive Raids List," October 7, www.centrolegal.org.

Chertoff, Michael. 2008. "Leadership Journal Archive: Myth vs. Fact: Worksite Enforcement," July 9, http://www.dhs.gov/journal/leadership/2008/07/myth-vs-fact-worksite-enforcement.html.

Cornelius, Wayne A. 1989. "Impacts of the 1986 US Immigration Law on Emigration from Rural Mexican Sending Communities," *Population and Development Review* 15, no. 4 (December): 689–705.

———. 2005. "Controlling 'Unwanted' Immigration: Lessons from the United States, 1993–2004," *Journal of Ethnic and Migration Studies* 31, no. 4: 775–94.

Department of Homeland Security. 2008. "DHS History: Who Became Part of the Department?" April 11, http://www.dhs.gov/xabout/history/editorial_0133.shtm.

Federal Register. 2008. "The Federal Register Online," November 14, FR Doc E8-26904, http://edocket.access.gpo.gov/2008/E8-26904.htm.

Fuentes, Jezmín, and Olivia García. 2009. "*Coyotaje:* The Structure and Functioning of the People-Smuggling Industry." In *Four Generations of Norteños: New Research from the Cradle of Mexican Migration,* ed. Wayne A. Cornelius, David Fitzgerald, and Scott Borger. La Jolla, CA: Center for Comparative Immigration Studies, University of California, San Diego.

GAO (U.S. Government Accountability Office). 2008. "U.S. GAO - Employment Verification: Challenges Exist in Implementing a Mandatory Electronic Employment Verification System," May 6, http://www.gao.gov/new.items/d08895t.pdf.

Gorman, A. 2008. "Escondido Tries to Rid Itself of Undocumented Immigrants," *Los Angeles Times*, July 13.

Heyman, J. M., and J. Ackleson. 2009. "U.S. Border Security after September 11." In *Border Security in the Al Qaeda Era*, ed. J. A. Winterdyk and K. W. Sundberg. London: Taylor and Francis.

Kimball, Ann, Yesenia Acosta, and Rebecca Dames. 2007. "Impacts of U.S. Immigration Policies on Migration Behavior." In *Mayan Journeys: The New Migration from Yucatán to the United States*, ed. Wayne A. Cornelius, David Fitzgerald, and Pedro Lewin Fischer. La Jolla, CA: Center for Comparative Immigration Studies, University of California, San Diego.

Leonard, A. B. 2009. "Feds Investigate Inglewood Police after Officer-involved Shootings," *Los Angeles Times*, March 13, http://www.calendarlive.com/tv/radio/la-me-inglewood-police13-2009mar13,0,4769291.story.

Lopez, Mark Hugo. 2009. "Hispanics and the Criminal Justice System: Low Confidence, High Exposure," Pew Research Center, http://www.pewhispanic.org/report.php?ReportID=106.

Meissner, Doris. 2006. "Immigration and America's Future: A New Chapter." Washington, DC: Migration Policy Institute.

Meissner, Doris, and Donald Kerwin. 2009. "DHS and Immigration: Taking Stock and Correcting Course," Migration Policy Institute, http://www.migrationpolicy.org/pubs/DHS_Feb09.pdf.

National Immigration Law Center. 2008. "Local Law Enforcement Issues," http://www.nilc.org/immlawpolicy/LocalLaw/locallaw-limiting-tbl-2008-12-03.pdf.

Pew Hispanic Center. 2009. "Pew Hispanic Center Research Topics: Demography," April 14, http://pewhispanic.org/files/factsheets/47.pdf.

Pham, Huyen. 2004. "The Inherent Flaws in the Inherent Authority Position: Why Inviting Local Enforcement of Immigration Laws Violates the Constitution," *Florida State University Law Review* 31: 965–1003.

Preston, Julia. 2007. "Judge Voids Ordinance on Illegal Immigrants," *New York Times*, July 27.

———. 2009. "Obama to Push Immigration Bill as One Priority," *New York Times*, April 8.

Reyes, Belinda, Hans P. Johnson, and Richard Van Swearingen. 2002. *Holding the Line? The Effect of Recent Border Build-up on Unauthorized Migration*. San Francisco, CA: Public Policy Institute of California.

Rotstein, Arthur H. 2009. "Border Deaths Up despite Apparent Dip in Crossings," Associated Press, April 8.

Sisco, Jessica, and Jonathan Hicken. 2009. "Is U.S. Border Enforcement Working?" In *Four Generations of Norteños: New Research from the Cradle of Mexican Migration*, ed. Wayne A. Cornelius, David Fitzgerald, and Scott Borger. La Jolla, CA: Center for Comparative Immigration Studies, University of California, San Diego.

Thompson, G. 2009. "Immigration Agents to Turn Their Focus to Employers," *New York Times*, April 30.

Tichenor, D. J. 1994. "The Politics of Immigration Reform in the United States, 1981–1990," *Polity* 26, no. 3: 337–38.

U.S. Citizenship and Immigration Services. 2009. "USCIS - Applicability Date for E-Verify Federal Contractor Rule Extended," http://www.uscis.gov/portal/site/uscis/menuitem.5af9bb95919f35e66f614176543f6d1a/?vgnextoid=f2ae9d63361b0210VgnVCM1000004718190aRCRD&vgnextchannel=75bce2e261405110VgnVCM1000004718190aRCRD.

U.S. Immigration and Customs Enforcement. 2008. "Delegation of Immigration Authority Section 287(g), Immigration and Nationality Act," August 18, http://www.ice.gov/partners/287g/Section287_g.htm.

Varsanyi, Monica W., ed. 2010. *State and Local Immigration Policy Activism in the U.S.: Interdisciplinary Perspectives*. Stanford and La Jolla, CA: Stanford University Press and Center for Comparative Immigration Studies, University of California, San Diego. Forthcoming.

Weeks, John R. 2009. "Who's Crossing the Border: New Data on Undocumented Immigrants to the United States," *Population, Space and Place*, May 6, pp. 1–25.

Zito, K. 2009. "Pelosi: End Raids Splitting Immigrant Families," *San Francisco Chronicle*, March 8.

A triple-fenced section of the border, in Cañón Los Laureles near Tijuana.
Photograph by María Teresa Fernández

4 Economic Crisis vs. Border Enforcement: What Matters Most to Prospective Migrants?

Scott Borger and Leah Muse-Orlinoff

One of the most notable differences between the field research conducted in Tunkás by the MMFRP in 2006 and in 2009 is the decrease in economically active Tunkaseños who reported that they planned to migrate to the United States in the next twelve months. While 30 percent of respondents in 2006 indicated that they intended to migrate to the United States in the coming year, that percentage fell to 11 percent of economically active respondents in 2009.[1]

As preceding chapters have demonstrated, the two biggest structural changes in the intervening years between the 2006 field research and the 2009 project were changes in U.S. migration policy—specifically, more aggressive border controls and increased domestic enforcement measures—and the contraction of the U.S. job market. Tunkaseños considering migration to the United States are taking both of these potential deterrents into consideration.

For example, increased vigilance on the border has pushed clandestine migrants to more dangerous crossing points, and deaths along the border continue to be all too common, as the case of María de los Ángeles Manzanero, presented in chapter 3, demonstrates. María, an experienced Tunkaseña migrant, died of hypothermia in the mountains of San Diego County during a clandestine crossing in 2007. We found that 44 percent of Tunkaseños knew of her death or a death resulting from some other border-crossing attempt, and many indicated that the physical dangers of the border crossing were among the most worrisome aspects of a clandestine entry to the United States. To mitigate the dangers of crossing and

---

1. The set of economically active respondents includes individuals between the ages of eighteen and forty who are currently receiving some kind of paid salary; it therefore excludes housewives and subsistence farmers.

to increase the chances of a successful entry to the United States, nearly all migrants from Tunkás hire a *pollero*, or people-smuggler (sometimes known as a *coyote*). The cost to hire a *pollero* increased dramatically from 1994 to 2009 and is now close to US$3,000. However, as previous MMFRP research indicates, migrants who cross with a *pollero* are almost universally successful at gaining entry to the United States (Martell, Pineda, and Tapia 2007; Sisco and Hicken 2009; Parks, Lozada, Mendoza, and García Santos 2009).

It is in the costs and logistics of hiring a *pollero* that we begin to perceive the interaction between economic conditions in the United States, border enforcement, and the possibility of migrating from Tunkás to the United States. A reduction in the number of jobs available to migrants naturally exerts its own deterrent effect, but labor market conditions in the United States also negatively affect the ability of Mexico-based potential migrants to undertake the expensive and risky journey in other ways. For instance, MMFRP data demonstrate that the vast majority of potential migrants finance their clandestine border crossings with monetary assistance from U.S.-based relatives and friends: 71 percent of Tunkaseño migrants reported that, on their most recent trip to the United States, a U.S.-based friend or relative provided all or part of the money they needed to travel from Tunkás to the border, hire a *pollero*, and support themselves until they found a job. As the U.S. labor market shrinks and settled migrants lose their jobs or worry about doing so, U.S.-based Tunkaseños become reluctant to advance the thousands of dollars needed to support the migration of their kin. As a consequence, even motivated potential migrants have a difficult time obtaining the capital necessary to migrate.

Given the clear interaction between the effects of migration policy and changes in the U.S. economy during 2008, one of our central tasks is to disentangle the relative importance of migration policy enforcement and the U.S. economic downturn as deterrents to clandestine migration. In other words, can the decline in the percentage of Tunkaseños who currently intend to migrate be better explained by reduced job prospects in the United States or by fear of border and interior enforcement efforts?

In this analysis, we test whether the decline in the pool of potential migrants planning to migrate from Mexico to the United States in the following calendar year is more strongly connected to increases in border enforcement or to the deterioration of the U.S. economy. In other words, were potential migrants more worried about getting caught on the border or about not being able to find a job in the United States once they crossed?

CROSS-SECTION TIME-SERIES MODEL

As noted in the introductory chapter, MMFRP communities are surveyed every few years, and this long-term data collection strategy allows for comparison across time. The models discussed in this chapter draw on data collected in Mexican migrant-sending communities in 2006, 2007, 2008, and 2009. This time line provides us with data on intentions to migrate during a period when the U.S. economy was expanding and showing strong growth in the housing, construction, and service sectors, as well as data on migration plans in a period when the United States was in a period of economic contraction.

Using dummy variables for the year of the survey, we compare reported migration plans from 2006 and 2009 to ascertain whether the changes in the U.S. economy had a deterrent effect independent of the changes in border enforcement policy. In other words, we control for changes in perception about border enforcement to determine whether the deterioration in the economy has contributed to the migration decisions of potential migrants.

We find that the number of respondents who planned to migrate to the United States dropped every year between 2006 and 2008.[2] Indeed, Model 1 shows that in 2008, potential migrants were 54 percent less likely than their counterparts in 2006 to respond that they intended to migrate to the United States in the next twelve months (table 4.1). By 2009, potential migrants were more than two times less likely to have plans to migrate in the coming calendar year than in 2006. Though this result suggests that economic conditions were a primary factor behind the decline in plans to migrate, stepped-up border enforcement policy during this period also

---

2. The analysis controls for basic demographic and social characteristics that have been demonstrated previously to contribute to a person's likelihood of migrating internationally. These control variables are gender, age, marital status, level of education, and number of relatives living in the United States prior to one's first migration. See chapter 1 for a more detailed description of the sociodemographic characteristics of Tunkaseño migrants.

could have discouraged people from migrating. To determine the effect of changes in border enforcement policies on plans to migrate, we include data about whether respondents thought that crossing the border without documentation was difficult and dangerous and whether they knew someone who had perished while trying to cross the border. As shown in Model 2, the decline in intention to migrate remains, strongly suggesting that even experienced and knowledgeable migrants are now reluctant to cross clandestinely.

Table 4.1. Logit Models: Intention to Migrate over Time

	Model 1 β	Model 2 β
Year 2009	−1.145*** (.177)	−1.230*** (.196)
Year 2008	−.432** (.174)	−.445** (.189)
Year 2007	−.136 (.169)	−.384 (.219)
Difficult to cross border		−.156 (.149)
Dangerous to cross border		.062 (.231)
Knows of a death of someone attempting to cross		.419** (.153)
Male	.264** (.130)	.258 (.137)
Age	−.022*** (.006)	−.024*** (.006)
Married	−.318** (.139)	−.293** (.146)
Education	−.007 (.016)	−.012 (.017)
Legal status	1.206*** (.196)	1.186*** (.202)
Network	.063*** (.019)	.068*** (.020)
Migrant	.999*** (.149)	1.022*** (.149)
Constant	−.810*** (.287)	−.771** (.351)
N	2,437	2,264
Pseudo R²	.136	.140

** 95 percent, *** 99 percent confidence levels. Robust standard errors in parentheses.

Independent Variables

Difficult is a dummy variable that equals 1 if the interviewee responded that it was difficult to evade the Border Patrol and equals 0 if the response was that it was easy. Death is a dummy variable equal to 1 if the respondent knew someone who had died trying to cross the border and 0 if the respondent did not know someone who had died.

Demographic and Control Variables

Male is a dummy variable, with male equal to 1. Age is the respondent's current age. Married is a dummy variable, with married equal to 1 and not married equal to 0. Education is the respondent's years of schooling; and Legal is a dummy variable set at 1 if the respondent reported having a permanent resident permit or citizenship in the United States and 0 if the respondent reported being undocumented. Network is the number of family members already in the United States. Migrant is a dummy variable set to 1 if the respondent has previous migration history and 0 if there is no international migration history.

Year Variables

The year variables are dummy variables for the year in which the survey was conducted and the year that migrants had no intention to migrate. The reference period is 2006. Figure 4.1 illustrates the response of intention to migrate over time relative to the 2006 reference period. The dashed lines are the 95 percent confidence bands, while the solid line is the estimated decrease in intention to migrate.

Figure 4.1 depicts a slight decline in plans to migrate (relative to intention in 2006) between 2007 and 2008, and a much more marked decrease between 2008 and 2009. This sharp drop-off coincides with the contraction of the U.S. economy and job market during 2008, suggesting that the lower probability of finding work in the United States was, indeed, a strong disincentive to migrate for many Tunkaseños. However, this analysis does not confirm whether changes in the economy provide the principal explanation for the reduction in planned migration, or whether the heightened immigration enforcement initiatives put in place at the end of the George W. Bush administration were the stronger deterrent.

Figure 4.1. Logit Model Estimates of Intention to Migrate Relative to 2006

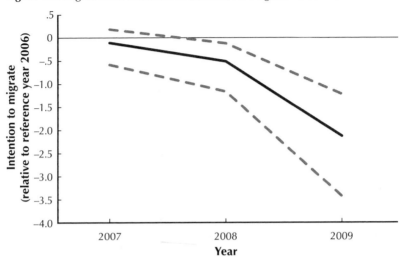

DIFFERENCE-IN-DIFFERENCE MODEL

To delve deeper into the relative importance of border enforcement and economic deterrents for intention to migrate, we employed a difference-in-difference approach. In both 2006 and 2009 we surveyed the same migrant-sending community—Tunkás. However, the economic climate in the United States was markedly different in 2006 and 2009. By surveying the same community in such different economic contexts, we can control for specific migration-related effects that are idiosyncratic to Tunkás. Moreover, this model uses a control group—documented migrants—that would not be affected by changes in border enforcement in order to ascertain whether the economy or border enforcement has a stronger effect on the likelihood of a potential migrant's intention to migrate in the following calendar year.

In Model 3, the control group is documented migrants. Tunkás-based migrants with documentation to legally enter the United States would not be affected by changes in border enforcement policy, so β_3, the documented-year09 interaction effect, would be negative (table 4.2). This effect controls for the fact that potential migrants are less likely to migrate in 2009 and that documented migrants are more likely than undocumented migrants to intend to migrate in any given year. If, controlling for these effects, documented migrants were also less likely to plan to migrate to the United States in 2009 than in previous years, then it could be argued that the decline in the U.S. economy is the most compelling explanation for the decrease in intention to migrate since 2006.

$$\text{Intent} = \beta_0 + \beta_1 \, {}^*\text{year09} + \beta_2 \, {}^*\text{documented} + \beta_3 \, {}^*(\text{documented}{}^*\text{year09}) + \beta_4 \, {}^*X + e$$

where β_4 is a vector of coefficients and X is a matrix of other factors that contribute to a person's intent to migrate.

Table 4.2. Difference-in-Difference: Effect of Economy or Border Enforcement

	Model 3 β
Year 2009	**−1.181***** (.202)
Legal	**1.491***** (.473)
Year09*legal	−.330 (.766)
Male	.302 (.215)
Age	**−.030***** (.009)
Married	−.297 (.217)
Education	.017 (.023)
Legal	**1.206***** (.196)
Network	**.189***** (.072)
Migrant	**1.096***** (.238)
Constant	**−.862**** (.389)
N	1289
Pseudo R^2	.174

** 95 percent, *** 99 percent confidence levels. Robust standard errors in parentheses.

Though the difference is not statistically significant, we find that legal migrants are indeed less likely to plan to migrate this year than previously. However, the results are statistically inconclusive on whether the current economic situation—even more than the increase in border enforcement—is substantially reducing the cohort of Mexican migrants with plans to migrate to the United States in the coming twelve months. One explanation for the statistically inconclusive result is the relatively low number of documented migrants in the international migration flow from this particular sending community, which is only in its first generation of migration to the United States.

Future MMFRP research in more mature communities of emigration, with a larger documented migrant population, will increase the precision of the estimates. In the meantime, it is evident that changes in the U.S. economy and the multiple interactions between labor market contexts, border enforcement policies, and the costs, both financial and physical, of clandestine border crossing are working in tandem to discourage migration from Tunkás to the United States. Even so, new unauthorized migrants continue to leave the town, albeit in smaller numbers than in the first half of this decade. And if history is any guide, as soon as the U.S. job market recovers and the demand for cheap labor from Mexico rebounds, more people from Tunkás and thousands of other migrant-sending communities in Mexico will make the perilous trek northward.

REFERENCES

Martell, Alpha, Maribel Pineda, and Luis Tapia. 2007. "The Contemporary Migration Process." In *Mayan Journeys: The New Migration from Yucatán to the United States*, ed. Wayne A. Cornelius, David Fitzgerald, and Pedro Lewin Fischer. La Jolla, CA: Center for Comparative Immigration Studies, University of California, San Diego.

Parks, Kristin, Gabriel Lozada, Miguel Mendoza, and Lizbeth García Santos. 2009. "Strategies for Success: Border Crossing in an Era of Heightened Security." In *Migration from the Mexican Mixteca: A Transnational Community in Oaxaca and California*, ed. Wayne A. Cornelius, David Fitzgerald, Jorge Hernández-Díaz, and Scott Borger. La Jolla, CA: Center for Comparative Immigration Studies, University of California, San Diego.

Sisco, Jessica, and Jonathan Hicken. 2009. "Is U.S. Border Enforcement Working?" In *Four Generations of Norteños: New Research from the Cradle of Mexican Migration*, ed. Wayne A. Cornelius, David Fitzgerald, and Scott Borger. La Jolla, CA: Center for Comparative Immigration Studies, University of California, San Diego.

A Tunkaseño works his parcel of land on the outskirts of the town.

5 Inhabiting Two Worlds: Tunkaseños in the Transnational Labor Market

MICAH GELL-REDMAN, ELÍ ANDRADE, ALPHA MARTELL, AND
ZOILA JIMÉNEZ PACHECO

On a bright Sunday morning in Inglewood, California, a steady stream
of cars pulled into the Rosewood car wash, where a group of mostly Yucatecan migrants were already mopping their brows as they hand-dried
minivans. Don Gerónimo, a Yucateco migrant who rose to the position
of manager after years of washing cars, surveyed the workers bustling
among the dripping vehicles. As the men bent over windshields and
crouched to shine tires, this quintessentially modern occupation recalled
the age-old labor of sowing and harvesting which most of them had left
behind in their home villages.

One of the workers, Pedro, left Tunkás for Inglewood at the age of
sixteen. He was happy with his job at Rosewood, where the boss had
not asked for any identification when he hired Pedro and the authorities
had never come to round up undocumented workers. In exchange for
relatively safe anonymity, Pedro spends hours on the hot asphalt without
allotted break times and often earning US$5 an hour, including tips—far
less than California's minimum wage. In the shadow economy of migrant
labor, Pedro belongs to two different worlds.

In one world, his wages and working conditions are substandard by
any measure. In the other, his source of income far outstrips opportunities
available in the urban centers and tourist destinations of southern Mexico,
and his earnings dwarf what he could make in Tunkás. This dramatic difference in earning potential—through more abundant job opportunities
and higher wages—is a powerful magnet attracting any worker who is
willing and able to risk crossing the border. But the "jobs magnet" does
not act in a vacuum. Existing laws and changing political imperatives for

immigration enforcement determine when firms can hire migrants. Further, migrants' own views of the rights available to them on the job may affect their working conditions.

In this chapter, we explore the forces and institutions that make up the transnational labor market. We first examine the wage-earning opportunities available to Tunkaseños in their home village of Tunkás, in the surrounding region, and in the Southern California communities to which they have migrated. Second, we investigate how the transnational labor market rewards Tunkaseños who accumulate human capital in the form of education, skills, and experience. Third, we ask what Tunkaseños can tell us about the role of labor rights in shaping the market for migrant labor in the United States. Finally, we discuss the policy tools available to the U.S. government for regulating this labor market and consider how these enforcement policies are changing.

THE LABOR MARKET IN SOUTHERN MEXICO AND TUNKÁS

In recent decades the labor market of the Yucatán Peninsula has been dramatically transformed as workers have steadily exited the agricultural sector for jobs in the service and industrial sectors in urban centers. This section describes the contemporary labor market for Tunkaseños in southern Mexico, that is, the opportunities for wage labor and subsistence available to Tunkaseños in their hometown and nearby cities. As we shall see, the overall pattern is one of strategic adaptation to changing labor market conditions, with families drawing from a portfolio of strategies to make ends meet.

The production of henequen, a fibrous plant used to make rope, was long the dominant economic activity in the Yucatán, and local indigenous populations labored as peons on henequen plantations until the plantation lands were seized for redistribution to the peasantry following the Mexican Revolution. In the 1970s, henequen production entered a steady and dramatic decline, forcing many small growers and laborers into agricultural activities that are no longer competitive in a "globalized" market (Castilla Ramos and Torres Góngora 2007). The net effect has been a steady exodus from agriculture. For Yucatán, the proportion of the economically active population working in agriculture dropped from 26 percent in 1995 to 11 percent in 2005 (INEGI 1995, 2008).

At the same time that agricultural work was becoming less attractive, growth in the industrial and service sectors was turning a few urban centers into regional job magnets. Beginning in 1972, the state government of Yucatán began to invest in *maquiladoras*[1] using predominantly low-skilled female labor. By 2000, there were 126 such plants in the state, most in the capital city, Mérida, and they were employing more than 5 percent of the state's workers (Castilla Ramos and Torres Góngora 2007). While the *maquiladora* sector has since diminished in importance, manufacturing has come to dominate the Yucatán economy, employing more than seven in ten of the state's workers. By contrast, the neighboring state of Quintana Roo is home to major international tourism destinations, including Cancún, Mexico's top tourist draw, and its economic activity is highly concentrated in services.

These structural shifts in the regional labor market have shaped the opportunities available to Tunkaseños in at least three ways. First, as the MMFRP's 2006 study of Tunkás demonstrated, service sector jobs have been a prime training ground for Tunkaseño migrants aspiring to migrate abroad (Rodríguez, Wittlinger, and Manzanero Rodríguez 2007). Second, Tunkaseños have felt pressure from the decreasing competitiveness of agricultural production, though work in agriculture remains the town's primary economic activity. Third, growth in nearby urban centers has made it possible for an increasing number of Tunkaseños to access wage-earning opportunities beyond the local labor market without incurring the greater costs and risks of international migration.

The market for labor in Tunkás contrasts sharply with that of the Yucatán Peninsula overall. The Tunkás economy depends heavily on the agricultural sector, which employs 51 percent of the economically active men. Tunkás's service and construction sectors are relatively small, employing 20 and 12 percent, respectively, of economically active men. As the following discussion of alternative labor market strategies makes clear, the sharp difference in labor force participation rates among men and women—85 percent of men are economically active but only 25 percent of women are employed outside the home—is key to understanding how families organize economic activity (see figures 5.1 and 5.2).

---

1. *Maquiladoras* are industrial plants that import materials for manufacturing or assembly and then export the finished products, usually to the United States, with the importer being taxed only on the value added in Mexico.

Figure 5.1. Men's Occupations in Tunkás

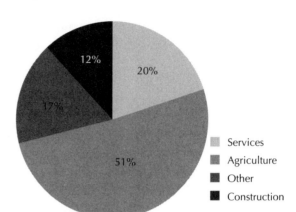

Figure 5.2. Women's Occupations in Tunkás

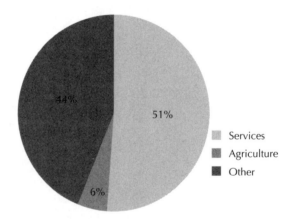

The percentages total more than 100 percent because of rounding.

The Precariousness of Agricultural Work

Agricultural employment in Yucatán, as in most of Mexico, is highly variable from year to year, as heavy rains and persistent droughts produce tremendously inconsistent crop yields. This section shows how Tunkaseños react to such instability in their household income. Most of their adaptive strategies occur in the local, agriculture-dominated labor market, but internal and international migration, driven by the search for higher wages, have become increasingly attractive options for Tunkaseños since the 1970s.

A Tunkaseño campesino's day begins early, often before sunrise, and ends around 3 in the afternoon, when he returns home for the *comida*. Men come home from the fields dressed in worn-out pants, T-shirts, *huaraches*, straw hats, and carrying machetes. Tunkaseños working in agriculture perform three main activities: apiculture (beekeeping), livestock raising, and corn production. Apiculture holds a special place in Tunkás's economy, and honey production has been an important source of income in the town since the 1960s. Yet beginning in the early 2000s, a combination of factors—a parasitic infection in the bee colonies that is expensive to treat, the invasion of Africanized bees, and climate change—has made beekeeping less profitable. In late 2008, honey production was threatened further when a sustained drought prevented the bees' favorite flowers from blooming, and an unseasonably cold winter kept the bees in their hives rather than collecting pollen. Beekeepers in Tunkás had to feed their bees expensive sugar water to keep them alive. This combination of reduced honey output and increased expenses forced Tunkaseño beekeepers to seek other sources of income. Manuel, a 54-year-old Tunkaseño apiculturist who learned bee care from his father, told us that he grows corn and raises cattle in addition to maintaining his thirty hives:

> If we had only one source of income, that would be a big problem because no matter how hard you work the land, if the land doesn't yield enough you have to look for something else to do in the meantime. And if this other thing doesn't work out either, then you have to look for yet one more thing to do. That way, earning a little from one activity, a little from another and another, you can survive, earning a living for your wife and children.

Yet sowing crops is hardly a guarantee against deprivation, and the combination of unpredictable weather and a lack of infrastructure makes corn cultivation a particularly precarious livelihood. In 2008, severe drought ravaged the cornfields. Nearly half of Tunkaseño farmers lost their crop, and eight of ten reported losing at least part. Anecdotal

A Tunkaseño grandmother of four weaves hammocks to supplement her household income.

evidence from our field survey suggests that this unexpected shortfall caused many campesinos to use what little they could harvest to feed their families; 64 percent adopted this pure-subsistence strategy. Though we cannot be certain how many of these agriculturalists would have sold surpluses in better years, we do know that their families were in an economically vulnerable position.

In response to such vulnerability, Tunkaseños often adopt informal strategies to generate income. These activities are mostly home-based and include raising turkeys and chickens for sale, weaving hammocks, selling home-prepared food, and performing domestic tasks for other households. In contrast to agricultural work, many of these informal income-generating activities place housewives at the center of the family's economic activity. Of the 70 percent of women in Tunkás who are primarily homemakers, many are active in the informal economy. Conrada, the wife of a campesino, described herself as a homemaker who spends her days taking care of household chores, cleaning the garden, and feeding the animals. But she also weaves hammocks, which her daughter takes to a reseller in Playa del Carmen:

Right now I get paid 20 pesos for each tube of thread I weave.
If I weave eight tubes, I make 160 pesos. If you can dedicate
sufficient time to it, you can finish a hammock in fifteen days.
But it's really tiring. I have to lean over and weave, weave,
weave. My eyes get tired, too. It's a lot of work for very little
pay. But how can I say no, if that's all there is to do?

Like many Tunkaseños, Conrada chooses to weave hammocks because
the town's formal labor market provides no viable options to remedy her
family's economic precariousness.

When a combination of agricultural production and informal, home-
based economic activity is not enough, many Tunkaseños look for labor
market opportunities in other parts of the Yucatán Peninsula. The tourist belt of Quintana Roo, as well as Yucatán's state capital, Mérida, offer
wages that attract Tunkaseño workers into the service and construction
sectors (see figures 5.3 and 5.4). For Tunkaseños, the possibility of traveling just two hours and more than doubling the wage they would earn in
Tunkás is obviously compelling. Samuel, an eighteen-year-old Tunkaseño
who learned basic construction skills from his father, found commuting
to Playa del Carmen preferable to remaining in Tunkás, where opportunities were scarce, and preferable to international migration, with its
associated risks.

Figure 5.3. Men's Occupations in Other Parts of Mexico

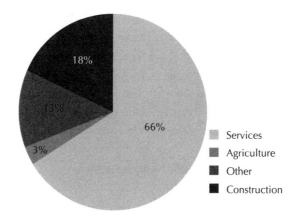

Figure 5.4. Women's Occupations in Other Parts of Mexico

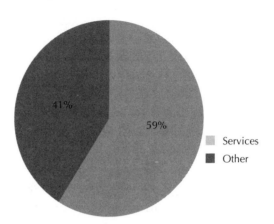

In addition to helping their families in Tunkás, internal migrants are able to develop their human capital in ways rarely available to those who remain home. Migrants gain experience and skills that expand their earning potential and put them on a different trajectory than their more stationary counterparts. Josué, who grew up working the fields with his father in Tunkás, was able to find steady work in the construction industry in Mérida. The cousin who helped him find the job also gave him a place to stay while away from home. Josué was later able to exploit the construction skills he developed in Mérida in Santa Ana, California.

THE LABOR MARKET FOR TUNKASEÑOS IN SOUTHERN CALIFORNIA

Between 1942 and 1964, much of the northward flow of Mexican migrants was channeled through the Bracero program, created to satisfy the labor needs of the U.S. agricultural industry (Calavita 1992). Government officials on both sides of the border ultimately bowed to the objections of U.S. organized labor and discontinued the program, but this simply shifted Mexican labor migration to unauthorized entry, a pattern that has persisted despite increased border enforcement (Martin 2004). The practical outcome of this political process is a transnational labor market that cannot be perfectly regulated by the United States or Mexico but that has diverse and important consequences for each nation.

The presence of Mexican migrants in the U.S. labor force has expanded steadily during the past three decades despite a vigorous ongoing debate over the impacts on the employment and wages of "native" workers (see Borjas 2003; Raphael and Ronconi 2007). By 2007, Mexican migrants alone made up almost 17 percent of workers in U.S. agriculture and 12 percent of workers in the construction industry (Pew Hispanic Center 2009a). In California, where most Tunkás migrants have settled, foreign-born Hispanics accounted for more than four of every ten construction workers in 2007 (Pew Hispanic Center 2009b).

As Tunkás becomes a more mature community of migration, a clearer picture is emerging of how Tunkaseños are incorporated into the U.S. labor market. The dominance of the service sector is unmistakable, but this masks a diversity of occupations within that sector. Tunkaseño migrants in service occupations work in car washes; bus tables, prepare meals, and wash dishes in restaurants; handle medical and financial records; and clean homes, offices, and amusement park rides. The difference in labor force participation by gender is striking. Just under 7 percent of male Tunkaseño migrants living in the United States are economically inactive, compared to nearly 63 percent of women.

What is the typical work environment for Tunkaseños in Southern California? Most (51 percent) are in workplaces where the boss speaks some Spanish, and a number of our interviewees were employed by fellow Yucateco migrants. Data from our qualitative interviews indicate that employment by "co-ethnics" can sometimes mean a more exploitative work environment. One employer told us explicitly that he hires Yucatecos because they are docile and easier to handle: "In this neighborhood, the customers sometimes insult my workers, but to avoid problems, the workers don't answer back." We do not have specific data on unionization in our interviewees' current places of employment, but 7 percent reported having been members of a labor union in the United States at some point—significantly lower than the overall rate of union membership for the metropolitan area that includes Los Angeles and Orange counties (17 percent) (Milkman and Kye 2008).

The most striking aspect of the typical Tunkaseño participant in the Southern California labor market is his or her precarious position within it. As reported in chapter 2 of this volume, more than 50 percent of Tunkaseño workers had their work hours reduced in the twelve months preceding our interviews, and many had been forced to pursue compensating strategies in the labor market. When one respondent was told by a car wash manager that no work was available, he offered to work for tips alone, a desperate strategy described in one word, *propinar*. In other cases, Tunkaseños' responses have been more contentious. For example, Ramón, who has worked in hotel kitchens for over two decades, participated in numerous demonstrations in 2008 protesting his employer's unwillingness to negotiate with union representatives over pay freezes and cutbacks in hours.

Nearly a third (31 percent) of our interviewees had changed jobs at least once between 2006 and 2008, often moving quickly within and between sectors. This tendency to switch occupations precipitously highlights a key ambiguity in the migrant labor market. Immigrant workers' position in the labor market is often precarious in the sense that it does not remain stable over time, but this very instability may allow them to adapt more quickly than their native counterparts to fluctuations in the business cycle.[2] The following profiles illustrate several of these adaptive strategies among U.S.-based Tunkaseños.

Some U.S.-based Tunkaseños have responded to pressures in the labor market by transitioning to different occupational sectors. When Mauricio was laid off from the factory job he had held for more than a decade, a month passed before a Tunkaseño friend found him a job in the kitchen of a sushi restaurant. In other cases, Tunkaseños moved from job to job within the same sector. In just three years, Yovany had bused tables and washed dishes in four different restaurants though his pay, benefits, and level of training had remained unchanged. Alicia, a 55-year-old Tunkaseña migrant, had never been active in the formal labor market in Tunkás, though in addition to raising her children she had always woven hammocks to supplement the family's income. When Alicia migrated to Southern California with her family, gender roles shifted quickly and she began working outside the home at her husband's request:

> Making flowers was my first job in Fullerton. Later I became the nanny for my grandchildren, five days a week,

---

2. See Papademetriou and Terrazas 2009 and Alarcón et al. 2008 for a discussion of this feature of the migrant labor market.

> eight hours a day. My daughter-in-law actually paid me.
> Two years later I got a work permit thanks to the fact that
> my husband got a green card.[3]

Since obtaining legal status, Alicia has worked nights in a food products factory, preparing and packaging crackers and pizza for $11.95 an hour. She works the graveyard shift from 7:30 p.m. to 6:00 a.m. so that she can spend days with her family.

Laura's family was well established economically in Tunkás, where she retains part ownership of a butcher shop and six taxis. Nevertheless, she left her homes in Mérida and Cancún behind to migrate to Anaheim after her husband died in a workplace accident in Mexico.[4] She first crossed the border in 1997 with a tourist visa, and through ties of friendship and family she landed a job as a janitor at Disneyland. Laura's story is atypical in that she moved quickly to more highly skilled work. Her educational background and business experience allowed her to find and keep work managing financial records. But her work life has been typical in its precariousness. When she found she could not work full-time and also care for her grandchildren, she quit her job and began preparing Yucatecan regional cuisine in her home kitchen to sell to friends and neighbors.

Olivia, a pioneer Tunkaseña migrant to the United States who has been living in Anaheim since the mid-1970s, manages an apartment complex that is home primarily to other Tunkaseño migrants. As the complex's manager and one of the Tunkaseño community's most well-connected members, Olivia has taught many newly arriving migrants to navigate an unfamiliar and often difficult environment, and she has also helped aspiring migrants make the connections required to cross the border. She plays a pivotal role in Tunkasenos' labor market insertion in the United States. At the same time, however, Olivia is also a long-term U.S.-based worker who has moved between the formal and informal economies. Though she worked at a factory for many years and currently manages the apartment complex, she also sells food to Tunkaseños and other Yucatecos in her house on weekends.

---

3. Heriberto obtained his green card through one of the legalization programs contained in the Immigration Reform and Control Act of 1986.
4. Laura's husband was a member of the Mexican railroad workers union, which pays her a monthly widow's pension.

The stories of Olivia and Laura highlight the central role that migrants' social networks play in labor market incorporation (Cornelius 1989). In fact, over 60 percent of our U.S.-based respondents found their most recent job through the recommendation of a friend or family member. These two women in particular have accumulated a form of social capital—connections to others in and around the U.S.-based Tunkaseño community—that allows them to access opportunities that would not otherwise exist, while in turn providing opportunities for others. As Olivia's daughter pointed out, "When my mother arrived in the 1970s, there was no *paisano* to help her…. Now she is the one who has helped most of the Tunkaseños who live here." Olivia's ability and willingness to connect job seekers with employers, and her role in generating new international migration from Tunkás, give her a pivotal function in the transnational Tunkás–Southern California labor market.

As Tunkaseño migrants are incorporated into the formal labor market, they learn how labor rights are defined in U.S. workplaces, and some have come in contact with serious labor-organizing efforts. Ramón, the longtime restaurant worker described above, has played a key role in unionization drives at two Anaheim restaurants where he has worked. At his current workplace, a restaurant in a major theme park, contract negotiations have essentially stagnated, leading to protests and the threat of work stoppages. Mauro, who also has decades of experience in the hospitality industry, reported that having a union contract at the hotel where he works in Santa Monica served as a buffer against the worst effects of the recent economic downturn. The stories of Ramón and Mauro contrast sharply with the experiences of many Tunkaseño migrants who work in car washes, where even the most basic protections, including the minimum wage, often do not apply (Cathcart 2009).

Human Capital in the Migrant Labor Market

When Tunkaseños migrate to Southern California, they encounter a labor market that depends heavily on social connections, requires migrants to be flexible, and transmits mixed messages about rights in the workplace. In this section we expand on the qualitative evidence presented above, drawing on our survey interviews with Tunkaseños on both sides of the border. We first consider the returns to an individual's investment in human capital—that is, whether the education, experience, and skills that

Tunkaseños bring to the labor market influence the wages they earn on both sides of the border. Second, we examine how the experience of international migration changes Tunkaseños' views of labor rights.

As the results in table 5.1 demonstrate, higher levels of education and more work experience in both Mexico and the United States are significantly correlated with higher wages: more educated and more experienced Tunkaseños earn more. This relationship holds when we control for the effects of the respondent being employed in the lowest-paying sector (agriculture), working part-time, and benefiting from a pro-male gender bias in compensation. Our only measure of skills independent of work experience is the respondent's ability to speak English, which is not significantly correlated with earnings when we include all respondents reporting wages in the analysis. But rather than concluding that English skills have no effect on earnings, we hypothesize that such skills are likely to be more or less valuable depending on sector and location. For example, while Artemio used his English skills regularly as a gregarious chef at a Cancún hotel popular with U.S. tourists, all of the chefs, busboys, and dishwashers in the restaurant where he now works in Inglewood, California, are monolingual Spanish speakers.

What can we infer from our finding that more highly educated and more experienced Tunkaseños earn higher wages? The standard interpretation would be that, holding all else constant, each additional year of schooling and experience will yield a concomitant increase in wages.[5] Of course, in the real world one cannot hold all else constant. Thus a more appropriate interpretation would be that those Tunkaseños with higher levels of education and experience have a variety of characteristics that make their labor more valuable to employers.[6]

The second question we explored in our survey interviews relates to labor rights and protections, a topic that goes to the heart of public debate over immigration policy. If employers who hire immigrants (especially the undocumented) derive an unfair competitive advantage from doing so, this creates an incentive to shift jobs away from native-born workers while denying migrants the capacity to protect themselves from exploitation in the workplace. In fact, recent legal scholarship has shown that

---

5. For a more detailed discussion of education and migration, see chapter 6.
6. See Cornelius, Tsuda, and Valdez 2003 for a comparative analysis of the influence of human capital on migrants' wages.

certain facets of U.S. law effectively prevent immigrant workers from seeking redress of grievances in the workplace (Lee 2009). One central but often overlooked aspect of migrants' workplace rights is the attitude of migrants themselves. We sought from both our U.S.- and Mexico-based interviewees their opinions about rights and protections in the workplace. We gave respondents examples of basic workplace rights (minimum wage, breaks, the right to organize) and asked if they thought those rights applied to documented and undocumented migrants in the United States. A large majority of both groups, 89 percent of migrants and 87 percent of nonmigrants, believed that immigrants with papers are entitled to basic rights in the workplace. On the question of labor rights for undocumented workers, both migrants and nonmigrants are far more skeptical, but the difference is significantly greater for nonmigrants. Specifically, 47 percent of those who have made at least one trip to the United States believe undocumented workers are not protected by labor rights, while 66 percent of those who have never crossed the border hold the same belief.[7]

Table 5.1. Effect of Human Capital on Log Earnings

Determinant	β
Years of education	**.062***** (.009)
Speaks English well or "a little"	.136 (.140)
Works in agricultural sector	**−.495***** (.090)
Male	**.462***** (.109)
Works fewer than 35 hours per week	**−.242***** (.087)
U.S.-based	**1.948***** (.113)
Work experience in Mexico	**.019***** (.007)
Work experience in U.S.	**.011**** (.005)
Constant	**3.126***** (.153)

$N = 451$. $R^2 = .6345$. ** $p = .01$; *** $p = .001$.
Standard errors in parentheses.

---

7. For our sample size and standard deviation, this difference in proportions is significant at the $p = .001$ level.

The multivariate logistic regression analysis reported in table 5.2 enables us to delve more deeply into Tunkaseños' views of the immigrant labor market. The dependent variable in this analysis is the respondent's attitude toward undocumented migrants' labor rights, that is, their answer to the question posed above. Those who have migrated to the United States are more likely to believe undocumented migrants have rights in the workplace, controlling for gender. Combining the respondent's own experience of a workplace raid with the knowledge of such raids through a friend or family member, we find that experience with, or knowledge of, raids does not make respondents significantly less likely to believe undocumented workers have labor rights. Further, migrants who have spent more time in the United States are more likely to believe labor rights are available to the undocumented.

Table 5.2. Determinants of Attitudes toward the Labor Rights of Undocumented Workers

Determinant	β
Cumulative experience in U.S.	**.053***** (.020)
Internal migrant	−.251 (.155)
International migrant	**.988***** (.225)
Male	.141 (.159)
Experienced worksite raid	−.154 (.194)
Constant	**−1.028***** (.121)

N = 914. Pseudo R^2 = .082.
Standard errors in parentheses.

To illuminate the logic behind this finding, consider what we know about Tunkaseños' attitudes toward the status of migrants generally. If undocumented migrants are forced to cross the border clandestinely at great peril, and if they are under threat from the authorities while engaged in everyday activities like grocery shopping or taking their children to school, it would be reasonable for anyone to assume no legal protections apply to them in the workplace. The change in attitudes comes from growing experience in, and knowledge of, the U.S. labor market, which may teach migrants that such protections do extend to undocumented workers despite the fact that a given employer may flout them.

THE CHANGING WORKSITE ENFORCEMENT REGIME IN THE UNITED STATES

Transnationally integrated labor markets are at the heart of the more general problem of immigration control in liberal democratic states (Cornelius and Tsuda 2004). The differences in labor market opportunities (wages and access to employment) between migrant-sending and migrant-receiving countries create incentives that make migration extremely beneficial for some actors, while those who do not benefit often find it difficult to coordinate their opposition. These contrasting positions correspond to two sets of factors that regularly prevent effective control of immigration: macro-structural factors and domestic political constraints.

Macro-structural factors refer to the incentives and institutions that have led many of the world's developed economies to depend on migrant labor and the ways in which this dependency has impinged on states' capacity to respond to public demand for more restrictive policies. In his study of U.S. agricultural firms employing migrant labor, Krissman (2000) concluded that it was only through a "labor system of not very benign neglect" that businesses were allowed to "maintain access to a low-cost immigrant workforce despite popular opinion or public policy." Cornelius (1998) found that, particularly in California, demand for foreign workers has become "structurally embedded," that is, rooted in the receiving country's economy and society in ways that are "largely impervious to the business cycle as well as government interventions."

Further, domestic political constraints make it "difficult to implement control measures effectively, particularly when special interest groups are able to capture policy making" (Cornelius and Tsuda 2004, 11). Special interest groups contesting immigration policies in the United States include employer groups, labor unions, immigrant advocates, and those who oppose immigration on national sovereignty grounds. Together, these form "densely organized webs of interest groups contesting policies," and the conflict and compromise between them influence the policy-making apparatus, the letter of the law, and enforcement practices (Freeman 1995).

This section explains how the political factors described above have influenced recent changes, both de facto and de jure, in the way the U.S. government regulates the migrant workforce and migrants' employers. The potential effects of some of these new initiatives remain unclear, and evidence from our field survey shows that some measures are likely to fall short of their stated aims.[8] An essential feature of the immigrant labor market is the extent to which employers are able to select workers on the basis of characteristics signaled by their citizenship status. This identification mechanism is a key reason why migrant workers, especially the undocumented, are selected into the lowest-paying jobs (Waldinger and Lichter 2003). The first step in understanding how U.S. worksite enforcement policy affects the labor market that Tunkaseños encounter in Southern California is to ask what tools exist for employers to identify workers' citizenship status. Intimately related to this first question, what rules actually prevent employers from hiring undocumented workers, and how effective are they?

It was not until 1986 that the federal government adopted policies designed expressly to penalize employers for hiring undocumented migrants. The Immigration Reform and Control Act (IRCA) enacted in that year fell short of requiring all workers to carry a national identification card, a provision viewed as potentially violating civil liberties (Gimpel and Edwards 1998, 162). Instead, the political compromise that produced the final bill instituted a system of employer sanctions centered on the I-9 form. Under this new sanctions regime, employers were required to record the identifying documents presented by job applicants on a form that could be audited, a measure some hoped would make hiring undocumented workers much harder and in turn weaken the jobs magnet (Fix 1991).

IRCA's first consequence was to produce a "widespread pattern of discrimination" among employers afraid of hiring anyone who appeared foreign-born (GAO 1990). Changes made to the law's implementation in its early phases reduced discrimination, but these had their own consequences. As Rolph and Robyn put it, checking documents specified by the Immigration and Naturalization Service gave employers "an affirmative

---

8. For a discussion of worksite enforcement in the context of interior enforcement of immigration laws more generally, see chapter 3.

defense against sanctions" (1991, 119). Compliance meant only that employers had to record whatever documentation workers presented them and were not compelled to verify the authenticity of these documents, so one can imagine a fully compliant employer with an entirely unauthorized workforce.

The logical response to this problem would be a nationwide, reliable, mandatory-use system for identifying workers' employment eligibility. In fact, such a system was proposed in the mid-1990s as part of a package of more stringent laws directed at immigrants living in the United States. The Basic Pilot Program provided an electronic system for using centralized government data sources to verify identity and authorization to work in the United States. The Basic Pilot has since been expanded, and during the 2006–2007 drive for comprehensive immigration reform legislation the Bush administration renamed the system E-Verify. Although worker verification is clearly an important part of effective worksite enforcement, questions remain as to the accuracy and fairness of the existing system, not to mention its potential effects on the macroeconomy were it to be applied to all workers (Rosenblum 2009).

More than twenty years after the first employer sanctions law was adopted and ten years after the first system of worker identification was implemented, our Tunkaseño survey respondents told us that it is still relatively easy for unauthorized workers to find employment in the United States. One-quarter of the U.S.-based respondents to our survey reported that their most recent U.S. employer requested no documentation at all, and nearly 40 percent believed their employer was sure they were unauthorized to work, regardless of the documents they presented (table 5.3). In addition, roughly 10 percent of Tunkaseños were required to give their employer only a Social Security number, with no other form of identification.

Worker identification remains a controversial plank of any comprehensive immigration reform proposal, in part because it is still a potential cause of discrimination on grounds of ethnicity and national origin. In its present state, E-Verify may falsely identify authorized workers as undocumented, and, independently, it may discourage employers from offering work to Hispanics and other ethnic minorities. A government report issued in 2008 revealed that in 7 percent of cases, the E-Verify system could not immediately identify a workers' status (GAO 2008). Increasing the number of entry visas for skilled and unskilled workers would likely decrease the demand for undocumented labor, but this faces strong opposition from some labor unions as well as social conservatives.

Table 5.3. Worksite Enforcement Data from U.S.-Based Tunkaseños

	Percent
Raid at most recent job	5.0
Family or friend caught in a raid	14.6
Boss threatens raid[a]	0.9
Boss requests no documentation	25.0
Boss "certain" of unauthorized status	39.8

[a] Derived from responses to the following question: "At your current workplace in the United States, has the boss ever threatened to report employees to immigration authorities?"

In the absence of a perfectly reliable, mandatory, uniformly enforced means for determining workers' legal status, it is not surprising that worksite enforcement has not significantly curtailed the practice of hiring undocumented workers. As late as 2005, the U.S. Government Accountability Office found that worksite enforcement was a "low priority" for the Department of Homeland Security (DHS), as evidenced by a decline in arrests of violators, employer fines collected, and man-hours dedicated to enforcement in the workplace (GAO 2005). By the end of 2006, however, the panorama had shifted. Having been rebuffed by Congress in its quest for comprehensive immigration reform, the Bush administration began a series of high-profile workplace raids, ostensibly to impress legislators with the consequences of their inaction.

Arrests of unauthorized workers by DHS agents increased threefold in 2006 and remained elevated for the duration of George W. Bush's term in office (figure 5.5). A substantial portion of these arrests resulted from high-profile raids of worksites employing many undocumented workers: 1,100 workers at the IFCO pallet supply company were detained in April 2006 (Lipton 2006); in December of that year 1,300 workers at Swift & Co. meat-packing plants were rounded up in coordinated raids across six states (Kammer 2009); and 400 workers at Agriprocessors were arrested in May 2008 (Preston 2008). While worksite raids have wide-ranging effects on local economies, communities, and migrant populations, here we consider their effect on the market for migrant labor generally and on Tunkaseño workers in particular.

Figure 5.5. Arrests of Unauthorized Workers

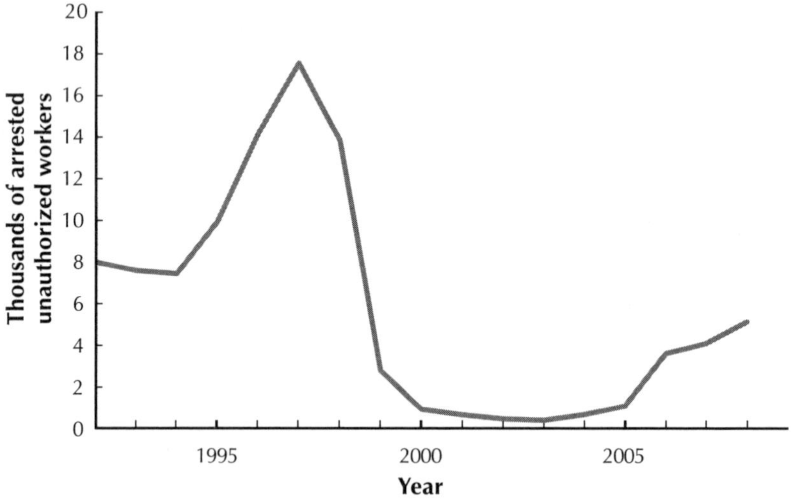

Source: Department of Homeland Security, Immigration and Customs Enforcement agency.

In a 2009 report on the Swift & Co. raids, the Center for Immigration Studies (CIS) argued that worksite raids had the potential to increase native workers' wages with minimal disruption to productive capacity (Kammer 2009). Before accepting the view of worksite arrests as a desirable enforcement tool, one should consider the following two flaws in CIS's analysis. First, the meat-packing plants in question do not have an unlimited source of potential labor, meaning that increased wages could be a short-term response to insufficient supply of labor rather than a long-term consequence of eliminating undocumented workers. Second, these plants were able to return to full productive capacity in part through the use of Somali refugees as replacement workers, a strategy with its own unintended consequences (Semple 2008). More generally, using worker arrests as a primary enforcement tool has troubling implications for rights in the workplace, especially if employers abide by the law inconsistently (see, for example, Greenhouse 2008).

Whatever one's opinion on the ethics of workplace raids as a primary enforcement tool, our survey suggests that the impact of raids on migrants' attitudes is minimal. Of those Tunkaseños who have experienced a workplace raid, 15 percent intended to migrate to the United States in 2009, compared to 9 percent who have not experienced a raid. Further, there is a negligible difference in perceptions of the current U.S. labor market between Tunkaseños who have experienced a raid (94 percent believe it is harder to find work in the United States now than one year ago) and those who have not (93 percent). Early indications from the Obama administration suggest a diminishing emphasis on enforcement, as DHS officials have pledged to focus on employers rather than workers in future raids (Thompson 2009), while the Supreme Court has reduced penalties for workers using fraudulent documents (Liptak and Preston 2009).

CONCLUSION

As we write this, leaders in the U.S. Congress are gearing up to propose new immigration reform legislation. If the public statements of interest groups are any indication, assumptions about how migrant flows influence the labor market and vice versa will be at the heart of the bill that legislators ultimately vote on. This chapter has shown that a focus on the far-reaching effects of the job magnet is well placed. A few observations about the transnational labor market derived from our field research provide further guidance.

The south of Mexico continues to emerge as a prime migrant-sending area, and policy makers would do well to bear in mind the precariousness that potential migrants face in communities like Tunkás. Approaches to immigration policy that ignore the lack of stable opportunities in the sending country are unlikely to succeed. Further, the inhabitants of rural communities like Tunkás view international migration as one option among many, and they will likely be responsive to the creation of new opportunities through intensification in agriculture or targeted development in nearby urban centers.

For those concerned primarily with the effects of migration on the U.S. labor market, our survey reinforces the well-established finding that migrants are responding to a structurally embedded demand for their labor. Tunkaseños are rewarded for investments in their own productive capacity, and we submit that the value of these investments, along with the increasing cost of migration, explain why the economic downturn has not provoked a flood of return migration to Mexico, as some expected. Where rights in the workplace are concerned, experience in the U.S. labor market teaches many Tunkaseños that rights are accessible to workers regardless of their legal status. Others, however, find themselves in environments where the most basic protections are not available.

Finally, our survey indicates that despite the intensity of the national-level debate over immigration policy since 2006, employers in a high-migrant-density area like Southern California have not significantly changed their hiring practices, often allowing migrants to obtain employment with little or no documentation. Given that any future comprehensive reform proposal is likely to include an electronic system of employment eligibility verification as the keystone of a new worksite enforcement regime, it is important to recognize that no identity verification system will be effective in those workplaces where no documentation changes hands in the first place.

REFERENCES

Alarcón, Rafael, Rodolfo Cruz, Alejandro Díaz-Bautista, Gabriel González-Konig, Antonio Izquierdo, Guillermo Yrizar, and René Zenteno. 2008. "La crisis financiera en los Estados Unidos y su impacto en la migración mexicana." Tijuana, Mexico: El Colegio de la Frontera Norte.

Borjas, George J. 2003. "The Labor Demand Curve *Is* Downward Sloping: Re-examining the Impact of Migration on the Labor Market," *Quarterly Journal of Economics* 118, no. 4 (November): 1335–74.

Calavita, Kitty. 1992. *Inside the State: The Bracero Program, Immigration, and the I.N.S.* New York: Routledge.

Castilla Ramos, Beatriz, and Beatriz Torres Góngora. 2007. "Hacia nuevas formas de organizar la IME de Yucatán: Análisis de dos empresas," *El Cotidiano: Revista de la Realidad Mexicana Actual* [Universidad Autónoma Metropolitana] 22, no. 142 (March–April): l.

Cathcart, Rebecca. 2009. "Carwashes Accused of Labor Violations," *New York Times*, February 10.

Cornelius, Wayne A. 1989. "The U.S. Demand for Mexican Labor." In *Mexican Migration to the United States: Origins, Consequences, and Policy Options*, ed. Wayne A. Cornelius and Jorge Bustamante. La Jolla, CA: Center for U.S.-Mexican Studies, University of California, San Diego.

————. 1998. "The Structural Embeddedness of Demand for Mexican Immigrant Labor: New Evidence from California." In *Crossings: Mexican Immigration in Interdisciplinary Perspectives*, ed. Marcelo Suárez-Orozco. Cambridge, MA: Harvard University Press.

Cornelius, Wayne A., and Takeyuki Tsuda. 2004. "Controlling Immigration: The Limits of Government Intervention." In *Controlling Immigration: A Global Perspective*, ed. Wayne A. Cornelius, Philip L. Martin, and James F. Hollifield. Stanford, CA: Stanford University Press.

Cornelius, Wayne A., Takeyuki Tsuda, and Zulema Valdez. 2003. "Human Capital versus Social Capital: A Comparative Analysis of Immigrant Wages and Labor Market Incorporation in Japan and the United States," *Migraciones Internacionales* 2, no. 1: 5–35.

Fix, Michael. 1991. "Employer Sanctions: An Unfinished Agenda." In *The Paper Curtain: Employer Sanctions' Implementation, Impact, and Reform*, ed. Michael Fix. Washington, DC: Urban Institute Press.

Freeman, Gary. 1995. "Modes of Immigration Politics in Liberal Democratic States," *International Migration Review* 29, no. 4: 881–913.

GAO (U.S. Government Accountability Office). 1990. "Immigration Reform: Employer Sanctions and the Question of Discrimination." Washington, DC: GAO.

————. 2005. "Immigration Enforcement: Weaknesses Hinder Employment Verification and Worksite Enforcement Efforts." Washington, DC: GAO.

————. 2008. "Employment Verification: Challenges Exist in Implementing a Mandatory Electronic Employment Verification System." Washington, DC: GAO.

Gimpel, James G., and James R. Edwards. 1998. *The Congressional Politics of Immigration Reform*. Boston, MA: Longman.

Greenhouse, Steven. 2008. "Meatpacker in Brooklyn Challenges a Union Vote," *New York Times*, September 1.

INEGI (Instituto Nacional de Estadística, Geografía e Informática). 1995. "Conteo de Población y Vivienda 1995," http://www.inegi.org.mx/inegi/default.aspx?s=inegi.

————. 2008. Encuesta Nacional de Ocupación y Empleo del Inegi, IV trimestre de 2008, http://www.inegi.org.mx/inegi/default.aspx?s=inegi.

Kammer, Jerry. 2009. *The 2006 Swift Raids: Assessing the Impact of Immigration Enforcement Actions at Six Facilities.* Washington, DC: Center for Immigration Studies.

Krissman, Fred. 2000. "Immigrant Labor Recruitment: U.S. Agribusiness and Undocumented Migration from Mexico." In *Immigration Research for a New Century: Multidisciplinary Perspectives*, ed. Nancy Foner, Rubén G. Rumbaut, and Steven J. Gold. New York: Russell Sage Foundation.

Lee, Stephen. 2009. "Private Immigration Screening in the Workplace," *Stanford Law Review* 61, no. 5: 1103.

Lipktak, Adam, and Julia Preston. 2009. "Justices Limit Use of Identity Theft Law in Immigration Cases," *New York Times*, May 5.

Lipton, Eric. 2006. "U.S. Crackdown Set over Hiring of Immigrants," *New York Times*, April 21.

Martin, Philip L. 2004. "The United States: The Continuing Immigration Debate." In *Controlling Immigration: A Global Perspective*, ed. Wayne A. Cornelius, Philip L. Martin, and James F. Hollifield. Stanford, CA: Stanford University Press.

Milkman, Ruth, and Bongoh Kye. 2008. *The State of the Unions in 2008: A Profile of Union Membership in Los Angeles, California and the Nation.* Los Angeles, CA: Institute for Research on Labor and Employment, University of California, Los Angeles.

Papademetriou, Demetrios, and Aaron Terrazas. 2009. *Immigrants and the Current Economic Crisis: Research Evidence, Policy Challenges, and Implications.* Washington, DC: Migration Policy Institute.

Pew Hispanic Center. 2009a. Analysis of the American Community Survey data, http://pewhispanic.org/files/factsheets/foreignborn2006/Table-26.pdf.

———. 2009b. Analysis of the American Community Survey public-use microsample, http://pewhispanic.org/states/pdf/CA_07.pdf.

Preston, Julia. 2008. "Meatpacker is Fined Nearly $10 Million," *New York Times*, October 30.

Raphael, Steven, and Lucas Ronconi. 2007. "The Effects of Labor Market Competition with Immigrants on the Wages and Employment of Natives," *Dubois Review* 4, no. 2: 413–32.

Rodríguez, Andrea, Jennifer Wittlinger, and Luis Manzanero Rodríguez. 2007. "The Interface between Internal and International Migration." In *Mayan Journeys: The New Migration from Yucatán to the United States*, ed. Wayne A. Cornelius, David Fitzgerald, and Pedro Lewin Fischer. La Jolla, CA: Center for Comparative Immigration Studies, University of California, San Diego.

Rolph, Elizabeth, and Abby Robyn. 1991. "Los Angeles: A Window on Employer Sanctions." In *The Paper Curtain: Employer Sanctions' Implementation, Impact, and Reform*, ed. Michael Fix. Washington, DC: Urban Institute Press.

Rosenblum, Marc. 2009. "The Basics of E-Verify, the US Employer Verification System," http://www.migrationinformation.org/Feature/display .cfm?ID=726.

Semple, Kirk. 2008. "A Somali Influx Unsettles Latino Meatpackers," *New York Times*, October 16.

Thompson, Ginger. 2009. "Immigration Agents to Turn Their Focus to Employers," *New York Times*, April 30.

Waldinger, Roger, and Michael I. Lichter. 2003. *How the Other Half Works: Immigration and the Social Organization of Labor*. Berkeley, CA: University of California Press.

The Ferrers, a family of internal migrants.

6 Leaving to Learn or Learning to Leave: Education in Tunkás

TRAVIS SILVA, CHARLENE CHANG, CARMINA OSUNA, AND
IVAN SOLÍS SOSA

> *I would like to better myself. I've lived through some very dif-*
> *ficult times, days when we had no money for food. That's why*
> *I want to go to Mérida to study and then find a job to help my*
> *father and younger brother, because there are hardly any jobs here.*
> *If I leave, my father will be left alone with my brother. This all*
> *motivates me to continue studying to improve myself. When the*
> *day comes that I get married, I'll be able to provide a good home,*
> *a stable home for my children.*—Mayra, a student aspiring to
> continue her education beyond high school

In just a few sentences Mayra has captured many of the challenges associated with educational attainment in rural Yucatán. At age thirteen, Mayra
is already thinking strategically about school. She believes that three years
of college-level studies in Mérida, the capital city of Yucatán state, will increase her ability to find higher-paying employment in nearby cities. Mayra would like to use education as a springboard to a good job, the path she
has identified as most likely to improve her family's economic situation.

At the same time, Mayra is realistic about the obstacles she faces in
leaving Tunkás to attend college, constraints that may even prevent her
from attending high school. Her family is poor and may not be able to
afford school supplies, let alone college tuition. Mayra provides care for
a younger sibling who could not go with her to Mérida. Mayra's words
sum up the experience of many of Tunkás's youth—high educational
aspirations mapped onto a realistic evaluation of the challenges and obstacles that lie ahead.

We set out to determine the prevalence of high educational aspirations among Tunkaseño youths and how young people in Tunkás perceive education as a way to improve their economic situation. Specifically, we sought to determine the extent to which education and immigration were linked in the minds and lives of Tunkaseños.

We find that Tunkaseños generally do not believe that high levels of education will directly increase their ability to obtain higher wages in their hometown. Importantly, however, we argue that Tunkaseños do believe that education has the potential both to complement the decision to emigrate and to support the upward mobility of subsequent generations of young Tunkaseños living in urban centers such as Mérida, Cancún, Los Angeles, and Orange County.

We first place Tunkás in context by reviewing the literature on education in Mexico, with special attention to the relationship between education and the workplace. We also discuss the international immigration literature as it relates to the education of immigrant children and children of immigrants. Moving to our findings, we start by discussing schools in Tunkás and then exploring how education colors the immigration experience for both internal and international migrants. We consider the educational outlook for second-generation Tunkaseños living in the United States and conclude with suggestions for future lines of academic inquiry.

PAST RESEARCH AND CURRENT TRENDS: A REVIEW OF THE LITERATURE

The Current State of Mexican Education

Mexico is nearing universal primary education completion, with 99 percent of school-age children attending grade school in 2007 (UNESCO 2009). Yet educational inequality in Mexico persists along a number of axes. Investment in education is higher in northern than in southern Mexico (Fuentes and Montes 2004). Expansion of educational opportunities in rural communities lags that in urban centers (Gutiérrez Guzmán 2000), leading to decreased primary attainment in the countryside (Mier y Terán Rocha and Rabell Romero 2003). Based on these and similar findings, several scholars have suggested that the unequal distribution of educational resources has been a key factor in the reproduction of social inequalities in rural Mexico, particularly among indigenous peoples (Schmelkes 2000,

2002). The sum of these works suggests that we would expect to find low levels of educational infrastructure and attainment in Tunkás, a small, rural, indigenous community.

Economic Utility and Internal Migration

Writing on wage inequality, López Acevedo notes the high returns to education in Mexico. Measured against the more developed United States and the whole of developing Latin America, education remains a very strong predictor of wage levels in Mexico (López Acevedo 2001). Yet, notwithstanding the link between higher education and earnings, unemployment and underemployment remain high among well-educated Mexicans (Muñoz Izquierdo 2006; Rothstein 1996). Economic returns to education in Mexico are potentially great, but they are only accessible if the college graduate can find a job commensurate with his or her education.

Particularly relevant to the rural context of Tunkás is the geographic dispersal of professional employment. As in most of the world, high-wage, high-skill jobs in Mexico are concentrated in urban areas. Empirical findings from Mexico substantiate claims of a rural-to-urban "brain drain." Internal migrants positively select in terms of educational attainment as they seek to convert human capital, in the form of educational attainment, into higher wages (Boucher, Stark, and Taylor 2005). The literature correctly predicts the presence of few high-skill, high-wage jobs in Tunkás itself.

Ethnographers have documented the interplay between education and youth migration in Yucatán. In tracing the history of migration from Kuchmil, another rural town in Yucatán, Castellanos (2007) notes that adolescents who completed secondary and tertiary education migrated to Cancún in search of wage labor. The pressures of a monetarized economy, coupled with a lack of employment opportunities in the local context, pushed both boys and girls to the Mayan Riviera for higher-wage opportunities. Re Cruz (1994) finds that most migrants from rural Yucatán arrive in Cancún to find their labor opportunities constrained by their low educational attainment, though internal migrants with higher levels of education are able to bypass the lowest wage jobs and secure a higher salary. The anthropological perspective shows how the migrant selection theory developed by economists functions in the context of rural Yucatán, where a high school education is significantly above the median attainment level.

International Migration and Education

It is well established that migrants are not a randomly selected cross-section of their communities of origin (Lee 1966; Borjas 1999). As noted above, internal migrants in Mexico are positively selected in terms of educational attainment, but several scholars have argued that Mexican migrants to the United States are negatively selected on the basis of education, because unskilled labor is not rewarded in Mexico (Borjas 1996; Massey and García España 1987). Still others have suggested that Mexicans are at least minimally positively selected in terms of education (Feliciano 2005).

Scholars have also devoted substantial energy attempting to explain the variation in educational outcomes in the United States among different immigrant and ethnic groups. Portes and Zhou's (1993) segmented assimilation model takes ethnic groups as a unit of analysis in explaining disparate assimilation outcomes among the "new immigrants" who have entered the United States since the policy reforms of 1965. A key concept is the "context of reception," or institutional welcome, that migrants encounter when they arrive in the United States. Portes and Zhou contend that the context of reception, from the macro level of government policy down to the micro level of individual interactions with native-born Americans, is highly deterministic of immigrant incorporation into "mainstream America." Portes and Zhou paint a fairly negative picture regarding Mexican immigrants, who should expect low levels of assimilation due to a dim portrayal of the reception that awaits this group.

Several theories compete to explain why different groups, in the aggregate, articulate different educational aspirations for the second generation. Ogbu (2003) proposes that collective group identity is critical in youths' formation of educational expectations. The segmented assimilation model argues that structural characteristics of the receiving community shape aspirations and expectations (Portes and Zhou 1993). Feliciano (2005) offers a variation on this theme by calling attention to parental socioeconomic status in the country of origin as a determinant of educational ambition. More micro-level determinants, such as parenting style and immigration status, have also been offered as potentially instructive in an analysis of varying educational outcomes (Kao 2004). The dialogue between these and similar works suggests that group and individual characteristics are both at play in explaining educational attainment among immigrant youth.

Beyond the immigrant selectivity and segmented assimilation debates, Jiménez and Fitzgerald (2007) argue for the need to compare educational outcomes of second-generation migrants in the United States with their peers in Mexico and to disaggregate birth cohort from immigrant-generation effects to appreciate the rapid educational mobility that migration to the United States affords most children of Mexican immigrants. This debate has important implications not only for the perceived "quality" of the immigration flow into the United States, but also for the educational attainment of the second generation in the United States.

Methodology

A holistic approach involving a multi-sited migration system is the basis for understanding the relationships between education, community of origin, internal migration destinations, and the wider international "diaspora" of Tunkaseños (Fitzgerald 2006). When discussing the history of education in Tunkás, we group respondents by ten-year age cohorts in order to capture generational changes. In analyzing the interplay between education and migration among youth, however, we examine a wider age range (15–28), following the rationale developed in chapter 7 of this volume. We draw on both quantitative and qualitative data to elucidate the attitudes and aspirations of youth, their parents, and their educators.

EDUCATION IN TUNKÁS

In Mexico's education system, elementary or primary school includes first through sixth grades, middle school or junior high goes from seventh to ninth grade, and high school encompasses tenth, eleventh, and twelfth grades. Tunkás has two kindergartens,[1] four elementary schools,[2] one middle school, and one technical high school. Both the middle and technical high schools teach agriculture as part of the curriculum. Such technical studies are not universal in Mexico, but they are not uncommon in rural areas.

---

1. In Mexico, there are three years of preschool, with the final year equivalent to kindergarten in the United States. In 2002, the third year of preschool became mandatory in Mexico, and the first two years became mandatory in following years. Nonetheless, students can still enter first grade without having ever attended a preschool provided they are the appropriate age.
2. One of the elementary schools is an "indigenous" school and offers some basic Maya instruction.

A handful of Tunkaseños take advantage of educational opportunities elsewhere in Yucatán. A few Tunkaseño youths travel daily to neighboring Cenotillo, which has a high school with a more academic curriculum. In terms of advanced studies, nearby Izamal offers some opportunities for technical studies. Transportation links between the municipalities potentially allow students to live in Tunkás and attend classes in Izamal. The nearest university is in Mérida, approximately two hours from Tunkás.

The educational infrastructure in Tunkás developed slowly. The first primary schools were constructed in the 1930s, the middle school sometime around 1960, and the technical high school in the 1980s. This timeline is roughly reflected in figures 6.1 and 6.2, which show the percentage of male and female Tunkaseños, respectively, who finish a given level of education by age cohort.

Figure 6.1. Educational Attainment of Men, by Age Cohort

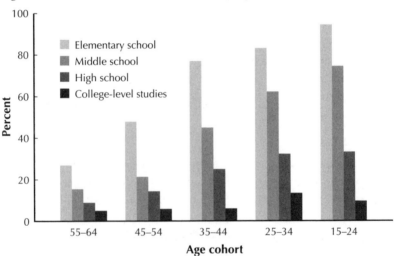

Recent generations of Tunkaseños have advanced further in their studies than previous generations. The greatest strides have been made in primary education. Among respondents between the ages of fifty-five and sixty-four, who would have attended elementary school in the 1950s and early 1960s, only a quarter of males and just over a third of females report having finished sixth grade. Attainment has increased steadily since then for both men and women. The most recent group surveyed, the 15–24 cohort, shows near universal attainment of a primary school education, with over 93 percent of respondents indicating that they had finished primary school.

Figure 6.2. Educational Attainment of Women, by Age Cohort

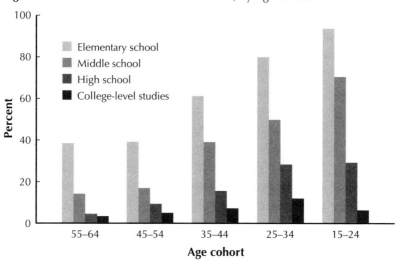

Middle school attainment (grades 7 to 9) has mirrored, but not entirely kept pace with, primary school completion. Completion rates in Tunkás for both men and women have increased over the past fifty years, though the rise has been steadier among men. Middle school only became compulsory in 1993, so we do not expect to find universal completion of ninth grade across all age cohorts. Nevertheless, 74 percent of male and 69 percent of female respondents between fifteen and twenty-four years of age report having finished middle school, a tremendous increase over the 14 percent reported by our oldest respondents.

There has been less growth in the number of Tunkaseños who have completed high school and university studies. Though younger respondents are more likely than their parents and grandparents to have completed these courses of study, we notice a much more modest advance for both men and women in high school and university completion (see figures 6.1 and 6.2). The youngest cohort has so far been unable to improve over their immediate predecessors in both high school and university attainment. We are cautious in making claims about this cohort's high school and university attainment, however, because some respondents are still enrolled in school. The impact of increasing out-migration from Tunkás on educational attainment in the town could also be affecting our youngest respondents' attainment levels in school.

The Gender Gap

Mier y Terán Rocha and Rabell Romero (2003) find that in the last half-century, Mexico has made great progress in closing the educational attainment gap between males and females, though boys continue to outpace girls in middle school completion. Muñiz (2000) theorizes that the persistent gender gap may be linked to a lack of labor market opportunities for women. Psacharopoulos and Patrinos (2002) argue that women who have completed middle and/or high school receive high economic returns to their education in Mexico, though there are very few well-paid employment opportunities. Because there are very few high-skill jobs in Tunkás, and given that internal and international out-migration remains a mostly male phenomenon among Tunkaseños, Muñiz's conjecture about the linkage between education and labor markets may help explain the persistently higher levels of education for boys in Tunkás, particularly after primary school.

The national gender gap is reflected in the data from Tunkás. At all four levels of education, men outpace women in attainment, though this gap is negligible at the elementary school level among the youngest respondents (whose experiences serve as the best proxy for education in the town today). The gender gap, illustrated in figure 6.3, shows changes in the attainment gap at each educational level by age cohort.

The information presented in figure 6.3 allows us to make three important observations. First, the gender gap appears to be closing within the youngest cohort at all educational levels. This is consistent with current enrollment figures in the middle and technical high schools, both of which slightly favor females, and with respondents' stated preferences for educational attainment. When asked how far children need to progress in school to qualify for a good job, Tunkaseños responded that, under ideal circumstances, both boys and girls should finish high school. The most recent chapter in the history of gender disparity in Tunkás's educational system appears to be one of converging attainment figures.

Figure 6.3. Relative Size of the Gender Gap in Tunkás, Males' Advantage over Females

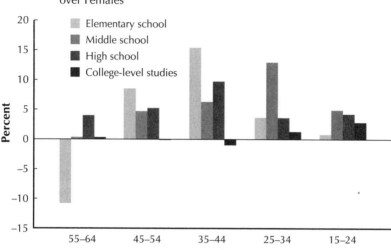

A second observation relates to two important data points: male attainment grew disproportionately quickly among the 35–44 age cohort in primary school and among the following cohort in middle school. Both cases occurred at a time when middle and high school access was expanding significantly across Mexico, and we hypothesize that males were privileged during the initial expansion of educational services in Tunkás. The Mayan family has a patriarchal structure in which men are expected to lead households and be primary breadwinners (Black 1988; Rosenbaum 1993). As Tunkás's middle and high schools grew in enrollment in the decade or so after being built, it is possible that families needing to prioritize resource allocation sent boys to school more frequently than girls. This logic spurred the development of social welfare programs such as Oportunidades, a government program that aims to lower the cost of education, particularly for girls (Adato et al. 2000).

Also notable is the one significant data point where female attainment is higher. Among the oldest cohort, students who began their formal education in the 1950s, substantially more women than men completed primary school, even though our survey data show that similar proportions of men and women in this cohort started elementary school. During this period, Tunkás experienced a moderate economic boom in the timber industry,[3] and we think it likely that families withdrew their sons from school to assist with woodcutting or to maintain agricultural plots while older family members worked in logging.

Financial Barriers to Educational Attainment

Respondents who are no longer in school most frequently stated that they abandoned their studies due to financial reasons, and those still in school often expressed the fear that financial constraints would block their educational aspirations. In this section we discuss how financial concerns affect educational attainment.

The cost of attending school is high. Students and their parents must provide supplies, uniforms, and, in the upper grades, textbooks. Even among the youngest survey respondents (the 15–24 cohort, excluding current students), 56 percent said they had to drop out of school because of insufficient financial resources, and only 34 percent replied that they had completed as many years of schooling as they had hoped. Government assistance from programs like Oportunidades is frequently used to cover educational expenses, and principals of elementary, middle, and high schools confirmed that this program is crucial in enabling many students to attend school. Oportunidades payments do not change significantly as students grow older, but the cost of education does rise from elementary to middle school and again from middle to high school, placing low-income students at a severe disadvantage.

There is some evidence that remittances from the United States help families defray the cost of education. When surveying respondents who receive remittances from international migrants, education-related expenses was the fourth most cited use to which those funds are put. Household maintenance, health-related expenses, and house construction were mentioned more frequently, but we believe that the results may underreport the importance of remittances for education, given

---

3. The boom quickly went bust as the region was deforested (Silva, Niño, and Solís 2007).

that many respondents may view education-related fees as a household expense.[4] Even though Sawyer et al. (2009) found that remittances do not generally affect educational attainment, money sent from abroad does help defray the costs of education for some families.

College-level studies are substantially more expensive than lower education levels, and very few Tunkaseños are able to pursue university or college-level studies (see figures 6.1 and 6.2). As Adriana, a sixteen-year-old prospective college student, told us:

> I would like to study and work, but they say it takes a lot. It's very tiring. For example, you work in the morning, and when school's out in the afternoon, you don't have enough time to do homework. It's exhausting but not impossible. If you want it badly enough, you'll make it. It would be really hard for me to go to college; I wouldn't want to accept help from others, because later they'd come and remind me of what they'd given me. It wouldn't be fair to ask my parents for something they don't have; they don't have the resources right now because they are both sick.

Many current high school students who expressed an interest in continuing their studies outside of Tunkás mentioned scholarships as the most realistic route to a university or college. However, there is little evidence that students are able to systematically access information about scholarships, and money remains a significant obstacle for youths wishing to attend university.

Financial constraints can affect educational attainment in another way, as students are compelled to drop out of school and go to work. Among respondents between the ages of fifteen and twenty-four who had left school, 23 percent did so either to work or to care for the home or family members. The case of Pascual and his sister Rebecca illustrates these points. Pascual, an intelligent young man who finished high school and began taking college

---

4. Among remittance recipients, 89 percent said the money went to household expenditures. We hypothesize that many respondents lumped education-related expenses into this category. Eighteen percent of respondents (who could list up to three uses of remittances) specifically cited educational expenses as a cost covered with these resources.

courses, was unable to finish university because of financial obligations to his family. He had to migrate internationally in order to support himself and earn enough to allow his younger sister Rebecca to continue her education. Pascual's experience is typical; many young Tunkaseños must cut short their own education in order to engage in wage labor. And his sister is representative of those students who rely on migrant remittances to pay school costs. This family's education and migration history depicts one way in which education and migration are linked for Tunkaseños.

An Agricultural Focus

Another barrier to meaningful educational attainment is tied to the structure of the Tunkás school system. Both the middle and high schools have an agricultural focus, a concentration that is not universal in rural Mexico. At first glance, an agricultural focus may seem appropriate in the context of a small town largely dependent upon subsistence farming. However, students and educators conveyed mixed feelings about the utility of the education offered at these two schools.

Students were generally upbeat about the agricultural program in Tunkás. When giving us a tour of their middle school, a group of female students led us past the classrooms to the chicken coop, tomato field, and corral. They proudly informed us that they sold the produce and animals raised at the school as a fund-raising activity. Students at the technical high school, the Centro de Bachillerato Tecnológico Agropecuario (CBTA), also enjoyed outdoor studies, though not necessarily to the exclusion of their more academic classes.

At the same time, several high school students expressed frustration at the quality of their classes. When asked if the high school prepares students for further study, Pedro, a current student, answered, "No, they only teach the basics. Sometimes they don't even come to teach because they have to commute from Izamal." Because the campus in Tunkás is technically an extension of a high school in Izamal, teachers must split their time between the two sites, a situation that negatively influences students' perceptions of the quality of the education they receive. Perhaps because of their agricultural focus, the middle and high schools have little time to teach more than basic skills in the classroom, which holds important ramifications for students wishing to pursue university studies.

The parents' ambivalence mirrored that of their children. Many parents were proud of the fact that Tunkás had a middle school and a high school (some larger towns in Mexico lack even a middle school). However, a notable segment of parents expressed reservations, especially about the high school. One mother rolled her eyes as she talked about teacher absenteeism at the technical high school: "Sometimes there's class, and sometimes there isn't." A few parents send their children to schools in nearby Cenotillo or Izamal, where agriculture is not a teaching focus.

Perhaps most critical were the educators themselves. The principals of the middle and high schools, both residents of Tunkás, disagreed on the extent to which their schools' technical, agricultural curriculum is appropriate for the town, clearly underscoring how the structure of the educational system in Tunkás can be controversial. Mindful of the town's historical reliance on agriculture, the high school principal believes that the technical program helps the town: "We've seen that the school has helped the people of the community. Many people from Tunkás who have studied here are now teachers in elementary and middle schools or have professional agricultural jobs."

The school principal related the successes of students who have been able to use Tunkaseño schools as a springboard to professional jobs elsewhere. By contrast, the middle school principal raised the issue of gender inequality when discussing the appropriateness of his technical school's curriculum:

> This is a technical school focused on agriculture. It teaches all students, both boys and girls, agricultural technology, how to work the land and how to care for animals, because that's the kind of work we have in this region. We don't have a workshop that prepares women for things like dressmaking, clerical work, or accounting. The truth is that we don't train them, we don't provide them with anything that would allow them to enter the workforce after completing middle school. The only thing we give them is the chance to continue their studies at the high school level. We are failing them. No, the system is failing them, not us. The system fails because we are not providing anything for the girls, just for the boys.

The middle school principal was very candid in evaluating his school's successes and failures. His observation that the curriculum privileges male students and disadvantages their female counterparts fits with Muñiz's (2000) theory that girls in Mexican schools, particularly in rural areas, suffer from a system that is not geared toward their needs as future wage earners.

Bilingual Education

Bilingual education is another feature of Tunkás's school system. Initially designed to introduce Spanish to communities where most people speak an indigenous language, the bilingual system now plays a different role. In Tunkás, students enter the bilingual preschool and elementary school speaking Spanish, and the goal of the bilingual schools' directors is to teach basic Maya to their students. However, Maya is not taught in the middle school or technical high school, so the opportunity for a bilingual education is somewhat restricted.

We asked the parents of students in the Maya-teaching elementary school why they prefer its educational program to that of the other elementary schools in the town. Their responses were largely focused on school policies and procedures; in fact, little was said about the bilingual program itself. Though the bilingual preschool has increased in size over the past few years, we did not find evidence that parents are deliberately choosing this school so that their children may learn Maya. And most parents in Tunkás expressed a preference for the large elementary school located in the town square over the bilingual elementary.

The director of the bilingual preschool believes that the students learning Maya would benefit if language instruction were extended to the middle school and high school. Because Spanish is spoken in nearly all Tunkaseño households, Maya is generally not being transmitted from generation to generation.

Because Spanish has become the dominant language in Tunkás, the bilingual education program holds important potential for preserving Mayan language and culture. Angelina López Pech, a teacher at the bilingual preschool, explained:

> The goal is to revalue and save the culture, to preserve ev-
> erything that is related to the culture. . . . Here in the town
> we realize that we are losing the Maya culture. Because of
> migration the people no longer value that culture. Many
> people are in the United States; many people go to Cancún.
> They imitate what they see in those places, they bring ways
> of living from other states and places. It's only logical that
> we're going to lose the beautiful culture that is Maya.

One hundred years ago, Maya was the only language spoken in
Tunkás. Some residents feel that first Spanish and now English, coupled
with immigration and advances in communications, have encroached
upon the cultural and linguistic traditions of Tunkás. Though parents did
not articulate the educators' goal, teachers like Angelina view bilingual
education as a way to preserve traditional ways of life.

Tunkás's complex educational system defies any attempt to evaluate it
in simple positive or negative terms. On the one hand, the town has made
tremendous strides in increasing and improving educational outcomes
over the past few generations. Curriculum is geared to the historical and
traditional needs of the town. However, many Tunkaseños appear am-
bivalent in their assessments of the value and quality of the educational
infrastructure. There is a sense that teachers are spread too thin. Further,
not all students will enter the agricultural sector though all must study
agricultural methods. As is true throughout Mexico, schools in Tunkás
continue to improve even as some community members express hopes
for a better system.

EDUCATION AND EMIGRATION

Tunkás is highly dependent on subsistence farming, and this presents a
particular challenge. A 2007 drought cost many residents their harvest
and made the need for diversification in the local economy painfully clear.
Jobs in the town are limited in number and earnings are low, a median
of US$32.14 a week among economically active nonmigrants. Aside from
agriculture, a few small businesses employ family members; some town
residents are informal entrepreneurs, selling food on the streets or in their

homes; and a few teachers live in Tunkás. In general, the wages that are available in the town are insufficient for most Tunkaseños.

We asked the town's youths (ages 15–28) if an individual could "get ahead" in life without leaving Tunkás. The vast majority, probably with an eye to the economy, said that remaining in the town was not feasible. Table 6.1 displays how the youth group responded to this question and how their responses differed by level of education.The data suggest that those with higher levels of education are slightly more likely (79 percent versus 71 percent) to feel that one must leave Tunkás to progress in life, indicating that young people of all education levels see little economic opportunity in Tunkás.

Table 6.1. Opinions on Needing to Leave Tunkás to Progress in Life, by Education Level

	Respondent's Educational Level	
Question: Does one need to leave Tunkás to progress in life?	Did Not Complete High School	Completed High School
Yes	71%	79%
No	29%	21%
N	626	196

Pearson's Chi-squared = 5.02, p = .025.

Since most of the young high school graduates believe they must leave Tunkás to be economically successful, it might be expected that many Tunkaseños are leaving the town to advance their education. Our data do not indicate that this is the case. Only 10 percent of all internal migrations were for education, and only 4 percent of all international migrants cited education as their reason for emigrating. Fewer than 9 percent of respondents reported having completed one year of education beyond high school, and only 5 percent reported having finished college. At first glance, there is scant evidence to support the notion that Tunkaseño youth systematically leave Tunkás to enroll in college.

These statistics may not tell the entire story, however. We conducted our Mexico fieldwork only in Tunkás, a town where we predicted there would be few highly skilled professionals. In so doing, we may have failed to capture people born in Tunkás who attended college and now live elsewhere in Mexico. Despite this potential under-sampling, our conversations with the families of college students and graduates—and, when possible, with college students themselves—revealed the obstacles facing Tunkaseños who want to pursue a university education.

One of the main barriers keeping Tunkaseño youths from attending the university in Mérida is a simple lack of information. Adriana, mentioned above, said she cannot rely on her family to pay for college and can only envision going to Mérida because she has relatives there. All of the Tunkaseños who are attending or have finished college have close ties with extended family residing in Mérida. But most Tunkaseños do not have family members in Mérida or other urban centers, so most of the town's young people lack access to this kind of crucial network.

Though the vast majority of Tunkaseño youths believe they must leave their hometown for internal and international destinations if they are to be economically successful, enrolling in college is difficult and relatively rare. Given that most Tunkaseños are unable to leverage a college education into a professional job close to home, the interface between education in Tunkás and subsequent immigration becomes critical.

EDUCATION AND IMMIGRATION

Rodríguez, Wittlinger, and Manzanero Rodríguez (2007) argue that internal and international migration flows from Tunkás should be considered a single system; we use this conceptual framework as a point of departure in our discussion of education and immigration. We also seek to build upon the finding that wages rise with increased years of education (see chapter 5, this volume) and hope to provide insight into why this is the case.

Our respondents share the belief that education assists migrants in their pursuit of economic opportunities. We asked respondents at which point in their lives it is most appropriate for young men and women to migrate to the United States; they responded that it is important to finish one's studies before migrating.[5] Fifty-seven percent of respondents

---

5. It is also possible that this response is capturing a concern among respondents that migrants will be unable to attend school once they migrate. We discuss how immigrant children navigate schooling in destination communities in a later section.

supported a boy's decision to migrate but preferred that the young man first finish his studies. The number was even higher, 64 percent, for girls. When posing the question, we did not define what was meant by "finishing their studies," leaving it to our respondents to decide for themselves. Though respondents certainly had different subjective understandings of what "studies" means, they agreed that finishing one's studies is important.

Current students share the same perception. Nidia, a seventeen-year-old student at the technical high school, told us that graduating from high school is particularly important for migrants entering the labor market outside of Tunkás:

> Well, the teachers say it's bad to stop studying and that students should finish technical school. Some young people don't even get to the technical high school; they leave in their second year of middle school. And when the question comes up as to why they want to go to the United States, the teachers say that if you don't finish high school, you can't get a job here and you certainly won't get one over there.

Nidia's interpretation of the situation is that Tunkaseño parents and children believe that being educated is crucial to their success as migrants.

Tunkaseños do more than pay lip service to this idea. Tunkaseños who emigrate do so after their schooling years. International migrants are older, at an average age of 22.7 years, while internal migrants are just 18.5 years old on average. As noted by Hawkins et al. (chapter 7, this volume), eighteen is the earliest age at which more respondents report being economically active than being students. When migrants leave Tunkás, they leave in search of jobs. The vast majority of migrants have already received all of their formal education before leaving their hometown.

Tunkaseño migrants are positively selected by educational attainment (see figure 6.4). Both internal and international migrant youths have attended school longer than their nonmigrant peers, and the median educational level for an international migrant is completion of high school. These statistics have important implications for the debate on the selection of immigrants.

Figure 6.4. Youths' Educational Attainment, by Current Place of Residence

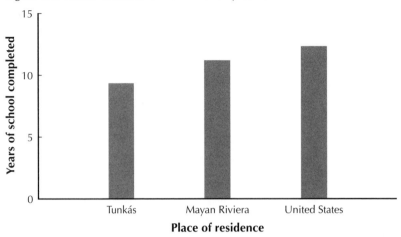

As noted above, scholars such as George Borjas and Cynthia Feliciano disagree on whether Mexican immigrants are positively or negatively selected on education. The dialogue between Borjas and Feliciano is clearly mapped onto the national context, and it would be inappropriate to support either position using only Tunkás as a reference point. The national milieu includes urban, suburban, and rural spaces, and it factors in many social conditions and opportunities that do not exist in rural Yucatán. However, our evidence suggests that the youths who emigrate from Tunkás are positively selected, and this is even more notable among those who migrate internationally. The positive selection of immigrants is the result of a variety of factors, not all of which are addressed in this chapter, though we do analyze the ramifications of this phenomenon among Tunkaseños.

Impact on Economic Opportunities

Educational attainment is linked to improved economic opportunities for migrants. We have discussed how Tunkaseño respondents have a sense that a higher level of education is beneficial when migrating internally or internationally. Gell-Redman et al. (chapter 5, this volume) show that when controlling for other factors, education is positively correlated with wage attainment. There is further evidence to support the notion that education is economically beneficial for migrants in the Mayan Riviera and California, and ultimately in Tunkás as well.

Table 6.2 shows the wage differential between migrants who started high school and those who did not for the four principal places where Tunkaseños live. The distinction is crucial because these results support the claim that migrants are positively selected on the basis of education credentials. The average nonmigrant does not enroll in high school, while internal migrants complete two years of education, on average, and international migrants typically finish high school before leaving Tunkás.

Table 6.2. Tunkaseños' Weekly Earnings, by Education Level and Current Place of Residence

Place of Residence	Earnings by Educational Level (U.S. dollars)		
	Did Not Start High School	Started High School	N
Tunkás	$47.06	$103.78	324
Mérida	$92.14	$112.50	29
Cancún	$116.04	$184.02	39
United States	$410.46	$540.73	93

In Tunkás and in each destination community, Tunkaseños who have attended high school earn more than their counterparts who have no education beyond the ninth grade. We first discuss this differential in the destination communities and then turn to salaries in Tunkás itself.

The wage differential is undoubtedly the product of many different forces, and we make no claim that education alone leads to higher wages. But as Gell-Redman et al. reveal, education does play a role. We asked our respondents to tell us which of the subjects they had studied in school were of most use in their daily lives. Their responses differ notably by location (figure 6.5).

Tunkaseños use their education differently depending on where they live. Both internal and international migrants report that the ability to read and write in Spanish is the most important skill they learned in school. For these groups, math is the second most frequently mentioned subject. Within Tunkás, Mayan language studies are relatively more valued than English; knowing some English becomes more valuable elsewhere in

Mexico. With this exception, the relative importance of each subject in school is constant within the Mexican context.

Figure 6.5. Perceived Utility of Subjects Studied in School, by Location

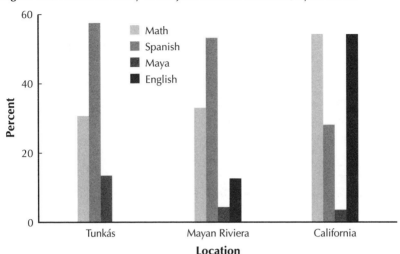

The story is entirely different among Tunkaseños living in California. In the United States, English is the most prized skill, followed by Spanish, and then math. Mayan studies, which in an absolute sense were not highly valued even in Tunkás, go virtually unmentioned as being of use in the United States. Internal Tunkaseño migrants acquire language skills in Cancún that later can help them in the United States (Rodríguez, Wittlinger, and Manzanero Rodríguez. 2007); we find that this process begins in the town's schools. The importance that Spanish language ability holds even in the United States is linked to the U.S. receiving communities in which Tunkaseños have settled, which are heavily Spanish speaking. In communities where business and leisure activities are conducted in Spanish, Tunkaseños' knowledge of Spanish remains important even though the economic utility of English is greater. Though better language skills cannot account for the entire wage gap between high school enrollees and non-enrollees, linguistic dexterity does matter to Tunkaseños. The differentiated responses based on location suggest that language skills have an impact on the economic lives of migrants.

The wage differential does not only exist in destination communities; it is present inside Tunkás as well. The gap between the salaries of high school enrollees and non-enrollees might initially seem to provide evidence of the presence of higher-wage jobs in Tunkás, jobs that individuals with more education and higher human capital would be able to access. This conclusion would be premature.

Migrants with higher levels of education are able to leverage their human capital into higher wages in destination communities. Of the 324 people whose weekly earnings in Tunkás are represented in table 6.2, 63 percent are returned migrants. In other words, the majority of the high school enrollees living in Tunkás today have at some point enjoyed a favorable wage differential in a destination community. Alfredo, a returned internal migrant, is a good example. Alfredo worked in construction in the Mayan Riviera for several years before returning to Tunkás to reunite with his family. He used the savings he had accumulated while a migrant to buy foundry equipment and now works out of his home, producing metal doors and fences for new homes in Tunkás and neighboring Cenotillo. He is considering another stint as an internal migrant to accumulate additional capital to build a shop and expand his business.

Better educated migrants earn more than migrants who never enrolled in high school in Mexico or in the United States. We hypothesize that language skills acquired in high school, particularly English, partially account for these higher earnings. When migrants return to Tunkás, they bring economic and social capital with them that they are able to parlay into higher wages. Most Tunkaseños believe they need to leave their hometown to find better economic opportunities; they also correctly perceive that education complements the decision to migrate within Mexico and to the United States.

THE SECOND GENERATION IN THE UNITED STATES

Most children of migrants from Tunkás were too young to be included in our survey, so we are unable to offer much quantitative analysis about the second generation's educational progress in the United States. We can, however, begin a preliminary discussion of the second generation using data from their parents' surveys and semi-structured interviews with both children and parents.

A number of Tunkaseños have migrated to the United States as children. Most came without documents, and over 80 percent of those who entered as children remain undocumented today. On average, an immigrant who came as a child spent more time in the U.S. educational system than in the Mexican one. Though our fieldwork did not capture their language competence, we presume that immigrants who came as children speak better English than their immigrant parents. Many have now reached adulthood, and most are economically active, though some are still engaged in part- or full-time studies. The story of the first children immigrants from Tunkás is not extraordinary; most have passed from childhood to adulthood and from students to workers in unremarkable fashion.

More important, however, is the age of immigrants who are children today. They are exceptionally young (four years old on average), generally undocumented, and likely to be educated entirely in the United States. The burgeoning population of second- and even third-generation Tunkaseños born north of the border expands even further the number of Tunkaseño children who will be educated in the United States. The critical difference between the native-born and foreign-born is legal status. For many parents and their children, legal status dominates any conversation about education.

Samuel, who has lived in the United States for nearly a decade, is the father of two. His daughter, Eréndira, now a fourteen-year-old high school freshman, migrated with him at a very young age and remains undocumented. Her brother, Joshua, is a second grader born in the United States and is thus a U.S. citizen. Samuel is very concerned about the challenges Eréndira faces as an undocumented student. Though she has a 4.0 grade point average and plays for her school's water polo team, Samuel doubts his daughter will be able to attend college in the United States. He supports her desire to become a physician, but he feels that she would be better off going to medical school in Mexico. Speaking about his daughter's aspirations, he said, "That's the dream. We'll have to see what happens. Because she was born in Mexico, the problem is with her papers." Though Eréndira would prefer to remain in the United States, both father and daughter are now making plans for her to attend college in Mexico.

Mixed-status families such as Samuel's are on the rise throughout the United States (Fry and Gonzales 2008), with clear implications for education. Eréndira may be denied the possibility of attending college and working as a professional in the United States, and the United States would then lose Eréndira's impressive human capital. As Tunkaseños continue to settle in the United States, more and more families will find themselves in similar circumstances.

CONCLUSION

Agriculture dominates Tunkás's economy; there are few opportunities for wage labor and even fewer high-skill, high-wage jobs. The majority of Tunkaseños believe that emigrating is the only successful strategy for upward mobility. At the same time, education can complement an individual's decision to migrate, with both internal and international migrants having more years of education than people who remain in the hometown. Tunkaseños place high importance on finishing their education in the hometown, and those who do so have a higher median wage in the Mayan Riviera and in the United States.

Students in Tunkás hold high educational aspirations. More Tunkaseños are completing high school today than ever before, and we encountered several community members who had completed postsecondary studies in Mérida or elsewhere in Mexico. Aspirations are tempered, however, by barriers to access; only 8 percent of our respondents had completed any college-level studies and fewer than 4 percent had the equivalent of a bachelor's degree. Those few who finish college find it impossible to obtain high-skill employment in their hometown, leading to a rural-to-urban brain drain. Given the scarcity of good job opportunities in Tunkás, the highly educated are unable to participate in the town's economy.

Language instruction is an important element of education in Tunkás. Two "indigenous" schools offer Maya instruction to students through primary school, but classes in Maya are not offered at the middle or high school, to the dismay of townspeople hoping to preserve the language in their home region. English is taught from seventh grade onward, and migrants confirmed the value that their English studies held for them as they settled in the tourist zone of the Mayan Riviera or in the United States. As the Tunkaseño diaspora continues, the children of migrants will be educated in increasingly urban contexts. Whether in Mérida, Cancún,

Los Angeles, or Anaheim, the second generation will come of age in a services- and information-based economy that is very different from the agricultural economy of Tunkás. These young people born outside of Tunkás and their parents are optimistic that increasing levels of education will assist the new generation as they enter the labor market, but this enthusiasm is tempered in the United States, where concerns about documentation status and access to higher education remain paramount for both students and parents.

Future Research

We view all migration from Tunkás, internal and international, as part of the same migration system. An advantage that our binational research protocol confers is the ability to conduct interviews in the community of origin and the major international destination community. However, we were unable to conduct fieldwork in domestic migrant destinations such as Mérida or Cancún and may have missed most of the Tunkaseños who have completed college. Future studies of migration in Yucatán may want to add these destinations to their fieldwork itinerary, and we strongly recommend giving attention to internal destination communities.

Future research may also opt to employ an interpretivist perspective to explain why students drop out of school as they transition from one educational level to another. Most students who begin the technical high school complete their course of studies there, but a question remains regarding why a significant portion of graduating middle school students do not transition to high school. And for the transition from high school to college, it is important to research the availability and accessibility of financial aid programs that might help Tunkaseño youths attain higher educational levels. We urge future researchers to adopt a "ground-level" approach when considering these questions.

Most pressing for policy makers and scholars of education and immigration in the United States is further research on the immigrant second generation in U.S. schools. The children of Tunkaseño migrants will grow up in the United States at a time when the proportion of Hispanic schoolchildren is increasing rapidly. Our binational framework will allow for a stronger comparison between the second generation and the nonmigrant children of their age cohort. Equally important, our method of looking at a destination community while focusing on immigration from a single point of origin in Mexico will allow researchers to analyze how dynamics in the community of origin might influence educational attainment in the United States. We are excited about the possibilities for the development of this framework in future research.

REFERENCES

Adato, M., B. De la Briere, D. Mindek, and A. Quisembin. 2000. "The Impact of PROGRESA on Women's Status and Intrahousehold Relations." Final Report. Washington, DC: International Food Policy Research Institute.

Black, Nancy. 1988. "Anthropology and the Study of Quiché Maya Women in the Western Highlands of Guatemala." In *Lucha: The Struggles of Latin American Women*, ed. Connie Weil. Minneapolis, MN: Prisma Institute.

Borjas, George. 1996. "The Earnings of Mexican Migrants in the United States," *Journal of Development Economics* 5: 69–98.

———. 1999. *Heaven's Door: Immigration Policy and the American Economy.* Princeton, NJ: Princeton University Press.

Boucher, Stephen R., Oded Stark, and J. Edward Taylor. 2005. "A Gain with a Drain? Evidence from Rural Mexico on the New Economics of the Brain Drain." ARE Working Paper 05-005. Davis, CA: Department of Agricultural and Resource Economics, University of California, Davis, http://repositories.cdlib.org/are/arewp/05-005.

Castellanos, Bianet. 2007. "Adolescent Migration to Cancún," *Frontiers: A Journal of Women Studies* 28, no. 3: 1–27.

Feliciano, Cynthia. 2005. *Unequal Origins.* New York: LFB Scholarly Publishing.

Fitzgerald, David. 2006. "Towards a Theoretical Ethnography of Migration," *Qualitative Sociology* 29, no. 1: 1–24.

Fry, Rick, and Felisa Gonzales. 2008. "One-in-Five and Growing Fast: A Profile of Hispanic Public School Students." Washington, DC: Pew Hispanic Center.

Fuentes, Ricardo, and Andrés Montes. 2004. "Mexico and the Millennium Development Goals at the Subnational Level," *Journal of Human Development* 5, no. 1: 97–120.

Gutiérrez Guzmán, Francisco Javier. 2000. "Education Levels of the Population and Its Distribution in 2000," *DemoS* 13: 20–21.

Jiménez, Tomás, and David Fitzgerald. 2007. "Mexican Assimilation: A Temporal and Spatial Reorientation," *Du Bois Review* 4, no. 2: 337–54.

Kao, Grace. 2004. "Parental Influences on the Educational Outcomes of Immigrant Youth," *International Migration Review* 38: 427–49.

Lee, Everet. 1966. "A Theory of Migration," *Demography* 3: 47–57.

López Acevedo, Gladys. 2001. *Evolution of Earnings and Rates of Returns to Education in Mexico.* Washington DC: Poverty Reduction and Economic Management Division, World Bank.

Massey, Douglas, and Felipe García España. 1987. "The Social Process of International Migration," *Science* 237, no. 4816: 733–38.

Mier y Terán Rocha, Marta, and Cecilia Rabell Romero. 2003. "Inequalities in Mexican Children's Schooling," *Journal of Comparative Family Studies* 34, no. 3: 435–54.

Muñiz, Patricia. 2000. "The Schooling Situation of Children in Highly Underprivileged Localities in Mexico." In *Unequal Schools, Unequal Chances*, ed. Fernando Reimers. Cambridge, MA: Harvard University Press.

Muñoz Izquierdo, Carlos. 2006. "Determinants of the University Young People Employability and Alternatives to Promote Them," *Papeles de Población* year 12, no. 49 (July–September): 75–89.

Ogbu, John. 2003. *Black American Students in an Affluent Suburb.* Mahwah, NJ: L. Erlbaum Associates.

Portes, Alejandro, and Min Zhou. 1993. "The New Second Generation: Segmented Assimilation and Its Variants," *ANNALS of the American Academy of Political and Social Science* 530, no. 1: 74–96.

Psacharopoulos, George, and Harry Patrinos. 2002. "Returns to Investment in Education: A Further Update." Policy Research Working Paper Series, no. 2881. Washington, DC: World Bank.

Re Cruz, Alicia. 1994. "Lo sagrado y lo profano de la identidad maya entre los emigrantes de Yucatán," *Nueva Antropología* 46: 39–48.

Rodríguez, Andrea, Jennifer Wittlinger, and Luis Manzanero Rodríguez. 2007. "The Interface between Internal and International Migration." In *Mayan Journeys: The New Migration from Yucatán to the United States*, ed. Wayne A. Cornelius, David Fitzgerald, and Pedro Lewin Fischer. La Jolla, CA: Center for Comparative Immigration Studies, University of California, San Diego.

Rosenbaum, Brenda. 1993. *With Our Heads Bowed: The Dynamics of Gender in a Maya Community.* Austin, TX: University of Texas Press.

Rothstein, Frances A. 1996. "Flexible Accumulation, Youth Labor, and Schooling in a Rural Community in Mexico," *Critique of Anthropology* 16, no. 4: 361–79.

Sawyer, Adam, David Keyes, Cristina Velásquez, Grecia Lima, and M. Miguel Bautista. 2009. "Going to School, Going to *El Norte*: Migration's Impact on Tlacotepense Education." In *Migration from the Mexican Mixteca: A Transnational Community in Oaxaca and California*, ed. Wayne A. Cornelius, David Fitzgerald, Jorge Hernández-Díaz, and Scott Borger. La Jolla, CA: Center for Comparative Immigration Studies, University of California, San Diego.

Schmelkes, Sylvia. 2000. "Education and Indian Peoples in Mexico: An Example of Policy Failure." In *Unequal Schools, Unequal Chances*, ed. Fernando Reimers. Cambridge, MA: Harvard University Press.

———. 2002. "La enseñanza de la lectura y la escritura en contextos multiculturales." In *VII Congreso Latinoamericano para el Desarrollo de la Lectura y la Escritura*. Puebla, Mex.: Red Latinoamericana de Educación Rural.

Silva, Travis, Amérika Niño, and Mirian Solís. 2007. "Tunkás: A New Community of Emigration." In *Mayan Journeys: The New Migration from Yucatán to the United States*, ed. Wayne A. Cornelius, David Fitzgerald, and Pedro Lewin Fischer. La Jolla, CA: Center for Comparative Immigration Studies, University of California, San Diego.

UNESCO (United Nations Educational, Scientific and Cultural Organization). 2009. "UIS Statistics in Brief—Education in Mexico," http://stats.uis.unesco.org/unesco/TableViewer/document.aspx?ReportId=121&IF_Language=eng&BR_Country=4840.

Four youths in Tunkás.

7 Values in Conflict: Youth in a Culture of Migration

BRIAN HAWKINS, YEDID MINJARES, LAUREN HARRIS, AND
JUAN RODRÍGUEZ DE LA GALA

> *The ones who come back from the United States have new ways of speaking and dressing. Some young people want to be like them, so they make plans to go over there. Many young people think it's easy to go there and work, but they're not thinking straight. They can't imagine what the work is like, but they say, "I'm leaving. The guys who've gone before already have houses and cars." A lot of people from here plan on finishing middle school and then leaving.* —Lourdes, a fifteen-year-old Tunkaseña

In the fall of 2001, 21-year-old Fernando and his brother secured tourist visas for entry into the United States by masquerading as successful Mexican ranchers. Their intent was to enter as tourists and then overstay their visas and find work, sending money back to family members remaining behind. Fernando has since started up his own successful business in Tunkás with the money he earned working in the United States. As an adolescent, Fernando never intended to migrate internationally for economic reasons, but he did want to experience the kind of adventures that many young returned migrants had recounted. It was not until he reached his twenties that his motives for migration shifted as he began aspiring to upward socioeconomic mobility for himself and his family.

Fernando's story is typical of a significant portion of male Tunkaseño youths. As an adolescent, the veteran migrants' glamorized stories and the lure of a U.S. lifestyle drew him to the idea of migrating to the United States. As he matured, his reasons for migrating came to align with his desire to support himself and his family, leaving behind boyhood dreams of adventure. His sisters and mother remained in Tunkás while Fernando and his brother shouldered the risks of living and working clandestinely in the United States. These patterns—the draw to the United States at a young age, a change in personal values over time, and the predominance of males in the migrant flow—are characteristic of the "culture of migration" in Tunkás.

Discussions surrounding the culture of migration generally posit this concept as something that positively influences the decision to migrate. Many authors view a culture of migration as a set of values that consistently reinforces participation in migratory flows. This conception certainly fits Fernando's case and many others in Tunkás. However, this conceptualization of migration culture does not account for the people in a community who choose not to migrate. While Fernando's story may be representative of a good portion of young Tunkaseño males, it does not represent those who have chosen to remain at home.

Does growing up in a culture of migration affect a youth's decision to migrate? If so, what accounts for the differences in migratory decisions across age and gender divides? Is it that some Tunkás youths are socialized into becoming migrants while others are not? If we do not recognize the interplay of culture, migration decision making, and youth, our understanding of Mexican migration to the United States will ultimately remain incomplete. The Tunkás case study is thus useful for providing a framework and point of comparison for understanding broader Mexican cultural processes as they relate to migration.

To answer the questions posed above, we first discuss what is meant by a culture of migration. Next we explore the similarities between the culture of migration in Tunkás and in other sending communities around the globe. We then posit the culture of migration in Tunkás as a series of values that influences youths' migration decisions and discuss a set of patterns that emerges in Tunkás as a result of a conflictive migration culture. Finally, we locate our work in the broader context of research on Mexican migration to the United States.

FRAMEWORK AND METHODOLOGY

"Culture" is defined in the Geertzian sense as a set of attitudes, values, and beliefs that inform action (Geertz 1973). The "culture of migration" might therefore be defined as a set of attitudes, values, and beliefs that inform the decision to migrate. Though definitions vary, this concept is found in migration research around the world.

For example, in his study of rural Romanian youth, Istvan Horvath defines the culture of migration as "the changes of values and cultural perceptions determined by previous migratory experiences within a given community that has a considerable migration history [where] enduring migratory practices can turn into referential behavioral repertories, orienting and motivating the choices social actors make" (2008, 773). Horvath constructs migration culture as historically rooted, because the historical precedence of migration changes the "values and cultural perceptions" that influence the decisions of "social actors" or, in this case, potential future migrants.

Douglas Massey and colleagues follow a similar vein, defining migration culture as a set of values that propels migration, where continued out-migration from a given community "changes its values and cultural perceptions in ways that increase the probability of future migration" (1993, 452). This persistence "becomes deeply ingrained into the repertoire of people's behaviors, and values associated with migration become part of the community's values" (Massey et al. 1993, 452). Likewise, Wayne Cornelius conceives of the culture of migration as "a set of interrelated perceptions, attitudinal orientations, socialization processes and social structures, including transnational social networks, growing out of the international migratory experience, which constantly encourage, validate, and facilitate participation in this movement" (1990, 24).

Finally, Syed Ali, in his study of migration culture among Muslims in India, defines the culture of migration as "those ideas, practices, and cultural artifacts that reinforce the celebration of migration and migrants. This includes beliefs, desires, symbols, myths, education, celebrations of migration in various media, and material goods" (2007, 39). While Ali includes material goods in his definition of migration culture, the emphasis remains on the attitudes, beliefs, and values that "reinforce" migration.

Although more explicit in some cases than in others, the common denominator in these researchers' conceptions is that migration culture reinforces, facilitates, and propels emigration from a given community. While some authors emphasize the culture of migration as rooted in the migratory history of a community and others focus on the prevalence of foreign material goods or experiences, none speaks of the cultural influences that weigh *against* a potential migrant's decision to leave. In short, existing accounts of the culture of migration suggest its inexorable promotion of out-migration when available evidence shows this is clearly not the case. In Tunkás, Tunkaseño youths reflect a broad range of competing values. Some young people state they wish to migrate for reasons related to upward mobility or adventure, while others express the desire to remain in the hometown to be with family or to continue their schooling. Understanding this community's "culture of migration" demands a retooling of received understandings of the concept.

Redefining the Culture of Migration

While Tunkaseño migration culture is indeed a set of values, beliefs, and attitudes rooted in a collective migration history that influences the decision to migrate, that influence is not entirely positive. Rather, the culture of migration in Tunkás is a historically rooted but still contested territory, in which conflicting values, attitudes, and beliefs continue to produce varied migratory decisions. As we show below, the migration option is not equally valued across all age cohorts and social divides in the community. Instead, the value of migration is constantly renegotiated in Tunkás, as each Tunkaseño considers its diverse impacts on the community, the family, and the individual himself.

Having defined the culture of migration in the Tunkaseño context as a competing set of values that can positively or negatively influence the decision to migrate, the next step is to identify those values. We sought to do this in a systematic fashion, constructing a set of distinct values and beliefs that might compose this culture. To assist us, we first review the literature on the culture of migration for the values that appear to be prevalent in other migrant-sending societies. We explore three case studies that highlight specific values in these societies' cultures of migration and apply them to the Tunkás context.

Values and Their Effect on the Decision to Migrate: A Literature Review

Horvath's study of rural Romanian youth provides a look at two contrasting values that affect a youth's decision to migrate—the value of upward economic mobility and the value of remaining at home. Horvath suggests that Romanian youth placed a certain value on individual economic success, and oftentimes this value's influence outweighed the stigma attached to working in a lower-tier job. However, in contrast to the positive influence that valuing economic success exerts on the decision to migrate, Horvath shows that "staying in the home community [is] a form of moral responsibility towards the rest of the minority society" (2008, 780). Given that the value of staying in the hometown and the value of economic success coexist in this community, it is clear that there can be competing values with respect to migration within a single society.

Ali's case study of Muslim youth in India also records two prevailing beliefs that guide the decision to migrate—the value of supporting one's family and the value of the migratory experience itself. Ali notes that an Indian youth who does not migrate must defend that decision lest he or she be seen as disappointing their families. Further, Ali shows how those who migrate rise in social status and are seen as heroes, where "the desire to migrate is not only based on the promise of financial security, but also is rooted in a sense of adventure," making the "migrant-hero . . . desirable for a marriage partner" (2007, 48, 54).

Finally, Kandel and Massey's study of Mexican schoolchildren in Zacatecas examines the interplay between education and migration as a means of upward mobility. These authors find a "cultural milieu in which young people invest more faith in foreign wage labor than in Mexican education as a strategy for socioeconomic mobility" (2002, 996). While this suggests that many Zacatecan students place more value on migration than education, we can assume the reverse exists for other students. In other words, if a young potential migrant places a high value on education, he or she may be less likely to migrate to the United States for work. This is a cultural belief that could negatively shape the migration decision.

The five cultural values drawn from these three case studies—individual economic success, supporting one's family, the migratory experience, staying home, and continuing one's education—provide a framework for investigating the culture of migration in Tunkás. We analyzed the prevalence of these five values in the community using both quantitative and qualitative measures.

The remaining question to consider was how Tunkaseño youths might become infused with the attitudes, beliefs, and values that make up the Tunkás culture of migration. We hypothesized that friends and family, major media (television, radio), and community institutions (school and church) served as sources on which a youth could draw in forming his or her value system. In keeping with situated knowledge and practice theories (Bourdieu 1990), the values that make up the culture of migration will be manifest in daily practices and migration decisions. Thus, by observing the migration-related behaviors of Tunkaseño youth, we gain insight into Tunkás migration culture.

Youth in Tunkás Defined

For the purposes of our research, a "youth" is defined as any Tunkaseño between the ages of fifteen and twenty-eight. The lower age limit accords with the age restriction (young adulthood) followed in our surveys. The upper limit is derived from survey data showing that twenty-eight is the median age at marriage for both men and women in Tunkás. We have further divided the youth category in two cohorts: fifteen to seventeen, and eighteen to twenty-eight. Seventeen is a socially significant dividing line between cohorts because it is the median age at first internal migration and the point at which we find more Tunkaseños working than in school. We set our "middle age" at ages twenty-nine to forty-one. The cutoff age of forty-one is the median age at which a Tunkaseño's first child reaches eighteen and generally either finishes school or migrates internally for the first time—signs of a transition into adulthood.

THE CULTURE OF MIGRATION IN TUNKÁS

We found that all five of the values identified in the literature were present in Tunkás. Three positively influenced the decision to migrate, and two tended to negatively affect the decision to migrate. The positively influencing values are supporting one's family, socioeconomic success and upward mobility, and the migratory experience. The value of completing a set level of education and the value of family unity in Tunkás are the dominant cultural factors discouraging migration.[1]

---

1. The value of completing a desired level of education and the value of spatial family unity may also propel international migration given that some Mexican youths go

Supporting the Family and Individual Socioeconomic Success

Of sixty-six respondents who said they intended to migrate to the United States in 2009, 76 percent planned to do so for the betterment of their family or for individual socioeconomic mobility, confirming the prevalence of these values in Tunkás. Specifically, this fraction gave the following as reasons for migrating: an opportunity for a better salary, a standing job offer or no current employment in Mexico, plans to construct a home in Mexico, or plans to set up a business in Mexico. As theories of the new economics of migration underscore, these seemingly individual economic reasons to migrate form part of larger household strategies built around values of household solidarity (Stark and Bloom 1985).

Research on remittances, for example, demonstrates that most remittances are to help families in the hometown cover daily household expenses (Suro 2003; Cantú, Shaiq, and Urdanivia 2007; Rodríguez de la Gala, Molina, and García 2007). Migrating in order to build a residence in the sending community is also directly tied to the value of supporting one's family, given that most families in Tunkás feel the need to construct homes that provide better security and protection from flooding and other natural disasters. Using the lens of the new economics of labor migration, migration as a way to invest in a business in the sending community can also be motivated by a value of family support, as there is a "contractual arrangement" between the migrants and the rest of the household to diversify options for family well-being, including investing in enterprises within the sending community (Stark and Bloom 1985; Massey et al. 1993). Migrating internationally in search of better wages, more job opportunities, and a chance to invest in a house or business at home shows a strong connection to a value of familial support.

Fifteen-year-old Lourdes illustrates the link between economic circumstances and the desire to sustain one's family: "There are no jobs here," she said, "so it's necessary to look in other places in order to support the family." Though she had not yet mentioned her plans to her mother, thirteen-year-old Eva expressed a desire to migrate to the United States with her fifteen-year-old sister in the near future in order to help her mother provide for the household.

---

to the United States for higher education or family reunification. However, our findings suggest that these values remain largely negative in terms of their influence in the Tunkás context.

Juan, twenty years old, told us about a cousin who plans to go with him to the United States. Juan's cousin, who intends to cross the border without documents, wants to migrate because "he can no longer afford to have what he wants." In other words, acquiring material possessions is his motivation for migrating. And Fernando, mentioned at the beginning of this chapter, first migrated to the United States to earn money to start his own business. He now owns a successful water-purifying enterprise in Tunkás and claims he would like to return to the United States some-day for additional financial gain. Joaquín Ramírez, a teacher at a middle school in Tunkás, emphasizes the prevalence of this value: "The majority of those I've talked with go to the United States with the idea of getting ahead economically." These cases exemplify how the value of individual socioeconomic mobility contributes to the desire to migrate.

Value of the Migratory Experience

The value of the migratory experience itself in the culture of migration in Tunkás also positively influences the decision to migrate. Pedro, a seventeen-year-old high school student studying in Mérida, was tempted after hearing some friends recount the experiences of their first migra-tion. "Yes," he said, "I did want to go, to see how it is, how migrants cross the border into the United States, what happens, what the desert is like." The lure of boyhood adventure affected Pedro's early ideas of what the migrant experience would be.

The apparent monetary gain, the alteration in clothing and behavior, and the risks that migrants encounter in a clandestine crossing all con-tribute to glorify the image that younger teens hold of migration, add-ing to the value of the migratory experience. Seventeen-year-old Isabel commented: "Many girls here think that the male migrants have more money and things like that in the United States. The girls seek them out when they return because they're attracted by the money." Manuela, also seventeen years old, added, "I think they're brave, crossing the desert." She noted that many young migrants who return to Tunkás have adopted a U.S. style of dress, and she concurred that this is attractive to girls and young women in Tunkás. Interview respondents in Tunkás consistently estimated that about half of the town's young girls are attracted to a mi-grant in modern urban dress because of the contrast with the traditional, more conservative style of clothing in Tunkás.

Three young Tunkaseño friends enjoying the town's festivities.

Pedro corroborated this perception: "Girls want to be with those who've returned" because "they see something new in them." He was careful to note, however, that "some people see return migrants and think badly of them; they look at them and think they're weird." Pedro reaffirmed that migrants bring a certain style of dress from the United States and others in the town imitate it, but he does not see this style as either "good" or "bad."

Furthermore, as Fernando elaborated, there is a selective storytelling process that occurs when young male migrants return home that gives a skewed and glorified vision of the migrant lifestyle. This selective storytelling, combined with the number of young women who are attracted by a return migrant's style of dress and elevated socioeconomic standing, leads some young boys to emulate the idealized image of a migrant. This imitation is not widespread, but it is a well-recognized phenomenon in the town. We discuss this imitative behavior below and how it plays out as a young man matures.

The Value of Education

While many young Tunkaseños are influenced by the stories recounted by returning migrants, others respond to factors that negatively influence the decision to migrate or factors that at least alter their initial plans. Fourteen

Students take a break from studying at the municipal library.

percent of Tunkaseños between the ages of fifteen and twenty-eight said they did not intend to migrate in 2009 because they are currently students. For many Tunkás youths, completing one's studies supersedes migration as a means of bettering one's individual economic situation or gaining status among one's peers. Lourdes, for example, told us she would like to contribute to her family's income, and her brother-in-law has invited her to the United States. However, she prefers to finish her studies before leaving Mexico:

> Sometimes when my brother-in-law calls, he tells me how nice it is there and asks me if I'd like to go with my sister. And I tell him, "Well, maybe." But truthfully, I'd like to finish my studies. He tells me I can study over there, but I don't speak English.

In short, this young girl's desire to pursue more education outweighs any external influences to migrate internationally, which would necessarily interrupt her academic studies. Many Tunkaseños viewed youth migration, specifically female youth migration, as acceptable only if certain conditions were satisfied (see figures 7.1 and 7.2). Forty-one percent of all respondents believe it would be all right for a young female to migrate to the United States if she first finished her studies; 48 percent said the same for young males. That nearly half of all Tunkaseños believe young people should finish their education before migrating internationally demonstrates the considerable value the community places on education (for more on the choice between education and migration, see chapter 6, this volume).

Figure 7.1. *Question:* "When Would It Be Acceptable for a Young Female to Migrate to the United States?"

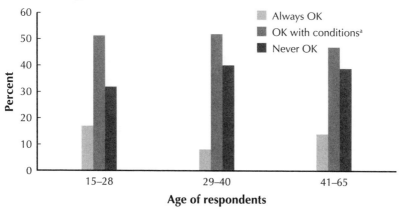

[a] Conditions include completing one's education, marriage, and having children.

Figure 7.2. *Question:* "When Would It Be Acceptable for a Young Male to Migrate to the United States?"

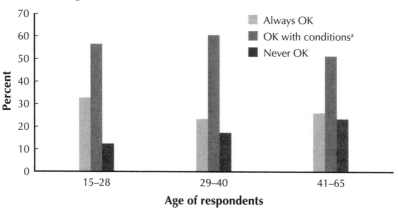

[a] Conditions include completing one's education, marriage, and having children.

The Value of Family Unity

A second factor that discourages migration is the importance of spatial family unity. Fourteen percent of respondents who did not intend to migrate to the United States in 2009 stated family reasons and having school-age children as motives for remaining in Mexico. Fifteen-year-old Blanca said that only economic necessity could convince her to leave Mexico. If she had a well-paid job in Tunkás, she would remain in the town with her family. The value of staying close to home heavily influences Blanca's desire to remain in Tunkás, and in different economic circumstances it would be the deciding factor in preventing her from migrating. Isabel demonstrated this commonly conflicting desire—if given the opportunity to migrate, whether to join a spouse in the United States or for the opportunity to work there, family unity always prevails:

> Well, I'd be overjoyed that since my husband is in the United States, I'd be able to go there, I'd be able to visit. But, on the other hand, I wouldn't see my family and I don't like that. Mostly I'd like to stay here in Tunkás, so, no, I wouldn't leave just for the chance of visiting someplace different.

In sum, while reinforcing positive decisions to migrate, the culture of migration in Tunkás also exerts an opposing force to negatively affect the decision to migrate. The culture of migration in Tunkás can thus be seen as swayed by two often-competing value sets with positive and negative migration-decision influences. On the positive end, there are the values of supporting the family, individual socioeconomic mobility, and the migratory experience itself (and the perceived status that comes with it). On the negative end, there is a value of education as a preferred means of mobility and the value of maintaining close physical proximity to one's family.

PATTERNS AMONG YOUTH WITHIN THE CULTURE OF MIGRATION

In this section we explore the ways in which the conflictive culture of migration in Tunkás translates into daily behaviors, social patterns, and migration decisions among youths. Transmission of the migration culture occurs through various sources, and the information they disseminate may serve to further the cultural conflict in Tunkás. Specifically, two distinct patterns emerge from the clash of values: a gender divide regarding who is more prone to migrate, and changes in a young male's value system over time.

Transmission of Values: Sources and Perceptions of Migration

We found the most significant sources of information about migration to be U.S.-based family members, informal relationships (with friends and co-workers), community institutions (school, church, and government), media (television, radio), and the community at large. We distinguish between sources that impart information *about* migration (such as community institutions or the media) versus information *for* migration (such as the household and informal relationships). Sources of information *about* migration present details about the dangers clandestine migrants may face (for example, Mexican news stations reporting migrant deaths along the border). Conversely, sources of information *for* migration directly facilitate migration decisions. For example, friends or family may provide contact information for people-smugglers and U.S. employers. To learn more about the influence of these various sources on youths' perceptions and beliefs about culturally acceptable migratory behavior, we asked respondents where they got information about migration in the last year (figure 7.3).

Figure 7.3. *Question:* "Where Do Young People Hear about Migration?"

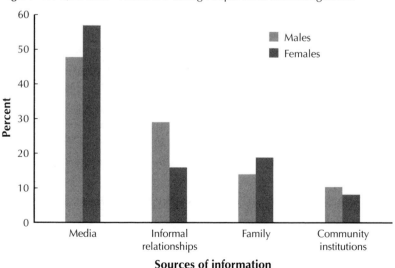

Migration in the Media

The media are clearly the most prominent source of information about migration for both young men and women. Fifty-seven percent of women and 48 percent of men in our 15–28 age group reported getting most information about migration from television and radio. In general, these sources portray migration in a negative light, warning of the dangers of crossing the border or the challenges of living in the United States. Blanca explained that many people in Tunkás were afraid of migrating "because the news sometimes tells of someone who was killed over there." Youths also receive news of the current economic crisis from the media and worry they will not be able to find jobs even if they do leave Mexico.

Migration Information from Friends and Family

The second most important sources of information—informal relationships and the family—illustrate an important difference between males and females: 29 percent of males report hearing the most about migration from informal relationships with friends or co-workers, compared to only 16 percent of females. Furthermore, slightly more females (19 percent) than males (14 percent) said they receive information about migration from the family. Because these sources provide information *for* migration, we suggest that friends and co-workers have more direct influence over young males, underscoring the strong role that peer networks play in informing migration decisions. Epstein and Gang (2006), who examine the "influence of others on migration plans," find that "herd behavior" has considerable influence on the migration decision. Those who want to migrate with friends and make their decisions based on their peers' plans evidence this behavior. Accordingly, we learned in our interviews that many young males plan trips with friends rather than with family. Enrique, a 22-year-old Tunkaseño, had migrated to the United States the previous year with eight friends from Tunkás. Two of the friends were returned migrants and knew both the dangers involved and the best strategies for a less risky crossing. Enrique told us, "we agreed that we would all go together, that no one would split off in order to cross over there. . . . We crossed the border as a group of friends from here, from Tunkás." Enrique's friends provided the support needed to ensure that he would make it to the United States. His story is typical of many young Tunkaseños, who rely on friends to help with the migration process.

The family—in both Tunkás and the United States—is a particularly important source of influence for girls. Though the data indicate that only slightly more females receive migration information in the household than do males, the young girls we interviewed confirm the significance of this source.

Family plays a dual role in young people's decision making because youths can feel pressured to remain close to the family and also pressured to migrate to help support the family. Females are often encouraged to stay while boys are encouraged to go. Parental attitudes toward migration vary widely in Tunkás. Many mothers stress the importance of spatial family unity, while fathers often speak of the value of the migratory experience. Claudia, the mother of an eighteen-year-old son, told us she did not want him to leave Mexico: "I think that youths can get ahead here . . . if, as they say in Yucatán, they make the effort to get ahead. They don't need to go to the United States. . . . They can succeed here." Further, Claudia is afraid of the dangers her son might encounter trying to cross the border and living away from home. She wants him to stay in Tunkás because, she said, "It's comfortable staying in your hometown."

Migration in the Community

Community institutions, such as schools or churches, exhibit relatively less influence over a youth's values associated with migration. Only 8 percent of females and 10 percent of males reported these institutions to be the prominent source of their information about migration. Nevertheless, many teachers encourage their students to finish their education before migrating. For instance, Joaquín Ramírez, a middle school teacher in Tunkás, says the majority of teachers "try to convince [their students] to continue studying, to finish the technical high school in Tunkás." But in reality, most only "finish middle school, and few have the opportunity to continue their studies." Ramírez also tells his students that finishing school offers "the only possibility for them to get ahead in life, without taking dangerous risks." There are also visible markers in the Tunkás community that are effective sources of information about the positive returns to migration. These include well-constructed, modern houses built with remittances, cars brought back by migrants, or nice clothing sent to family members. All are status symbols and reflect the values of supporting one's family and achieving individual economic success.

These various sources of information create mixed perceptions about migration, conveying several of the values discussed earlier. These values are transmitted differently depending on age and gender. In following sections, we focus on the ways in which men and women in different age groups absorb these values to create an array of migration decisions.

Gender Differences

The international migration of young Tunkaseños is mostly a male phenomenon. Seventy-eight percent of respondents in our 15–28 cohort who have international migration experience are young men. The median age for the first international migration experience among females in Tunkás is thirty-one, falling outside the youth cohort. Furthermore, 60 percent of female respondents with plans to migrate to the United States in the next year already have a husband residing there. These data reflect the gendered nature of the migration decision, with young girls placing greater value on remaining with the family, while young men place more value on supporting their family, on the migratory experience itself, and on individual economic success.

The value of remaining with family is also connected to the fear that many young girls express when talking about international migration. When asked why they were not thinking of migrating internationally, 37 percent of young females said they did not have documents or were afraid of crossing the border; this compares to 25 percent of young males. This fear is reinforced by television news and parental attitudes. The Mexican news media often portray clandestine border crossing as life-threatening, and thus as an activity better chanced by younger males. Thirty-six percent of respondents said it is never acceptable for a girl or young woman to migrate to the United States, while only 17 percent said the same for boys or young men (see figures 7.1 and 7.2). Eva's case is typical; she would like to see new places and also help her mother financially, but she has been reluctant to even discuss these plans because of her mother's concerns about safety.

Three generations of Tunkaseñas.

The combination of parents' expectations and fears, along with the value that young women place on staying with the family and on education, results in more young girls migrating internally than internationally (see figure 7.4). The gender divide decreases significantly when we look at internal migration; of all respondents in the 15–28 cohort who have internal migration experience, 56 percent are males and 44 percent are females. Gabriel, seventeen years old and about to finish high school, explained that students in Tunkás who want to continue their education beyond high school must go to Mérida because there is no higher education institution in Tunkás. He noted: "Few girls go to the United States. . . . The girls go to Mérida or some other place, but they don't leave Mexico." By going to Mérida a Tunkás girl can abide by the values of staying near or with family in Mexico while pursuing education as a means of upward mobility, thus both adhering to her parents expectations and fulfilling her own educational aspirations.

Figure 7.4. International and Internal Migration Experience, by Gender

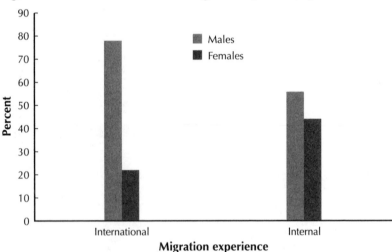

It should be noted that though the value of remaining with the family seems more widespread among girls, the same does not apply regarding the value of education as an alternative to migrating. We find just as many boys as girls expressing an interest in higher education.[2] However, certain values that reinforce the decision to migrate do dominate the young Tunkás male mind-set and are less frequently seen among young women. These include the values of contributing to the economic support of

---

2. For more on this topic, see chapter 6.

the family, succeeding economically as an individual, and the migratory experience itself.

When Emanuel was asked why his friends are in the United States, he initially responded that they were there to send money to their families. He said this is the most common reason for a male from Tunkás to migrate to the United States. But when we asked him whether his friends left Tunkás for the United States because they want to have a house, to have material things, to prepare themselves for marriage, or just for the adventure of it, he answered, "just for the adventure of it." Emanuel's response demonstrates that it is a mixture of wanting to support the family in Tunkás and an interest in the adventure associated with the migration experience that is propelling young men to leave to the United States. We found no young women who expressed an interest in the migratory experience, and fewer girls than boys espoused economic responsibility to the family as a reason for migrating.

Gabriel provides an interesting look at the interplay between the value of education and the value of supporting his family. Gabriel's father has been in the United States for eight years and has seen his children only rarely. When we asked Gabriel if he had any interest in going to the United States, he said he needs to stay with his mother and sisters because he is the only remaining male in the household. He would rather go to Mérida, where he can stay close to his family while he advances his education, one he believes will bring future socioeconomic mobility.

Gabriel's case is unique in that the value of supporting the family combines with the value of education to yield a negative migration decision. This case demonstrates that the culture of migration in Tunkás has ambiguous effects on youth emigration, and it is a caution against any generalization that would relegate the values that enforce out-migration to males and the cultural forces that inhibit migration to females. Though this pattern is apparent in Tunkás, we must be wary about making sharply separated gendered categories. Though we find the values that propel out-migration to be more common among young males, they are not unique to them, and there is a significant amount of overlap between the sexes and the value systems they express. Thus youths' international migration from Tunkás is mostly, but not exclusively, a male phenomenon.

Maturing Motives for Migration: From Adventure to Breadwinning

As young male Tunkaseños mature, their value system and their reasons for migrating often shift. From ages fifteen to seventeen,[3] many boys express an interest in going to the United States largely for the migratory experience itself. Although economic success or family support are still important factors, they are subordinate to the desire for "adventure" and a perceived increase in social status. From ages eighteen to twenty-eight, the value of the migratory experience begins to fade, giving way to more conventional notions of supporting the family or personal economic gain, values that persist as young people transition into adult roles as spouses, parents, or full-time workers (Goldschneider and DaVanzo 1985, 546).

The desire for adventure among the younger cohort is heightened by the money and the stories returning migrants bring back to Tunkás. Fernando related the impact veteran migrants had on his decision-making process: "Some get here and tell you that all they did was go from party to party, but they don't tell you, 'I had to wake up at six in the morning to go to work.' And the young men think, 'parties, parties!' We only went out two or three times in the United States, no more than that." Like Fernando, some youths hear very selective accounts of the migration experience and may not comprehend the difficulties involved in living and working clandestinely abroad. Furthermore, young Tunkaseños witness the rewards of migration as remittance-receiving families build nice homes or returning migrants come back to Tunkás with cars. During the town fiestas, many returned migrants attract the community's praise and attention, increasing the likelihood that boys and young men will want to imitate them.

Shortly after discussing the selective storytelling that occurs in Tunkás, Alberto related how he had changed. "That's why I'm telling you this," he said, "because I went through the same thing." He was referring to the change that many young males experience over time as they switch from dreams of adventure to the reality of needing to support oneself and one's family.

By the age of eighteen, most Tunkaseños have left school and found jobs. Of the eighteen-year-olds whom we interviewed, only 35 percent

---

3. The age cohorts presented are not absolute cutoffs for this phenomenon; they are presented for the sake of analysis.

continue to study (compared with 48 percent in Mexico as a whole in 2005), and 59 percent had begun working. It is around this age that many Tunkaseños leave home for nearby Mérida or Cancún on an internal migration that often serves as a "training ground" for later international migration (Rodríguez, Wittlinger, and Manzanero Rodríguez 2007). Through these experiences—leaving school and leaving home—young males become more independent and more able to support themselves and/or their families.

We attribute the attitudinal and behavioral shifts in young males to the pressure of taking on adult roles as spouses, parents, or full-time workers (Goldschneider and DaVanzo 1985, 545–46). As young male Tunkaseños marry, have children, and take full-time jobs, they become increasingly independent and refocus their attention on these new obligations. Yolanda told us about her husband, Ernesto, who was fifteen when he left for *el norte*. Ernesto feels he did not take full advantage of his migration experience because he was too young to be concerned about such future responsibilities as supporting a family or building a house: "I only thought about going to parties and dances, meeting girls." Ernesto is typical of many young men who first migrated for the sake of the migratory experience itself. However, when he acquired "adult roles," he became more concerned with migration as a means of supporting his family.

Furthermore, as youths grow older, they may pay more heed to the negative aspects of migration. Juan, the twenty-year-old mentioned previously who intends to migrate with his cousin, already has international migration experience and had left for the United States at a young age. When speaking of his experience, he noted: "Before, I didn't really think things through. Everything looked so easy, but now . . . you begin to think more clearly about how things are in the United States . . . that if *la migra* picks you up, they'll deport you back to Yucatán." As Juan grew older, he became less interested in the migratory experience and more conscious of his need to avoid *la migra* if he were to continue supporting his family with remittances.

Finally, many young people acquire the freedom and sense of responsibility to make the migration decision when they finish school. Joaquín Ramírez, the teacher mentioned earlier, explained:

It's not very common for young people to migrate before finishing middle school because they feel they must still obey their parents, but once they finish school they feel they can make their own decisions as doors begin to open, so if a friend says "let's go," they go.

How the motives for migration shift over time as a young person matures into adulthood is an important consideration when evaluating the reasons young males decide to migrate. Although the quantitative data reduce their migration logic to simple economic motivations, our qualitative evidence shows there is another significant component—the value of the migratory experience—an influence to which the 15–17 age cohort is especially susceptible.

CONCLUSION

The culture of migration in Tunkás defies the conception prevailing in the literature that a migration culture consistently reinforces the decision to migrate. We identified five value sets in three case studies and measured their prevalence in Tunkás. These included the values of individual socioeconomic success, of supporting one's family, of the migratory experience itself, of education, and of staying in the home community with one's family.

These cultural factors interact and compete among the youth we interviewed, resulting in a varied pattern of migratory decisions. We found international migration by young Tunkaseños to be mostly a male phenomenon, since young males respond to the values that positively influence the decision to migrate, especially the value of the migratory experience itself. Young women, on the other hand, express more interest in staying with the family, providing a partial explanation for the gendered nature of international youth emigration from Tunkás. Further, some young males display a change of values over time, the value of the migratory experience giving way to more traditional values, such as supporting family members who remain in the hometown.

We also found wide variation in the ways the community at large perceives return migrants, a fact that intensifies the interplay of migration-related values in Tunkás. Because most Tunkaseños receive their information about migration from the media, which tend to focus on deaths along the border and the Border Patrol's mistreatment of migrants, this is clearly an influence for a negative migration decision. Also negative is the opinion some Tunkaseños, particularly the older members of the community, express about the changes that return migrants exhibit in their behavior and style of dress. However, return migrants who have achieved economic success and invest in their families and the community are seen positively, and some Tunkás youths feel strongly attracted to the migrant lifestyle.

Thus the culture of migration in Tunkás does not only promote outmigration, and this fact holds important implications for future research. Would the same be true of a community of comparable size but with a longer international migration history? Exploring the differences between Tunkás and a community with deeper migration roots may shed greater light on the interplay between a community's migration culture, its migration history, and young people's migration decision making. One could determine the presence and persistence of key findings from our study, such as the presence of a conflictive migration culture, a gender divide with respect to youth migration, and a change in young males' values as they mature. Further, although we have shown that the value system of many young Tunkás males changes over time with respect to migration, we have not explained why. What contributions could childhood and adolescent psychology make toward explaining this phenomenon? Such a line of inquiry would open the door to further interdisciplinary study of the culture of Mexican migration.

REFERENCES

Ali, Syed. 2007. "'Go West Young Man': The Culture of Migration among Muslims in Hyderabad, India," *Journal of Ethnic and Migration Studies* 33, no. 1: 37–58.

Bourdieu, Pierre. 1990. *In Other Words: Essays Towards a Reflexive Sociology.* Stanford, CA: Stanford University Press.

Cantú, Brisella, Fawad Shaiq, and Anjanette Urdanivia. 2007. "Migration and Local Development." In *Impacts of Border Enforcement on Mexican Migration: The View from Sending Communities,* ed. Wayne A. Cornelius and Jessa M. Lewis. La Jolla, CA: Center for Comparative Immigration Studies, University of California, San Diego.

Cornelius, Wayne A. 1990. *Labor Migration to the United States: Development Outcomes and Alternatives in Mexican Sending Communities.* Washington, DC: Commission for the Study of International Migration and Cooperative Economic Development.

Epstein, Gil S., and Ira N. Gang. 2006. "The Influence of Others on Migration Plans," *Review of Development Economics* 10, no. 4: 652–65.

Geertz, Clifford. 1973. *The Interpretation of Cultures: Selected Essays.* New York: Basic Books.

Goldschneider, Kobrin, and Julie DaVanzo. 1985. "Living Arrangements and the Transition to Adulthood," *Demography* 22, no. 4: 545–63.

Horvath, Istvan. 2008. "The Culture of Migration of Rural Romanian Youth," *Journal of Ethnic and Migration Studies* 34, no. 5: 771–86.

Kandel, William, and Douglas S. Massey. 2002. "The Culture of Mexican Migration: A Theoretical and Empirical Analysis," *Social Forces* 80, no. 3: 981–1004.

Massey, Douglas S., Joaquin Arango, Graeme Hugo, Ali Kouaouci, Adela Pellegrino, and Edward J. Taylor. 1993. "Theories of International Migration: A Review and Appraisal," *Population and Development Review* 19, no. 3: 431–66.

Rodríguez, Andrea, Jennifer Wittlinger, and Luis Manzanero Rodríguez. 2007. "The Interface between Internal and International Migration." In *Mayan Journeys: The New Migration from Yucatán to the United States,* ed. Wayne A. Cornelius, David Fitzgerald, and Pedro Lewin Fischer. La Jolla, CA: Center for Comparative Immigration Studies, University of California, San Diego.

Rodríguez de la Gala, Juan, Vanessa Molina, and Daisy García. 2007. "Migration and Local Development." In *Mayan Journeys: The New Migration from Yucatán to the United States,* ed. Wayne A. Cornelius, David Fitzgerald, and Pedro Lewin Fischer. La Jolla, CA: Center for Comparative Immigration Studies, University of California, San Diego.

Stark, Oded, and David E. Bloom. 1985. "The New Economics of Labor Migration," *American Economic Review* 75, no. 2: 173–78.

Suro, Roberto. 2003. "Remittance Senders and Receivers: Tracking the Transnational Channels." Washington, DC: Pew Hispanic Center.

Tunkaseño children gather after school in the town plaza.

8 The Family Dynamics of Tunkaseño Migration

KELLY NIELSEN, ARADHANA TIWARI, DAVID PASQUINI,
· LIZETTE SOLÓRZANO, AND MAY WEJEBE

Though many factors may influence the decision to migrate away from one's hometown, the process begins and ends with the family. Migration can be an individual action, but more often than not the migration decision involves a cost-benefit analysis of the possible impacts on the migrant and the migrant's family. Creating a higher living standard for one's family, a primary driver of many migration decisions, is often a collective decision that holds multiple consequences. The family, as well as the migrant, endures a great deal of stress in attempting to become a competitor in a highly globalized world. This raises the question, to what degree is familial stability being compromised for a "better life"?

Increased enforcement at the U.S.-Mexico border, in combination with the global economic crisis, has exacerbated the stress on individual migrants and their nonmigrant family members. We find that international migration creates more challenges for the family than does internal migration. Mixed migration—where some family members migrate to other parts of Mexico and other members go to the United States—can lessen the deleterious impacts of international migration on the family, but not all families share the benefits of mixed migration equally. This chapter explores the various strategies families employ to maintain relationships despite increased U.S. border control, the rising costs of transportation and communication, and the economic crisis. This chapter also considers how families negotiate separation under different patterns of family migration—internal, international, and mixed—with particular attention to the kinds of disruptions the families experience. Finally, the chapter analyzes how migration challenges familial stability and how the migration process affects all members of a family across multiple facets in both positive and negative ways.

FAMILY TREE: PAST STUDIES OF MIGRATION AND THE FAMILY

Much of the research on family and migration has been guided by the new economics of migration theory, which posits that migration decisions are strategic, rational family or household decisions that attempt to minimize risk while maximizing income (Massey et al. 1993). Likewise, De Jong and Gardner (1981) assert that the family is central in understanding migration decisions because these are not individual decisions; they are the result of bargaining between the migrant and family members. Not all researchers are in agreement on this point, however, Hondagneu-Sotelo (1994) challenges the household strategies model, finding that men often make the decision to migrate without the consent of or input from their wives or others in the family.

The broad scope of the impacts of migration on Mexican families is undeniable. According to the Pew Hispanic Center (2009), there were 12.7 million Mexican immigrants living in the United States in 2008. Given that each individual in the migrant flow is part of a family unit, at least some of whose members remain in Mexico, one can begin to imagine immigration's wide-reaching impacts on Mexican families.

What Is the "Family"?

Three key concepts dominate the discussion of family life and familial arrangements: the individual members who comprise a "family"; the concept of a "household," which provides a particular geographic or spatial referent for these individuals; and the idea of "home," which can refer to the physical household or be used as a symbolic representation of house and family space.

Mexican and U.S. scholars have defined "family" as a basic economic, social, and reproductive unit (Skolnick and Skolnick 1994; Murdock 1960; Sánchez Azcona 1976). Specifically, families have been defined as two adults in a socially acceptable sexual relationship and the children who are products of that sexual relationship and/or adopted children (Murdock 1960; Sánchez Azcona 1976).

Some scholars include the concept of "household," defining family as a married couple or a group of kinfolk that may or may not live in the same household (Skolnick and Skolnick 1994; Ortiz 1984). Households, unlike families, are often defined in spatial terms. Ortiz (1984) says that daily social contact always takes place in particular physical spaces; therefore, the idea of household contains a specific notion of space. Family and household do not signify precisely the same concept, but they do provide an important way to conceptualize the family.

Furthermore, "home" is frequently used in connection with families or households. But is there a difference between a home and a household? Munro and Madigan define home as encompassing both the physical and the social: "The house itself is home, as are the social relations contained within it" (1999). Thus "home" is at the intersection of family and household as the symbolic space within which an individual constructs her/his conception of family and where she/he can arrange a household to reflect this conception.

However, families do not always fall into definite types. Even when family types can be defined, these are further differentiated by the multiple living arrangements family members create or by what—or where—family members consider "home." In the United States, the "nuclear family"—a provider, a caregiver, and dependents—is often accepted as the most fundamental and traditional form of family unit (Skolnick and Skolnick 1994).[1] Further complicating the notion of a "traditional" family is the fact that families may or may not live in the same household, as when families are separated by divorce or migration. In short, there is no universally legitimate family arrangement or single definition of family.

Our definition of family acknowledges all three conceptualizations—family, home, and household. Because geographic separation between family members in the context of migration in Tunkás challenges the spatial immediacy associated with household and home, we use the affective, communicative, and economic ties that bind family members who are dispersed across geographic spaces. We focus on families separated by internal and international migration, specifically cases where the separa-

---

1. However, even nuclear families vary tremendously and can include same-sex parents with children, families reconstituted following divorce, and parents with adopted children.

tion occurs between migrants and their parents, spouses, and children who remain in Tunkás.

These three relationships—migrants and parents, migrants and spouses, migrants and children—allow us to explore the complexity of family dynamics when a family member leaves. Each separation represents a different level of "split": an upward split refers to the migrant and parents; horizontal split refers to the migrant and spouse; and downward split refers to the migrant and children. These types of family separation frame our discussion of migration's impacts on the Tunkaseño family.

We first discuss the types of family separation—upward, horizontal, and downward—observed in internal, international, and mixed migration families. We then analyze family disruption across a family's economic, communicative, and affective ties in both internal and international migration. We next consider whether mixed migration can mitigate some of the disadvantages of strictly internal and strictly international migration. We conclude with a discussion of implications for future research on families and migration.

TYPES OF MIGRATION AND FAMILY SEPARATION

Internal Migration

Migration, both internal and international, is an increasingly common fact of life for Tunkaseños. Of the 1,030 respondents in our 2009 survey, 45 percent reported having lived somewhere other than Tunkás at some point, and 42 percent currently living in Tunkás reported having at least one relative living in another part of Mexico (figure 8.1). These numbers show the extent to which migration has reached into the community and the amount of family separation that takes place: mothers and fathers from sons and daughters, husbands from wives.

The familial nature of migration magnifies the number of people migration involves. For example, 62 percent of the surveyed married internal migrants living away from Tunkás reported that their spouse lives in Tunkás, and 69 percent indicated that their children live in Tunkás (table 8.1). Conversely, 10 percent of Tunkaseños residing in Tunkás reported that their spouse lives in another part of Mexico, and 10 percent have at least one parent outside the community. Finally, we found that 34 percent of respondents living in Tunkás have children in other parts of Mexico, and 47 percent of Tunkaseños living in other parts of Mexico have at least one parent in the home community. In short, internal migration has produced Tunkaseño family dispersal across Mexico, particularly the Yucatán Peninsula. In the majority of cases, internal migration means family separation at one or more levels—upward, downward, or horizontal. It is not uncommon for spouses to be several hours of travel apart, for children to see one or both parents only occasionally, or for parents to see their children only when they come home for the annual fiesta. Internal migration affects each split level differently, but it is clear that these effects reach a large fraction of the community.

Figure 8.1. Separation Pattern of Tunkaseño Migrants and Their Families

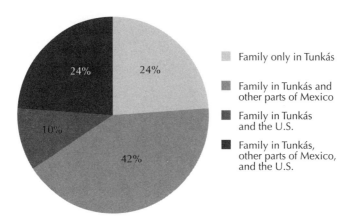

- Family only in Tunkás
- Family in Tunkás and other parts of Mexico
- Family in Tunkás and the U.S.
- Family in Tunkás, other parts of Mexico, and the U.S.

Table 8.1. Separation among Internal Migration Families

	Separated from Spouse	Separated from One or More Children	Separated from One or Both Parents
Respondents living in Tunkás	10% N = 559	34% N = 606	10% N = 672
Respondents living in other part of Mexico	62% N = 98	69% N = 89	47% N = 173

Note: Totals are for married respondents, respondents with children, and respondents with parents, respectively.

International Migration

Like other Yucatecans, Tunkaseños joined the statewide surge in international migration that began in the early 1990s (Lewin Fischer 2007, 16). Twenty-four percent of the respondents currently living in Tunkás said they had a relative in the United States.[2] Today, approximately 17 percent of the Tunkaseños we surveyed live in the United States, concentrated in the Southern California cities of Inglewood and Anaheim.

Most Tunkaseño international migrants are married with children, and international migration, like internal migration, implies family separation. For instance, 49 percent of migrants to the United States report that they had to leave their children in Mexico on their first trip to the United States. Of this subgroup, 90 percent said they left their children behind with their mother. Arturo explained that he left his wife and children in Tunkás because of the dangers involved in crossing the border without documents: "I didn't take them with me because of the problem of the border crossing. Since we didn't have papers, we didn't have an easy way to enter the country. . . . We had to go through the mountains, and I didn't want to put my family at risk." Had there been a safer and easier way for Arturo to enter the United States with his family, he might have chosen to keep his family together.

For many couples, international migration means years apart. We asked international migrants whether during the last five years they had spent more time in Mexico or the United States. Of the respondents who spent the majority of the past five years in the United States, 66 percent had spouses who had never migrated. Eleven percent of the respondents living in the United States had left a spouse behind in Tunkás, and 14 percent had children there (table 8.2). Nine percent were separated from both a spouse *and* at least one child who remained in Tunkás, and 54 percent reported a parent in the home community. In total, 81 percent of respondents living in the United States reported having at least one family member in Tunkás.

Despite the comparatively short history of international migration from Tunkás, Tunkaseños who migrate to the United States tend to remain there for long periods. The median time a migrant remained in the

---

2. When asking about the whereabouts of the respondent's relatives, the 2009 survey referred only to spouses, children, siblings, parents, and grandparents.

United States on their most recent trip was six years. Of the Tunkaseños with migration experience whom we interviewed, 57 percent spent more time in the United States than in Mexico during the last five years, and nearly 45 percent of the interviewees said that their most recent trip to the United States had lasted longer than they had anticipated. Nonmigrant respondents with migrant spouses in the United States reported spending a median of 3.5 years away from their husband or wife. Clearly, families with international migrants are spending long periods apart, separated by an international border that is increasingly difficult to cross.

Table 8.2. Separation among International Migration Families

	Separated from Spouse	Separated from One or More Children	Separated from One or Both Parents[a]
Respondents living in Tunkás	3.8% N = 500	10.7% N = 532	4.1% N = 614
Respondents living in the United States	11% N = 99	14% N = 104	54% N = 151

Note: Totals are for married respondents, respondents with children, and respondents with parents, respectively.

[a] Because we did not collect data on children under the age of fifteen, this figure does not reflect the full extent to which children are separated from migrant parents. As a proxy, we looked at married respondents living in Tunkás with children under the age of fifteen and whose spouse lives in the United States (N = 261) and found that 3.8 percent of respondents fit these criteria. However, because this does not take into account the number of children under age fifteen, we believe that the real figure is much larger.

The combination of extended stays in the United States and split families means that families may endure long years of separation, with little or no interruption. On average, Tunkaseño international migrants who spent the majority of the last five years in the United States returned to their hometown approximately 1.5 times during that time. Those who spent the majority of the last five years in the United States and were undocumented averaged less than one return visit during that period.

The causes for extended separations are many, but financial need and the costs and risks associated with entering the United States without documents are particularly significant. When migrants do return to

Tunkás, they most often reported that it is to reunite with their families; when asked why they returned to Tunkás, 40 percent of these respondents gave family reunification as the most important reason and it was also the leading second choice. In short, the impacts of international migration, which is a relatively recent but transformative phenomenon in Tunkás, are being felt in the economic, affective, and communicative spheres of family life.

Mixed Migration

Well over two-thirds (71 percent) of respondents living in Tunkás who reported having a relative in the United States also indicated that they had at least one relative in another part of Mexico. There are several reasons that may explain why families opt for a combination of internal and international migration. Rodríguez, Wittlinger, and Manzanero Rodríguez (2007) identified a process of "stepwise migration" from Tunkás, first to an internal destination and then on to the United States. In a mixed-migration family, several members may have first migrated internally before a portion of them left for the United States. Another possibility is that the older generation of migrants may have gone to internal destinations while younger family members left directly for the United States. This is increasingly the case as Tunkaseños have developed networks to aid new migrants in the journey north.

Alternatively, the needs of a family may have led one or more members to stay in Mexico while spurring others to go to the United States. For example, Señora López's brother migrated to Cancún and was able to support his wife and children on the income he earned working in a fish market. Her husband, on the other hand, had to go to the United States, where higher salaries enabled him to pay for their son's cancer treatments. Señora López told us that her husband left "to send money for my son who died." Finally, it is possible that mixed migration families are employing a strategy that takes advantage of the higher wages available in the United States as well as the benefits of having someone close by in an internal migration destination. Whatever the reasons, the mixed migration arrangement may be the best alternative when more than one family member leaves Tunkás.

MIGRATION AND FAMILY DISRUPTION

Each type of migration—internal, international, and mixed—affects the family differently. These differences become apparent when we look at each migration model through the communicative, emotional, and economic realms of family life.

This section reveals that, relative to international migration, internal migration has a *low degree* of disruption for Tunkaseño families. Proximity and ease of communication lower migration's financial and emotional costs to the family, while the higher wages migrants can earn elsewhere in Mexico deliver economic benefits that cannot be obtained if the family stays together in Tunkás. In other words, the communicative, affective, and economic outcomes of internal migration may be less problematic for families than the outcomes of international migration. This is the case at all three levels of family split: upward, downward, and horizontal.

On the other hand, increased migration to the United States has lengthened the period of separation for the growing number of families involved in the process. The great distance between Tunkás and Southern California, and the significant risks and costs migrants shoulder when covering this distance, have serious consequences for families involved in international migration. For these reasons, international migration leads to a *high degree* of disruption for families. The greater distances and the barriers to movement across those spaces exacerbate the problems associated with separated families. Communication, either by telephone or face to face, is difficult and expensive when a migrant leaves Mexico for the United States. And the longer that families are separated, the more chances there are for disruptive factors such as adultery, abandonment, and divorce. Despite the disruption, families continue to commit to international migration, whether out of dire necessity or the ambition to enhance one's socioeconomic standing.

Economic Impact on Internal and International Migration Families

The single greatest driving force in the decision to migrate internally or internationally is economic necessity. The economic incentives for migration become much higher when migrants have a family to support. As one Tunkaseño explained, "Mexican families benefit from migration. If they send fifty dollars, that equals many pesos here, and that really helps us." These comments echo the sentiment of many Tunkaseño migrants about the importance of sending remittances, especially dollars.

In addition to seeing remittances as a way to meet a family's needs, relatives and migrants often interpret money sent in cards, payments of school fees, and care packages as demonstrations of love and care (Horst 2006). Remittances not only keep families in the sending communities financially secure, but they also reduce the stress on migrants, who know that their families' needs are being met.

As with families throughout Mexico, migration has generated positive economic outcomes for Tunkaseño families. Both internal and international migration have brought financial gains to remittance-receiving families. The wealth index for Tunkás shows that nonmigrant families had less wealth than migrant families (table 8.3).[3] The difference between internal and international migration families was less pronounced; the wealth of the latter was higher but by only a marginally significant amount.[4]

Table 8.3. Wealth Index Scores for Tunkaseño Families

	Nonmigrant Families	Migrant Families	Internal Migration Families	International Migration Families	Mixed Migration Families
Wealth index	53.3	**62.6*****	**61.7*****	**65.6*****	**65.0*****

*** Significance level relative to nonmigrant families, $p < .001$.

For many Tunkaseño families, internal migration provides substantial economic benefits. For instance, Señor and Señora Ferrer's children give them money when they can afford to. According to Señora Ferrer, "My children have expenses, so they usually don't send us anything. But when we visit them in Playa del Carmen, if they have some money they give it to us. If they don't have any, well, I understand that they

---

3. This finding was statistically significant at a $p < .001$ level.
4. Given the modest wealth gains made by families that undertake international migration, the decision to go to the United States rather than stay within Mexico raises complex questions about the motivations for families to participate in international rather than internal migration. Though we offer some suggestions as to why a family would choose migration to the United States over migration to other parts of Mexico despite the marginal gains associated with U.S. migration, our main focus is on the benefits and disruptions associated with the two types of migration.

have family expenses and can't help us." Because the Ferrers are able to support themselves on the husband's pension, they used the money they received from their migrant children to pay for a new kitchen and some furniture, as opposed to using it to cover basic expenses, as many remittance-receiving families must do. In other words, the Ferrers are a remittance-independent household,[5] not a remittance-dependent or remittance-complementary household. Similarly, Doña Fermina receives money from her son in Mérida only when she has moments of particular need. As Doña Fermina explained, "My son in Mérida sends money only when we have difficult times, but not continuously, because he also has a family to support. He works, but he is a pastor; he doesn't make much money. He gives us two or three hundred pesos, but not regularly." Lily and her siblings, on the other hand, send money to their mother regularly. All but one of them live in Mérida; twice a month they get together to pool money to send back to Tunkás, which their mother uses for basic expenses and only occasionally to improve the house. For many upwardly split families, remitting was irregular or occurred less frequently than in horizontally or downwardly split families. Yet whether remittances are used for home upgrades, emergencies, or subsistence, internal migration has provided important financial resources for these families.

Horizontally and downwardly split families typically require, or at least receive, a steadier stream of remittances. Doña Magdalena has raised all fourteen of her grandchildren in Tunkás, but the economic responsibility for their care remains with their parents, who live in Mérida. Doña Magdalena explained that her daughter "sends the money for food for the girls, clothes, school supplies, everything. She covers all their expenses." Señor Torres, a migrant living in Cancún, described the incessant economic demands put on him by his three primary school–aged daughters, who need a constant supply of clothes, books, and art supplies. For both Doña Magdalena's family and the Torres family, internal migration has allowed the family to earn sufficient money to cover basic expenses.

Overall, internal migration's economic impact on families is largely positive. Nevertheless, for many families the gains come at the cost of family unity. As Juanita Puc, a nonmigrant whose daughter lives in

---

5. In chapter 2 of this volume, the authors found three types of households that receive remittances: remittance-dependent, remittance-complementary, and remittance-independent.

Cancún, recounted about the birth of her granddaughter: "Her parents brought her to me when she was only fifteen days old; they left her as a baby. They left her, and my daughter went to Cancún. My daughter couldn't care for her child because she worked. She had to leave the baby in Tunkás so that she could work."

While financial reasons drive both internal and international migration, the financial reasons for going to the United States can differ from those that lead to internal migration. Although 57 percent of international migrants surveyed cited better salaries and more jobs as the primary reasons for going to the United States the first time, the need to earn higher wages reflects a variety of objectives. For example, Señor López migrated to the United States for the first time to earn money to build a house for his wife and three children. After a year and a half, unsatisfied with his new life in the United States and wanting to be reunited with his family, he returned to Tunkás. However, soon his son was diagnosed with cancer, and Señor López returned to California to earn money to cover his son's medical expenses. Because of the high costs associated with international migration and his son's mounting medical bills in Mexico, Señor López was not able to return home until his son died. He came home just long enough to bury his son and then left once more for the United States in order to pay the remaining medical bills and repay loans he had taken to cover the costs of migration. Señor López spent a total of ten years away from his family. Like the López family, many families find international migration a necessity, but the long periods of family separation associated with international migration can be a factor in the erosion of economic support for dependent family members in the home community.

The reasons why a family in Tunkás might lose financial support from a migrant family member vary. Migrants can become victims of drug and alcohol abuse, arrest, violence, accidents, or economic downturns, any of which can make them less likely or unable to continue earning and sending money home. Señora López expressed a commonly shared fear that infidelity will cause migrants to stop supporting their spouses and children in Tunkás: "They leave a wife abandoned here and then hook up with another woman over there. The woman over there gets his money, so he doesn't send any here to his family." When this occurs, there are multiple disruptions to the spouse and children in the home community.

The nonmigrant spouse may have to increase her workload or enter the labor market for the first time to support the family. Given the limited options for work in Tunkás, she may borrow money or other resources from family members or neighbors. Children may have to start working sooner than they would otherwise have done, possibly forcing them to drop out of school. The spouse and older children may decide to migrate themselves in order to support the rest of the family, thereby causing new family separations and disruptions (see chapter 2 for more on coping strategies people employ when they stop receiving remittances).

Upwardly split families dependent on or used to receiving money from migrant children can face tremendous challenges when remittances are reduced or disappear altogether. Fernando, a Tunkaseño in his mid-forties living in Garden Grove, California, was planning to stop sending money to his parents in Tunkás because he had recently had his work hours reduced in the restaurant where he works as a chef. To tide his parents over until his restaurant hours picked up again, Fernando sold land he owned in Tunkás. Not all migrants, though, have the resources to maintain the family until conditions improve. Elderly parents who require medicines or medical attention may find themselves without health care if something prevents a migrant child from sending money. Some migrants' parents rely on remittances for basic subsistence. Matilde explained how her son's change of job reduced the amount of money he could send her:

> I have a son in Los Angeles who used to send me money every two weeks. He sent me something every two weeks, but now he sends me money once a month because he's working less. He had two jobs—one during the week and one on Saturdays, and what he earned on Saturdays was what he sent to me, and what he earned during the week he kept to pay his rent and everything else, his expenses. So now he doesn't send me money like before. Now he sends me a thousand pesos each month.

Elderly parents whose migrant children are no longer able to send remittances may not have the option of entering the workforce or migration stream because of their age. In some cases, another child may have to migrate or other migrant children may have to increase the amount of support they contribute to their parents.

At all three levels of family split, the economic effects of migration can range from a statistically significant gain for families to a financially devastating situation for those left behind. International migration, though, has greater potential for economic disruption. Paula, discussing her brother and sister-in-law who live in the United States, pointed out the economic precariousness that can come from being undocumented. "Sometimes, but not always, they send money. They say that work in the United States is scarce, and since she entered illegally maybe she's not earning much." As discussed in chapters 3 and 5 of this volume, undocumented workers also may have fewer protections in the workplace or lose their livelihood if they are caught in a workplace raid by Immigration and Customs Enforcement (ICE). Outside the workplace, undocumented migrants risk arrest and deportation, putting a sudden end to their ability to earn and cutting off the remittance stream to the rest of the family. Paula continued, "People just want to better their situation a bit, but sometimes immigration officials deport them and they come back here. The money that they put together to go, often borrowed money, becomes a heavy debt burden." A combination of loans to cover the costs of migration and troubles with immigration status can turn hope for financial gain into legal troubles and crushing debt.

In addition to economic problems linked to legal status, the long separations associated with international migration may induce migrants to use alcohol or drugs to relieve their loneliness or other emotional stresses, undercutting their ability to remain employed and, hence, their ability to continue remitting. Further, the long periods apart from family make it more likely that a migrant will settle permanently in the United States and even start a new family, abandoning the family in Tunkás or dividing the migrant's earnings between the two families.

In sum, there is a clear economic gain to families from migration. However, there is also the potential for economic disruption, and this is most pronounced for international migrants and their families because immigration enforcement measures endanger a migrant's ability to earn and remit money and imply long family separations, which can undermine a migrant's willingness to continue sending money home.

Finally, any loss of income, whether partial or total, can affect a migration family's ability to communicate. This is especially true for international migration families because of the high costs of telephone communication and, especially for the undocumented, of crossing the international border. In the case of diminished earnings or job loss, a migrant may decide to phone less frequently or delay a return visit to see his or her family. The following section reveals that, like the economic impacts of migration, communication poses challenges for families at the various split levels and between internal and international migration.

Communication in Internal and International Migration Families

Communication for internal and international migrants, both by telephone and face to face, is a key aspect of a life of family separation. Regular and sustained communication via e-mail or phone calls can strengthen family networks and help family members feel they can call on others for support (Wilding 2006), and it can sustain intimacy with distant children (Parreñas 2005; Horst 2006; Parella 2007). On the other hand, international communication technology can amplify the emotional strain caused by separation (Dreby 2007).

In addition to telephoning, split families attempt to maintain face-to-face communication, with varying degrees of success, largely because of the high financial costs and potential risks involved whenever an undocumented migrant must attempt an additional border crossing into the United States after a return home. As discussed in chapter 3 of this volume, enhanced border enforcement is keeping migrants bottled up in the United States.

Communication between internal migrants and their families in Tunkás is facilitated by proximity. Internal migrants have a much easier time traveling to their sending communities because barriers to movement—costs, risks, and time involved—are all much lower than for international migrants. For example, Señor Torres returns from Cancún to see his wife and four children every three months. For some internal migrants, the cost of returning determines the frequency of visits, while others' work demands can make it difficult to make even the short journey home. When talking about her daughter in Cancún, Juanita Puc explained: "She almost never comes. She has to work. Sometimes she has to cover for a friend or something, so she doesn't come. Sometimes she comes once a month, every two months, a month and a half, when she can, and she comes to see her daughter." In some cases, both cost and work schedule combine to keep families apart. Paula's sister returns only every month or so, "because bus tickets are expensive," and she usually stays for only a day. "One day, sometimes two. She rarely stays more than a day. For example, on this last occasion, I talked to her and she said she was going to work on her day off so she'd have two days free."

In addition to the fact that proximity makes regular visits home easier for internal migrants, it is also less expensive for families to communicate by phone with relatives in other parts of Mexico than with family members in the United States (Muse-Orlinoff et al. 2009). As a result, internal migration families can talk more regularly and more casually. The Ferrers, for instance, talk to their children in Playa del Carmen nearly every day, and they often call just to say hello. Doña Magdalena, who lives in Tunkás, has a phone for the sole purpose of talking to her children in Mérida. However, households with telephones are still in the minority.

The low rate of home telephones among families with members elsewhere in Mexico is a substantial barrier to regular communication in internal migration families. Sixty-nine percent of Tunkás-based respondents with relatives in other parts of Mexico did not have a telephone in their home, which means they must use a public phone or a neighbor's phone. In these cases, communication between the migrant and family members is less private. It also places a burden on people in the sending community who have to wait at a specific place at a specific time in order to receive a promised call.

For family members separated by international migration, communication is largely shaped by two factors: distance and national boundaries. Together, these factors make the cost of communicating very expensive. As discussed above, the costs of traveling to the international border are high, as are the risks of an undocumented crossing, and the vast majority of Tunkaseños (84 percent) cross without documents. These costs raise a high barrier to family unity, discouraging migrants from returning regularly to Tunkás and hence reducing their opportunity for face-to-face communication with family members.

We found that U.S.-based respondents with documents had visited Tunkás an average of three times in the previous five-year period, but undocumented respondents were able to return to Tunkás an average of only 0.7 times in five years. As noted previously, the median time a nonmigrant respondent was separated from his/her U.S.-migrant spouse was 3.5 years. In these long periods apart, families rely on the telephone to stay in touch. During the nearly ten years that Señor López was in the United States working to pay for his terminally ill son's medical treatment, he had to substitute phone calls for face-to-face communication with his family. However, his work schedule limited the times when he could converse with his family:

> I worked all week. I got out of the factory at 3:00 or 3:30 in the afternoon. I'd go home, make something to eat, and then at 4 or 5 o'clock I'd go to work again at the factory until 11 p.m.—a lot of work. At night on weekends they'd call me to wash trucks from 8 in the morning till 5 in the evening. Then another job from 10 p.m. until 6 a.m.

His wife and children in Tunkás could only await his calls; the timing of the calls and their frequency depended on Señor López's work schedule and the amount of money he could devote to the cost of phone calls. Under such conditions, the qualitative difference between communication by phone and in person is clear to see.

When it comes to the communication sphere, the high degree of disruption for international migration families is not limited to those in extreme circumstances like the López family. Many migrants must work long hours at multiple jobs to cover the high living costs in the United States and still have money left to send to their families, and these time demands can significantly reduce the amount of time families have to communicate. The high cost of international phone calls further reduces the total amount of communication since these calls are typically much briefer (Muse-Orlinoff et al. 2009, 88).

For international migration families, limited communication can have different impacts depending on the split level. For example, spouses (horizontal split) often serve as "hubs" in communication networks, the individuals responsible for receiving and transmitting information to others

(Muse-Orlinoff et al. 2009, 112–17). Their responsibility for sharing information with others and relaying messages to others means they have less time to talk about their own lives or maintain their emotional ties with the spouse. Calls are more likely to be devoted to dealing with family business such as the children's schooling, parents' health, or household budget. Communication between downwardly split family members can be even more limited than between spouses. In addition to getting a narrower slice of the communication time pie, children may be left out of the direct communication altogether, passing and receiving news, orders, or intimacies through the parent or grandparent "hub." This means that the information children receive is dependent on the content of the communication that takes place between the migrant and the hub. Children who cannot communicate regularly with an absent parent may feel a sense of abandonment or a loss of discipline in their lives. After José's wife left for the United States, his son would get upset when his father arrived home from work late. According to José's sister, Paula, "Now José can't go to the United States to work, because the child cries for his father. When he sees that José is late, he begins asking why his father hasn't come home."

The disruption of communication at both the horizontal- and downward-split levels is generally greater than at the upward-split level. Problems such as infidelity or divorce, which disrupted communication may foster in horizontally split families, are not an issue between migrants and their parents. On the other hand, parents in the home community may suffer from highly disrupted communication in times of emergency, particularly as they get older. In addition, elderly parents, like children, may find themselves forced to rely on a communication hub, such as a daughter-in-law, and the lack of direct communication over an extended period can take an emotional toll. In sum, international migration can result in high-degree disruption for families at all three split levels, but this outcome is especially pronounced at the horizontal and downward splits.

As we discussed earlier, communication in internal migration families has a lower degree of disruption than that found in international migration families. The lower cost of domestic telecommunications means that internal migrants can afford to maintain communication at all three split levels. Furthermore, internal migrants are better able to return home regularly or in times of emergency. Nevertheless, visits can still be months apart, and communicating by telephone is not always a sufficient solution for families. As Juanita Puc showed when talking about her internal-migrant daughter and her granddaughter in Tunkás, internal and international migration families can face similar challenges, in this case when it comes to the children's response:

> Yes, my granddaughter talks with her mother. If the girl is being stubborn and won't obey, her aunt scolds her. But my granddaughter does obey her mother—but not her aunt, with whom she's a bit stubborn. So she sometimes gets a spanking.

In sum, migrating, whether internally or internationally, disrupts communication, and this disruption is often emotional in nature. Communication is key to understanding emotional care because nurturing affective ties includes keeping communication open between family members. Communication engenders the trust and sense of inclusion within the family that are crucial for keeping a family united, especially in the context of migration. The following section discusses the ways in which migration is emotionally disruptive for Tunkaseño families, an effect that is inextricably linked to the disruption in communication.

Emotional Care among Internal and International Migration Families

As noted above, many studies of family in the context of migration have approached the topic by defining the family primarily as a household, that is, as both a spatial and an economic structure. This structural approach ignores the emotional component that differentiates families from other groups or social structures. It is important to understand the emotional sphere of the family because migration's effects often play out more clearly in this sphere—in arguments, separation, divorce, and so on. In examining how migration influences families' affective ties, we found a high impact on familial affective ties in an international migration context and a lesser impact in an internal migration context.

We found that migration—both internal and international—places an emotional care-taking burden on those who are left behind, regardless of family split type. For example, Magdalena raises her fourteen grandchildren in Tunkás while the children's parents work in Mérida. Explaining her responsibilities as caregiver, she said, "I bathe them, dry them . . . put them in their hammock, give them their bottle. I tie a knot at the end of the hammock so they don't fall out." And there is José, whose wife left him and their children in Tunkás to go the United States. José continued to work to support his children while a large share of the childcare and housework fell to his younger sister. When asked who took care of the house, José replied:

> My younger sister. In the morning I go to work and she takes my son to school, takes him lunch, and brings him back home. When I come home at three o'clock I take over caring for the house and my children. I'm still at work when she gets here, so she takes care of the children and I arrive home later.

José has decided against leaving Tunkás himself because of the burden this would place on his sister. "If I leave, the responsibility would all fall on my younger sister, and she already takes care of my elderly mother and my niece." Clearly, both internal and international migration increase nonmigrants' care-taking responsibilities.

Overall, however, we found that internal migration produces a low degree of disruption for families relative to international migration, possibly because internal migration allows for ongoing familial emotional care through visits and communication. For example, the Ferrer family, an upwardly split family with extensive internal migration, told us that visiting is a major part of their communication. The relative proximity of the migration destination and the absence of an international border allow parents and children to visit each other often. Señora Ferrer said, "Yes, we go there every month . . . we go and come back every month." The family members engage in constant communication, which engenders trust and camaraderie among them. Though the family is split by internal migration, the members' emotional well-being is apparent in their display of unity.

Unlike families split by internal migration, families split by international migration show a higher degree of disruption, in large part because there are fewer opportunities for visits and phone communication. International migration inhibits migrants' ability to visit and communicate with family members in Tunkás, making it more difficult for migrants to remain connected to family members and informed about events and family news across the long distance.

This is especially true for undocumented immigrants, who tend to be separated from their families for longer periods. Because of the dangers of border crossing and high U.S. living costs, undocumented international immigrants can rarely bring their families with them to the United States. The resulting long separations can undermine trust among family members and families' emotional well-being. Like Hirsch (2003), we found migrant men who felt lonely or socially isolated during their U.S. sojourns and sought sexual relationships with women in the United States. Ramona, whose husband migrated to the United States for four years without ever returning to Tunkás, told us that she and her husband lost their trust in each other during his absence. Ramona explained that family members told her he was having an affair with another woman in the United States, and Ramona's husband was told that Ramona was having an extramarital affair in Tunkás. When he returned to Tunkás, their marital ties were frayed. As Ramona recalled:

> I would ask my husband, "What good is it that you're over there if we're still poor? Better to be together here in Tunkás, working out our problems together." Being away just brings problems . . . only problems. They told me he had another woman. Somebody told him that I had another man. . . . Just problems. And that's how a family falls apart.

Such emotional challenges cannot easily be resolved in a phone conversation, and without closer contact cases like these end in loosened or severed marital ties. The negative impacts of geographic distance between family members become more apparent in the context of international migration, as this case has revealed.

The loneliness that family members experience during migrants' long absences also leads to arguments that weaken ties in families with a downward split. Tunkaseño migrants report that the worst aspect about life in the United States is the loneliness. Pedro mentioned that he returned to Tunkás after a three-year absence because he was lonely and missed his family very much. His son missed him too, and was angry at Pedro for not returning to Tunkás. Remembering, Pedro said, "I was lonely. . . . My son would ask when I was going to come home, and sometimes he didn't want to talk to me. . . . I'd tell him that I couldn't return yet because I still had to work to buy our house. That's why I went north." The loneliness experienced by both father and son ultimately led to Pedro's decision to return to Tunkás.

Migration can also result in separation or divorce, particularly affecting a horizontally and downwardly split family. For instance, some Tunkaseño nonmigrants report that returning migrants are often violent and some are addicted to alcohol or gambling. When Ramona's husband returned to Tunkás, he spent his money drinking and gambling and no longer supported their children financially or emotionally. She explained: "When he left, he didn't drink. But when he came back, he drank and played cards a lot. It affected my family so much that we don't relate to one another as we used to. It's likely my marriage will end because everything has changed so much." In this case international migration was extremely disruptive for the family. Affective ties were broken, and a family may be dissolved as a result.

Ramona's experiences are not unique among Tunkaseño migrant families. Migrants are more likely than nonmigrants to be divorced or separated—15 percent of migrants versus 9 percent of nonmigrants.[6] Arturo, an international migrant who left his family behind during his trip to the United States, mentioned that for four years (the duration of his trip) he "abandoned" his family, in the sense that work commitments prevented him from returning to visit them. During this time, his wife began a relationship with someone else and initiated divorce proceedings. Arturo attributes the divorce to his immigration. In fact, he said he would never return to the United States and risk another relationship: "No, I would not go back. It was a terrible experience, and I'm not the only one." His words suggest that infidelity is common among families separated by international migration.

Low- and High-Degree Disruption of Internal and International Migration

Separation is clearly a source of disruption in internal migration families, but when compared to the impacts of separation in international

---

6. This difference is statistically significant at the .05 level.

migration, the disruption is obviously of a lesser degree. Internal migration has offered Tunkaseño families economic gains that are only marginally below those accruing from international migration. Moreover, absent an international border, internal migrants can visit their families more regularly, and because of lower domestic telecommunications costs, they can have more frequent and longer phone conversations. Internal migrants and their families are less lonely and better able to sustain mutual trust because they see each other more often and know that family members are reachable in an emergency. In other words, a lower level of disruption in communication reduces the potential for emotional disruption, which can, in turn, lower the potential for economic disruption. Similarly, low economic disruption reduces disruption in the communication and affect spheres; and low affective disruption can prevent disruption in the communication and economic spheres.

While this same integrated process holds for international migration families, disruption, when it occurs, is high in degree. Given that the majority of Tunkaseño migrants to the United States are undocumented, U.S. immigration enforcement increases their economic precariousness. Furthermore, the time, distance, and enforcement barriers that separate members of international migration families can produce a high degree of communicative and affective disruption. Loneliness and distrust increase because international migrants and their families see and speak with one another less frequently. In consequence, the potential for emotional and economic abandonment rises as migrants unable or unwilling to make the journey to Tunkás settle permanently in the United States and shift their focus away from those left behind. When asked whether he knew of other cases of family disintegration as a result of migration, José responded, "There are many cases where couples separate and don't get back together. . . . The majority break up."

In both internal and international migration families, the type of disruption members experience varies by their family's split level. Spouses separated by internal and international migration both face the possibility of infidelity and divorce, but spouses trying to maintain a marriage across an international border are likely to communicate less and must work harder to preserve strong emotional ties. Children can develop disciplinary problems or feel abandoned, while a migrant's parents may not have the support they need in times of emergency. In either case, international migration, which hinders efforts to maintain a sense of family unity, exacerbates the problem.

Families with more than one migrant member may be poised to take advantage of the economic benefits of international migration by having one member in the United States, while simultaneously mitigating the degree of disruption by having another family member migrate internally. This mixed model of family migration offers a potential strategy for families for whom family unity in Tunkás is not an option. The following section outlines some experiences of families that have members both within and outside of Mexico.

FAMILY NEAR AND FAR: THE CASE OF MIXED MIGRATION

When more than one family member leaves Tunkás, is there a trade-off between internal and international migration? Do migrants want to risk family disruption for the economic gain of international migration, or is it preferable to maintain strong family ties by migrating internally even though financial returns are lower? While internal migration imposes less of an emotional burden on migrants and their families, it may be insufficient to satisfy their economic needs or goals. On the other hand, international migrants may earn more in the United States, but they increase the risk of disrupting family dynamics. But what if families choose both internal *and* international migration?

Mixed migration may be a preferred middle ground for some families. Members of mixed-migrant households report having greater wealth than individuals who never migrate or only migrate internally (table 8.3). In economic terms, mixed migration reduces dependency on a single family member who sends remittances. When compared to a family with two international migrants who send remittances, a family with an internal migrant and an international migrant experiences less communicative and affective disruption. However, even with the benefit of international remittances and the affective comfort that comes with having some family members close to home, mixed migration families still experience emotional distress, and high levels of disruption can occur in mixed migration families just as they do in families divided by international migration. We found that the degree of disruption is contingent upon the level of the split. Mixed migration may be less disruptive for upwardly split families in which a migrant's parents remain in Tunkás, but it brings only minor emotional benefit to a Tunkás-based nonmigrant whose spouse is the international migrant.

Carmen's family has a mixed migration arrangement at the upward split, but they have maintained strong family ties despite the separation. Carmen lives in Tunkás with several of her daughters, one son and another daughter live in Mérida, and another son lives in the United States. Carmen explained that her children residing in Mexico often help her financially, as does her son in the United States. She also mentioned that her internal-migrant children visit her every month or so. Her son in the United States, however, has not been able to visit. Her eyes glistened with tears as she told us how she worries about him because he is undocumented. Her experience of an upwardly split, mixed migration family has been painful, but it has not weakened the ties between family members. The family is very united; they communicate often and come together when Carmen needs help.

In contrast, Maira's mixed migration family, with horizontal and upward splits, has experienced deep disruption. Maira's husband, who works in the United States, has not returned home in six years and calls only twice a month. Maira's oldest son, who is also in the United States, has not returned since he left Tunkás two years ago, though he calls more frequently than her husband. Maira's younger son is in Playa del Carmen; he returns about every two months to visit her in Tunkás and calls about twice a week: "My son in Playa calls me more than the others." After her husband and sons migrated, Maira was alone in Tunkás. She lives in a small rented room and admitted that she has felt great emotional pain and loneliness since their departure. However, her husband's absence has been especially difficult because of his infidelity; the couple actually separated for a time while her husband continued an extramarital affair. At the horizontal split, then, Maira has felt the emotional pain of other nonmigrants married to international migrants. However, her son in Playa del Carmen, who communicates with her more frequently and visits on a more regular basis, provides some comfort to ease her loneliness.

In fact, with mixed migration, one split level may mediate the disruption and pain caused by the split at another level; our findings suggest that upward splits mediate disruptions produced by horizontal splits. Again referring to Maira's experiences, her son in the United States is the one who informed her about her husband's infidelity; and he also told his father that his actions were wrong and that he should not abandon his wife. Though Maira and her husband did separate, she has now reunited with her husband and is trying to salvage her marriage. Maira's story points to the possibility for transparency and a system of checks and balances in mixed migration. Having family members in close proximity to both herself and her husband—younger son closer to Maira and older son closer to her husband—mediated the emotional distress associated with her husband's infidelity. In this way, the family's upward split helped mediate the disruption and emotional distress Maira incurred due to the horizontal split.

CONCLUSION

This chapter has shown how migration shapes the dynamics of Tunkaseño family life. Whether internal, international, or mixed, migration has disruptive effects on Tunkaseño families. Yet economic necessity has continued to push Tunkaseños toward internal and, more recently, international destinations. Although a Tunkaseño family's economic situation usually improves when one or more family members migrate, the gain seldom comes without negative consequences. In economic terms, the benefits of internal migration are similar to those of international migration, but migrants living and working within Mexico suffer less from the economic and emotional disruptions associated with international migration. Remittance streams enable migrants and their families to satisfy basic needs and give them an increased sense of security which, in turn, leads to reduced disruption in both the communication and affective spheres.

In both internal and international migration, distance prevents family members from communicating as often as they would if they were living together, and phone calls cannot substitute for face-to-face contact, making it more difficult to maintain relationships over long distances. When one adds in the high cost of international phone calls, maintaining close ties with family members back home becomes even more difficult.

For many migrants, separation from family is emotionally draining. For Tunkaseños, both internal and international migration carry negative implications for the emotional well-being of the family, with international migration being the most disruptive. International destinations expose migrants to an array of dangers and increase the likelihood that they will be unfaithful, violent, abuse drugs or alcohol, and even abandon their Tunkás-based families. While internal migration is a less disruptive choice than international migration, it also increases the burden on those left at home, who must care for children and elderly relatives. Lower degrees of affective stress can prevent disruption in the communication and economic aspects of family life.

Analyzing Tunkaseño families by split levels has helped us approach the complex study of the family. By employing various split levels, we have been able to see how migration decisions and impacts ultimately depend on the situation of each family. For example, a downward split would require more in remittances because of the high costs associated with raising children, so these migrants may be more likely to go to the United States, where wages are higher. International migration produces a high degree of disruption for families at all three split levels, but it is most damaging for horizontal- and downward-split families. Mixed migration tends to mitigate the deleterious impacts of international migration and can often serve as an intermediate option between internal and full-scale international migration.

Because international migration from Yucatán is a very recent development, it is important to compare and contrast it with internal migration in order to fully understand how the migration process affects families. Very few studies address the links between internal and international migration. A 2007 study of internal and international migration that sought to identify any relationship or link between the two phenomena concluded that "the difficulties in finding the missing link that would tie internal and international migration in the Mexican case are probably due to the fact that such a link does not exist" (Canales and Montiel 2007, 38).

Despite Canales and Montiel's conclusion, 24 percent of the families interviewed in our study in Tunkás have members in both international and internal destinations. To explain this contradiction, we must remember that international migration from Yucatán, and from Tunkás in particular, began only recently. Internal migration, especially to Quintana Roo, has a much longer history. Our findings suggest that mixed migration may provide a strategy to lessen the economic and emotional costs of migration. The example provided by Maira's family suggests as much. Maira's younger son wanted to join his father and older brother in the United States, but his father did not allow it. As Maira recalled: "My younger son asked his brother for help to cross the border, but his father doesn't want him to leave me all alone." As mentioned earlier in this chapter, Maira's younger son migrated internally instead. The family consciously arranged a mixed migration scheme, with the younger son going to Playa del Carmen, in order not to leave Maira alone in Tunkás.

To assert that mixed migration is, in fact, a rational strategy that Tunkaseño families employ is a claim that exceeds the scope of our study. We can say, however, that people making mixed migration decisions are active agents giving consideration to factors—perhaps family concerns and economic need—that are sufficiently compelling to encourage adopting a mixed migration strategy.

REFERENCES

Canales, Alejandro, and Israel Montiel. 2007. "De la migración interna a la internacional: En búsqueda del eslabón perdido." Presented at the ECLAC workshop "Migración Interna y Desarrollo en México: Diagnóstico, Perspectivas y Políticas," April 16, Mexico City, http://www.eclac.org/celade/noticias/paginas/3/2835/ACanales.pdf.

De Jong, Gordan F., and Robert W. Gardner, eds. 1981. *Migration Decision Making: Multidisciplinary Approaches to Microlevel Studies in Developed and Developing Countries.* New York: Pergamon Press.

Dreby, Joanna. 2007. "Children and Power in Mexican Transnational Families," *Journal of Marriage and Family* 69: 1050–64.

Hirsch, J. S. 2003. *A Courtship after Marriage: Sexuality and Love in Mexican Transnational Families.* Berkeley, CA: University of California Press.

Hondagneu-Sotelo, Pierette. 1994. *Gendered Transitions: Mexican Experiences of Immigration.* Berkeley, CA: University of California Press.

Horst, Heather A. 2006. "The Blessing and Burdens of Communication: Cell Phones in Jamaican Transnational Social Fields," *Global Networks* 6, no 2: 143–59.

Lewin Fischer, Pedro. 2007. "Yucatán as an Emerging Migrant-Sending Region." In *Mayan Journeys: The New Migration from Yucatán to the United States,* ed. Wayne A. Cornelius, David Fitzgerald, and Pedro Lewin Fischer. La Jolla, CA: Center for Comparative Immigration Studies; University of California, San Diego.

Massey, Douglas S., Joaquin Arango, Graeme Hugo, Ali Kouaouci, Adela Pellegrino, and Edward J. Taylor. 1993. "Theories of International Migration: A Review and Appraisal," *Population and Development Review* 19, no. 3: 431–66.

Munro, Moira, and Ruth Madigan. 1999. "Negotiating Space in the Family Home." In *At Home: An Anthropology of Domestic Space*, ed. Irene Cieraad. New York: Syracuse University Press.

Murdock, George P. 1960. *Social Structure*. New York: Macmillan.

Muse-Orlinoff, Leah, Maximino Matus Ruiz, Chelsea Ambort, and John E. Cárdenas. 2009. "Long-Distance Lives: International Migrant Networks and Technology in the United States and Mexico." In *Migration from the Mexican Mixteca: A Transnational Community in Oaxaca and California*, ed. Wayne A. Cornelius, David Fitzgerald, Jorge Hernández-Díaz, and Scott Borger. La Jolla, CA: Center for Comparative Immigration Studies, University of California, San Diego.

Ortiz, Víctor Manuel. 1984. *La Casa: una aproximación*. Mexico: Universidad Autónoma Metropolitana de Xochimilco.

Parella, Sonia. 2007. *Los vínculos afectivos y de cuidado en las familias transnacionales: Migrantes ecuatorianos y peruanos en España*. Barcelona: Universidad Autónoma de Barcelona.

Parreñas, Rhacel Salazar. 2005. *Children of Global Migration: Transnational Families and Gendered Woes*. Stanford, CA: Stanford University Press.

Pew Hispanic Center. 2009. "Mexican Immigrants in the United States, 2008," http://pewhispanic.org/factsheets/factsheet.php?FactsheetID=47.

Rodríguez, Andrea, Jennifer Wittlinger, and Luis Manzanero Rodríguez. 2007. "The Interface between Internal and International Migration." In *Mayan Journeys: The New Migration from Yucatán to the United States*, ed. Wayne A. Cornelius, David Fitzgerald, and Pedro Lewin Fischer. La Jolla, CA: Center for Comparative Immigration Studies, University of California, San Diego.

Sánchez Azcona, Jorge. 1976. *Familia y sociedad*. Mexico: Editorial Joaquín Mortiz, S.A.

Skolnick, Arlene S., and Jerome H. Skolnick. 1994. *Family in Transition*. 8th ed. New York: Harper Collins College.

Wilding, R. 2006. "Virtual Intimacies: Families Communicating across Transnational Contexts," *Global Networks* 6, no. 2: 125–42.

Two young residents of Tunkás.

9 Sweet Dreams and Bitter Realities: Nutrition and Health Care in Tunkás and the United States

PAOLA PÉREZ, MARÍA LUISA REYES, PETER SEO, AND
LEAH MUSE-ORLINOFF

A person who migrates experiences transitions not only in language, culture, and work opportunities, but also in the composition of their diets. In addition, as remittances from migrants in the United States begin arriving in home communities, nonmigrant family members are often able to afford better-quality products and a greater variety of foods. However, poverty and ecological challenges in both sending and receiving contexts continue to limit the kinds of foods available to migrants and their relatives. In a context of economic crisis, when family incomes are more precarious than usual, these choices are even more constrained.

Various potentially serious health conditions are correlated with suboptimal nutrition; diabetes, anemia, high cholesterol, and heart attacks often result from dietary patterns shaped by a lack of healthy foods. To manage these conditions, Tunkaseño migrants and their compatriots who remain in Tunkás must receive ongoing medical care. However, a lack of infrastructure, high costs, and fear of apprehension by U.S. immigration authorities can constrain access to adequate medical intervention.

This chapter explores the connections between diet and health conditions among Tunkaseños in Tunkás and California and describes the medical facilities to which Tunkaseños on both sides of the border turn for treatment. We begin by describing what Tunkaseños eat in Mexico and the United States and then examine the medical treatment available to Tunkaseños suffering from diet- or nutrition-related illnesses. We conclude with a discussion of traditional health care practices, which some Tunkaseños continue to utilize for both diet-related and spiritual ailments.

THE TUNKASEÑO DIET

Several studies of migration and nutrition focus on the connection between migrant settlement in the United States and obesity (see, for
example, Kaplan et al. 2004; Romero-Gwynn et al. 1993). For instance,
according to Romero-Gwynn and Gwynn (1997), the longer a migrant
spends in the receiving society, the greater his or her chance of developing a diet-related illness. These studies, part of the literature that seeks
to explain the "Latino health paradox," find that Latino migrants in the
United States are healthier than groups with similar sociodemographic
characteristics and enduring exclusion from quality healthcare (Abraído-Lanza et al. 1999). Because migrants also tend to be healthier than
nonmigrants from the same community of origin (Oristian et al. 2009),
many researchers contend that a positive selection effect leads to the out-
migration of the healthiest individuals; these migrants are, it is argued,
best suited to withstand the physical hardships of a clandestine border
crossing and the difficult labor and living circumstances they encounter
in the United States.

However, these studies do not typically include a systematic consideration of the dietary or nutritional context of the sending community. In
this section we argue that the lack of complete and quality nutrition in
Tunkás has a negative effect on the health of Tunkaseños in Mexico, while
access to a greater variety of food in the United States may in fact improve
Tunkaseño migrants' overall health.

For many residents of Tunkás, the daily diet consists of tortillas, beans,
chilies, meat, and sodas. Although Tunkás is an agricultural town, most
Tunkaseños' daily food consumption is limited by their financial situation, the unavailability of certain products, and a lack of understanding
about what constitutes a healthy diet.

Aside from the corn and beans that Tunkaseños harvest from their
family plots and the herbs and spices they grow in their patios, few fruits
and vegetables are grown in Tunkás and hence are absent from most
Tunkaseños' diets. As one Tunkaseña woman commented, "Well, I eat
what we have available here, and it isn't much. When I go to Playa del
Carmen, I eat fruits and vegetables." Moreover, what fruits and vegetables are available are expensive. Señora Andrea, the owner of a small grocery store, explained that Tunkaseños rarely buy vegetables because of

the cost. A potato costs four pesos, while a package of Maruchan or Cup O' Noodles costs five, so many customers opt for the packaged product, which is easier to prepare and more filling.

Meat is a very important part of the Tunkaseño diet, but only for families that can afford to slaughter an animal regularly. Tunkaseño families often raise pigs, turkeys, and chickens for sale or personal consumption. These animals require little space, so they can be raised in patios and yards, and they eat just about anything. As one Tunkaseño explained, "We just give the pig leftovers, and that's enough." By contrast, Tunkaseños do not consume much beef. One of the town doctors explained that there is no land for grazing cattle, and the lack of pasturage makes pork the more popular meat in Tunkás.

Not only is pork a key component of the Tunkaseño diet, Tunkaseños also use rendered pork fat, known as *manteca*, for cooking. Señora Andrea noted: "People say that *manteca* gives food more flavor . . . and it costs less than oil." Micaela reported that her family generally uses oil at home but purchases lard when money is short. Unfortunately, as is discussed later in the chapter, the extensive use of lard in cooking has serious health consequences for Tunkaseños.

Another meat consumed in Tunkás is venison. Although venison is not a major part of the diet, many Tunkaseños hunt deer for both local consumption and sale. According to Dr. Gómez, "Several families hunt deer and they share the meat. . . . Because it doesn't cost them anything, they can eat venison once or twice a week." Although it is illegal to hunt deer, venison remains an attractive source of protein, especially for families with limited financial resources.

Tunkaseños do not consume milk or fruit juice at levels recommended in nutritional guidelines, mostly because of the high cost of these products. As one shopkeeper put it, customers "buy juice once every two weeks, on payday." Furthermore, 28 percent of Tunkaseño households do not have refrigerators and thus are not able to store milk or juice safely.

Water consumption is also low among Tunkaseños because of the shortage of potable water. Local *cenotes* are contaminated, and one of the town's doctors asserts that the water that is piped to Tunkaseños' houses is not adequately purified. As a result, many Tunkaseños experience chronic diarrhea, salmonella, typhoid, and skin infections. Bottled water is expensive, and few Tunkaseños have the wherewithal to install better water purification systems in their homes.

Because they are relatively cheap and available, sodas are the most popular drink for Tunkaseños. Unfortunately, sodas contribute to Tunkaseños' high rates of diabetes and high blood pressure, and their prevalence frustrates local health providers who note that Tunkaseños would be better served by purchasing water rather than soda. Finally, there are several cantinas in the town, and about a dozen stands installed around the plaza during the fiesta did an active business selling beer and liquor. Indeed, alcoholism is a problem in some Tunkaseño families.

The diets available to Tunkseños living in the United States are healthier on the whole than those in Mexico. In the United States people have access to a wider variety of meats, and Tunkaseños purchase beef, pork, poultry, and fish at supermarkets in Anaheim and Inglewood. In addition, migrants' higher salaries make it easier for them to purchase these products.

People in Tunkás cannot afford to include milk and fruit juices in their diet, but Tunkaseños in the United States do drink milk and juices. Francisco, who lives in Inglewood, mentioned that he only consumed milk once a week when he was growing up in Tunkás, but after he migrated to the United States milk became an important item on his grocery list.

Although some women in Tunkás sell prepared food from their houses, it is easier to purchase prepared food in the United States than in Tunkás. Though there is some evidence that frequent consumption of fast food has negative health consequences for Mexican migrants in the United States (Oristian et al. 2009), other experts argue that the presence of fruit vendors in neighborhoods where Yucatecan migrants settle increases their access to fresh fruits and vegetables and, in fact, helps Yucatecans living in impoverished Los Angeles neighborhoods obtain a more healthful diet (Rosales 2009).

Potable water is also more widely available to Tunkaseños in the United States, who can drink water from the faucet without risk of diarrhea or other water-borne diseases. On the other hand, Tunkaseños in the United States continue to consume a good deal of soda, and some migrants drink considerable amounts of alcohol.

Even though we initially hypothesized that Tunkaseños living in Mexico would have a healthier diet than those living in the United States, our results show that Tunkaseños in the United States actually enjoy a more balanced diet. When people from Tunkás migrate to Southern California or other parts of the United States, they encounter a large variety of foods which their increased incomes allow them to purchase. Unlike the limited availability of fruits and vegetables we found in Tunkás, U.S. markets have plentiful fresh produce, regardless of the season.

TUNKASEÑOS' HEALTH CARE OPTIONS

A person's diet and overall health are related, and a balanced and nutritious diet can prevent many of the chronic illnesses that are most common in Tunkás, such as diabetes and high cholesterol. However, given the challenges to maintaining a healthy diet, illnesses do occur, and access to good health care becomes critically important in keeping Tunkaseños healthy. Two types of health care services are available to Tunkaseños: Western-style medicine, which involves doctors, nurses, and medical practitioners at clinics and hospitals; and traditional health practices, which are provided by specially trained community members who heal physical and spiritual ailments with plants, herbs, and spiritual remedies.

The town's clinic, located on the central plaza, has two doctors, a dentist, and three nurses. The doctors work at the clinic full time but do not live in the town. In addition to providing routine care,[1] the clinic has an operating room for performing simple procedures and delivering babies. The clinic staff maintains detailed patient records and submits an annual report on the town's health condition to the Mexican Department of Health. According to these reports, diabetes is the second most frequently diagnosed illness in Tunkás, with 352 cases identified in 2008.[2] Diarrhea and gastrointestinal diseases followed, with 246 and 234 diagnosed cases, respectively.[3] Fourteen percent of Tunkaseños included in our study

---

1. The local health service provides ambulance transportation to hospitals in Izamal (about a thirty-minute drive from Tunkás) and Mérida. These hospitals treat patients with serious, chronic, or life-threatening illnesses that cannot be adequately treated at the clinic.
2. Respiratory illnesses such as colds and flu were the most commonly diagnosed ailment. The clinic reported 1,554 cases in 2008.
3. The clinic reports higher incidences of certain illnesses than the self-reported health information obtained through our survey. This discrepancy may emerge because a person with the same problem has visited the clinic multiple times; each visit is recorded as a separate event, which would inflate the numbers reported by the clinic.

reported suffering from high cholesterol, 11 percent from anemia, 8 percent from diabetes, 23 percent from stomach problems (including gastritis and chronic diarrhea), and 18 percent from parasites (figure 9.1).

Figure 9.1. Self-Reported Incidences of Nutrition-Related Illnesses among Tunkaseños

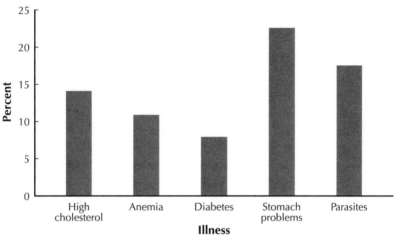

In all, just under half of Tunkaseños (47 percent) reported having been diagnosed with or suffering from a diet- or nutrition-related illness. When the data are broken down by migration status, we find that a higher percentage of Tunkaseños who live in Tunkás suffer from nutrition-related ailments than their U.S.-based counterparts (figure 9.2), supporting our hypothesis about the connection between better food options in the United States and better health conditions among migrants.

Another explanation for the prevalence of gastrointestinal illnesses—particularly chronic diarrhea and parasites—is the lack of adequate hygiene in food preparation or storage. Kitchens in Tunkás are often small buildings outside the primary residence, so meal preparation takes place only a few feet from the household's turkeys, chickens, and pigs, whose activities cause feces and other contaminants to become airborne and then be deposited on foods prepared on outdoor fireplaces. The notable lack of potable water exacerbates residents' susceptibility to gastrointestinal problems, and nearly a fourth of homes (23 percent) lack indoor bathrooms. Even in homes that do have a sewage system, the intermittent availability of hot water makes it difficult to maintain adequate hygiene.

Figure 9.2. Tunkaseños Reporting a Nutrition-Related Illness, by Place of Residence

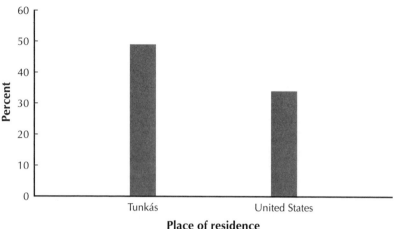

Place of residence

Pearson Chi-square = 10.63; $p < .001$.

A lack of information about proper nutrition may also contribute to the prevalence of diet-related illnesses among Tunkaseños. A nutritionist comes to the clinic once a month to give *pláticas* (short seminars) about healthy eating. However, the nutritionist's primary concern is preventing malnutrition among children, not educating adults on healthful eating. According to the clinic's nurse, the nutritionist "gives demonstrations on bottle feeding and distributes nutritional supplements." The government's Oportunidades program also provides occasional informational sessions about good hygiene and nutrition. These presentations address the entire family, but not everyone attends these meetings, and the recommendations that are made can be hard for Tunkaseños to follow. As Micaela noted, "it's difficult to do what the doctor says because it's hard to find good food here. But we do what we can." Though they may be difficult to implement, the recommendations go to the core of the many factors that account for the prevalence of diabetes in Tunkás: alcoholism, obesity, and a diet heavy in lard, soda, and meat, but light in fruits and vegetables. Dr Carlos Escalona, from the health center in Tunkás, said that many cases of diabetes could be prevented if people ate fish instead of pork and cooked with vegetable oil instead of lard. Unfortunately, by the time a patient visits the doctor with the symptoms of diabetes, it is often too late to reverse the disease.

In addition to a healthy diet, exercise is an important part of nutritional well-being. However, many Tunkaseños fail to follow a healthy daily exercise routine. Though most Tunkaseños walk everywhere rather than driving, routine walking does not constitute cardiovascular exercise. According to the staff of the rehabilitation center in Tunkás, Oportunidades has launched campaigns to encourage Tunkaseños to exercise and include a physical workout in their daily routine, but the campaign has had only limited success. As Dr. Gómez noted, "We at the clinic try to promote exercise, but we've got a lot of older people who can't move easily, and besides, the people are not accustomed to doing exercise."

We constructed a multivariate model to explore some of the factors linked to diet-related diseases among Tunkaseños. We tested for a relationship between certain sociodemographic characteristics and the illnesses discussed above (high cholesterol, diabetes, anemia, stomach problems, and parasites). The reference category is 0 (diagnosed with none of these illnesses), and the test was conducted on respondents who indicated that they suffer from at least one of these five diseases (table 9.1).

In the model, advanced age was directly related to a greater incidence of nutrition-related diseases, and the relationship was statistically significant. As people age, their overall health often declines, so it is not surprising that older respondents in both Tunkás and the United States were more likely to report nutrition-related ailments than were younger Tunkaseños. However, age was the only statistically significant explanatory factor for U.S.-based respondents; gender, marital status, the consumption of fast food or frozen meals, and relative wealth were not statistically important explanations for the occurrence of nutrition-related diseases among Tunkaseños living in the United States.

In Mexico, however, many of these factors were related to the likelihood that respondents had been diagnosed with a nutrition-related disease. Women were more likely than men to suffer from one of the diet-related illnesses; respondents who eat out regularly reported higher incidences of these diseases; and both relative wealth and receipt of re-mittances were positively related to the likelihood of a respondent report-ing that he or she had been diagnosed with at least one of the diet-related illnesses we included. This last point—that more prosperous Tunkaseños suffer more frequently from diet-related illnesses—hints at the relation-ship between household income and meat consumption. That is, families that can afford to eat more meat are more likely to suffer from ill health as a result of their consumption patterns. On the other hand, the relative fre-quency of diet-related illnesses among women may have less to do with differential nutrition and more to do with more regular medical visits (which increase the likelihood of a diagnosis) and female-specific health patterns, such as anemia during pregnancy.

Table 9.1. Factors Explaining Nutrition-Related Illnesses among Tunkaseños

	Mexico-Based	U.S.-Based
Age	.02*** (0.00)	.04** (.02)
Male	−.59*** (.15)	−.54 (.42)
Married	−.15 (.16)	.08 (.40)
Eating out	.06** (.02)	.03 (.04)
Wealth	.01** (0.00)	0.00 (0.00)
Remittance recipient	.67*** (.18)	—
Landowner	.27 (.15)	—
Chi-square	57.01	8.08
Pseudo R^2	.05	.05*
N	817	134

$*p < .05; **p < .01; ***p < .001.$
Robust standard errors are in parentheses.

Finally, although we hypothesized that having access to land for grow-ing crops might be a way for some Tunkaseños to incorporate fresh fruits and vegetables in their diet, there was no statistically significant relation-ship between land tenancy and the prevalence of diet-related illnesses.

OBTAINING TREATMENT: DOCTOR VISITS IN TUNKÁS AND THE UNITED STATES

Whether or not they suffer from chronic nutrition-related illnesses, all Tunkaseños require access to health care. We initially hypothesized that Tunkaseños would have a harder time obtaining medical attention in Tunkás than in the United States, given that Tunkás is a small, rural town. However, we found that it is easier to get medical care in Tunkás, for several reasons. First, the town's clinic treats patients who cannot afford to pay for care, removing the economic constraint on health care. Second, many U.S.-based Tunkaseños worry about being apprehended by immigration authorities if they utilize public health care facilities such as hospitals and emergency rooms, and they forgo medical attention for this reason.

Because health care is easier to obtain in Mexico, respondents who live in Tunkás reported visiting the doctor more frequently in the year prior to our survey than did their U.S.-based counterparts: Tunkaseños in Tunkás visited the doctor an average of 4.3 times in 2008, while Tunkaseños in the United States sought medical attention an average of 2.8 times during the same period (table 9.2). These differences persist when the data are disaggregated by gender: both male and female respondents in Mexico visited the doctor more frequently than did male and female respondents in the United States. However, in both countries, women reported visiting the doctor more frequently than men. Women in Mexico visited the doctor substantially more often than did women in the United States; the difference in the mean number of women's doctor visits in the two countries is statistically significant at $p < .01$.

Table 9.2. Difference in Number of Doctor Visits, by Gender and Place of Residence

	Average Number of Doctor Visits		Difference in Means (gender)	N
	Female	Male		
Live in Mexico	5.1	3.4	**1.7*****	863
Live in U.S.	3.4	2.6	0.8	146
Difference in means (location)	**1.5*****	0.8		
N	505	493		

*** $p < .01$ confidence interval for hypothesis that means are statistically different.

WHO HAS ACCESS TO MEDICAL CARE?

Medical coverage programs that facilitate access to health care are an important element in explaining the use of health care options in Tunkás and the United States. For instance, there has been a hue and cry in the media about undocumented Mexicans coming to the United States to obtain free or inexpensive health care, yet we find that Tunkaseños actually have better and more regular access to health care in Mexico than in the United States.

The clinic in Tunkás treats all Tunkaseños who need medical attention, regardless of ability to pay. However, most of the clinic's patients are registered in one of several government-sponsored medical insurance programs. According to the clinic's records, 598 patients were covered by Seguro Popular in 2008, 30 had ISSSTE coverage, and 32 received care under the IMSS program.[4] All of these programs were designed to help low-income Mexican families reduce the costs of medical care and improve the overall health status of Mexican citizens.

Seguro Popular is a federal-level medical insurance system for low-income Mexicans. It was launched in 2001 to protect the population most at risk of health problems due to low income levels and to reduce the number of families living in poverty as a result of burdensome medical expenses. Individuals are eligible for Seguro Popular coverage if they are not insured under another federal health care program, if they fall below a certain income level, and/or if they have at least one child between the ages of eighteen and twenty-five who is pursuing higher education.

The inter-institutional Oportunidades program attempts to lower the extreme poverty existing in Mexico by increasing educational attainment and improving health care. Oportunidades provides regular economic transfers to families who need financial assistance to help cover their children's educational expenses. In exchange, the children and their mothers must commit to regular medical visits and nutritional counseling. The program also helps families headed by single mothers; the health of these single mothers is of particular importance because deteriorating health among single-parent caretakers can lead to an increased burden on children, at the cost of their educational opportunities.

---

4. IMSS is the Mexican Social Security Institute, and ISSSTE is the parallel institution for government employees.

Several programs help low-income Tunkaseño families in the United States access medical attention. However, the process is difficult, and the undocumented status of many U.S.-based Tunkaseños complicates the situation still further. Fear of deportation can prevent undocumented migrants from seeking needed medical attention (Sack 2008), and visiting the hospital was the fourth most common response we received when we asked respondents to identify what most worries undocumented migrants living in the United States. Nevertheless, we found no statistically significant difference in the frequency of doctors' visits between documented and undocumented Tunkaseños living in the United States.

Medicaid and Medicare both require patients to present documents confirming legal residency in the United States. As discussed in chapter 2, 20 percent of Tunkaseños living in the United States currently rely on some form of public medical assistance (Medicaid, Medi-Cal, or Medicare) for their health care, and 40 percent of Tunkaseño migrants have used these programs at some point during their stay in the United States.

Other programs such as LA ORSA (Los Angeles Outpatient Reduced-Cost Simplified Application) and a few private clinics in Inglewood and Los Angeles are alternative sources of medical care for illegal immigrants. LA ORSA provides outpatient care to uninsured and low-income residents of Los Angeles County. Applicants must demonstrate residency by presenting water, electricity, or gas bills. However, they need not prove legal residency in the United States. Once accepted in LA ORSA, participants can receive care from two dozen private and public clinics without having to present any documentation.

Many of the U.S.-based Tunkaseños we interviewed have private insurance through their employer; 40 percent of respondents living in the United States reported that they have insurance provided by their employer or the employer of a family member. Although just over 40 percent of U.S.-based Tunkaseños pay out of pocket for medical care, we found that Tunkaseños share information about private doctors who are willing to treat patients at a reduced cost. One doctor in Anaheim charges $50 for a consultation regardless of the nature of the complaint. Such doctors are not listed in any media; information about them travels among Tunkaseños by word of mouth.

While undocumented Mexican migrants used to return to Mexico to receive health care, increased border security and the associated high cost of reentry discourage this approach. Concomitant with the bottling up of undocumented migrants in the United States in response to enhanced border security, there may be a bottling up individuals who are in need of medical attention but are unable or afraid to seek treatment. During the health care reform debates of 2009, advocacy groups, including the National Council of La Raza, sought to ensure that any universal health care option would be accessible to the millions of undocumented migrants living in the United States; however, at the time of writing there was as yet no specific health care reform legislation being voted on by the U.S. Congress.

TRADITIONAL HEALTH CARE

Tunkaseños sometimes turn to traditional medicine out of preference or when scientific medical treatments are not available. While traditional healing does not replace Western-style medicine, it does provide a parallel line of health care to Tunkaseños; the individuals who utilize traditional health care services typically do so in conjunction with visits to scientific medical practitioners.

Traditional health practitioners include *curanderos* (healers), *hueseros* (bonesetters), *parteras* (midwives), and *brujos* (individuals supposedly possessing magical powers obtained through a pact with the devil).

Doña Socorro, one of the four *curanderos* practicing in Tunkás, has twenty-five years of experience treating patients for *mal de ojo, susto, miedo, viento,* and *dolor de cabeza. Mal de ojo* results when an individual causes illness or other misfortune to befall another person through a glance accompanied by evil intent. It is generally believed that children are more susceptible to *mal de ojo*. Doña Socorro is able to determine if someone is suffering from *mal de ojo* simply by looking in the person's eyes:

> When they bring a child to me, it's because one of the eyes gets smaller. First it's big, then it's tiny. To cure it you prepare herbs. You grind them, add anis, and rub the concoction on the child from the top of the head to the tips of the fingers. Then you wrap the child in a cloth until they sweat it out.

One of the most frequent traditional ailments in Tunkás is *susto*, or fright. Doña Socorro explained that *susto* invades a small child's body when he or she is scared. To cure *susto*, Doña Socorro makes a sachet of lemon and orange tree leaves and *epazote*, and places it in the child's bed. Another treatment for *susto* is an infusion of *much* (lemon leaves) and tamarind leaves, which is strained and given to the patient to drink.

Empacho is a traditional illness diagnosed among young patients. *Empacho* "is caused by having food stick to the stomach lining . . . by forcing a child to eat food he does not like or want, [or giving] children too much to eat" (Trotter and Chivara 1981, 91). *Empacho* is cured with a purgative or an infusion of herbs. According to Trotter and Chivara, "in some cases the healer massages the part of the back behind the stomach with warm olive oil and pulls on the skin. The skin is said to make a snapping noise when the trapped food particles are loosened" (1981, 92).

Traditional healers also treat patients who have cancer, advanced diabetes, and chronic degenerative diseases. Doña Socorro asserted that a mixture of tarantula poison (extracted from the spider with a needle) and milk cures cancer and diabetes. Doña Socorro's grandparents taught her the art of curing when she was a little girl, and she would like to pass her knowledge to a daughter or another close relative, but few are interested. The remuneration she receives for her services may be a dissuading factor for potential apprentices; Doña Socorro has no set fee for her treatments and healings, and she often treats patients for next to nothing, noting that what she does is "an obligation to the community."

Doña Luz, a *partera* in Tunkás, began practicing midwifery nineteen years ago after her mother helped her through her own pregnancy and delivery. Doña Luz uses massage to position the baby for delivery and helps women during birth. "After the infant is born, I look after the woman, I dress her, I clean her, and I visit her on the third day. I visit her three times a week." Doña Luz charges a fixed amount of 300 pesos per birth. Like Doña Socorro, Doña Luz would like to pass on her knowledge, but "no one wants it."

Regina, another local health care provider, emphasized that her knowledge is a "gift." Regina specializes in bone alignment, and she believes that only someone born with the gift can become a *huesero*. Regina, who is now around thirty years old, learned to align bones from her father when she was only nine, and she began working as a *huesera* five years later. She works on "broken bones and sprains, fixes hips, and provides healing massages (*sobas*) to women's uteruses." Patients come to Regina instead of a chiropractor because she is able to help heal damaged tendons, while, according to her perspective, chiropractors "only snap bones."

Regina, who now lives in Cancún, travels to Tunkás every two weeks to treat her patients. She charges her Tunkás patients less than those in Cancún: in Cancún she charges 100 pesos (about US$8.50) to treat a specific muscular pain, and 200 pesos ($16) for the whole body, compared to 70 and 100 pesos, respectively, in Tunkás. Like Doña Socorro, Regina occasionally does not charge any fee, because "sometimes people just need help." If Regina feels that a patient is in need of more intensive medical treatment, she sends them to the doctor.

Although Tunkaseños' use of traditional medicine is limited in the United States by the lack of practitioners and changing preferences in medical treatment, some Tunkaseños do seek out the traditional healers who have migrated to the Los Angeles area. As in Tunkás, however, traditional care is typically a complement to, rather than a substitute for, Western-style medical attention.

Two traditional health care providers from Tunkás—a *sobador* and a *curandero*—now live in Los Angeles. Like their counterparts in Tunkás, they draw on knowledge accumulated over generations and attempt to assist everyone who comes to them for help. Don Simón, the *sobador*, learned the art of healing massage from his grandfather and has been providing massages to patients in Tunkás and the United States for over thirty years. Don Simón treats all parts of the body though, unlike Regina, he does not work on broken or damaged bones.

Like Doña Socorro and Regina, Don Simón does not charge a fixed fee for his services, instead accepting "whatever the person wants to give" in exchange for treatment. His stated lack of interest in the financial aspect of his practice suggests that, like the traditional healers in Tunkás, he adheres to the principle of curing as a civic obligation rather than a way to earn an income. He explained, "A lot of patients go to the doctor, and the doctor tells them that nothing's wrong. Then they come to me and I treat them, and they get better." However, like traditional healers in Tunkás, if Simón sees a patient that he cannot treat adequately—cases of shattered bones, for instance—he sends them to a doctor or specialist.

Despite the long history of traditional health care practices in Tunkás, just thirty-five Tunkaseños (4 percent of our sample) reported having visited a traditional healer in 2008, and only seven indicated that they prefer a traditional healer to a clinic doctor. Most traditional healers report that when people are suffering from a serious problem, they go first to seek advice from one or more doctors, but eventually they turn to the traditional practitioners. That is, the number of people who seek traditional remedies as a first option is declining.

Findings from our 2009 survey in Tunkás and California suggest that international migrants virtually never use the services of traditional health practitioners. This stated lack of interest contrasts with results from the previous MMFRP study in Tunkás, which showed a marked preference for traditional health care among international migrants: in 2006, 29 percent of international migrants reported preferring traditional health care providers to doctors or clinics, and the researchers speculated that this preference was "a coping mechanism that enables them to integrate their cultural identity with their new reality [and represented] a spiritual connection to Tunkaseño land and culture" (Prelat and Maciel 2007, 216). Despite the presence of two traditional healers from Tunkás in the Los Angeles area, Silverio, a young man born in the United States to Tunkaseño parents, stressed his preference for Western-style medicine: "I don't believe in that stuff [traditional healing]. If I get sick, I go to a doctor at the clinic and I buy medicine. I don't go to a *curandero* because I don't believe in what they do. They aren't trained to cure people. That's why I don't go."

Several factors may explain this preference. First, respondents may have opted not to acknowledge use of traditional health care practices for fear of social censure from the field researchers; they may have thought that an expressed preference for Western medicine would be more "appropriate." Second, increases in medical infrastructure and government support for federal and state health initiatives such as Oportunidades and Seguro Popular over the past several decades have made Tunkaseños more accustomed to and comfortable with Western-style medical attention and its associated care givers. Furthermore, the relative scarcity of traditional healers among the Yucatecan community in the United States limits access to traditional practitioners. Finally, because many of the traditional health care providers are of advanced age and are not finding apprentices interested in learning their skills, the number of *curanderos*, *parteras*, and *hueseros* is dropping in many Yucatecan communities, and young people are increasingly familiar only with treatment delivered by scientific medical providers.

Nonetheless, some Tunkaseños continue to seek out traditional healers, though usually in conjunction with scientific medical care. Thus the two systems appear to be complementary rather than competitive, at least from the perspective of the traditional healers; doctors at the clinic remain dubious about some of the *curanderos'* practices.

CONCLUSION

Migration creates many challenges for families and households. Prolonged separations, family disruption, and new forms of social exclusion can make life difficult for Tunkaseño migrants in the United States and their relatives in Tunkás. However, financial and employment opportunities in migrant destinations remain a strong lure for Yucatecos and Mexicans more generally. This chapter has examined another set of challenges and benefits inherent in migration, specifically, the changes in diet among migrants and the constraints on their access to health care in the United States. We argue that migration can lead to a more healthful diet, given the greater variety of products available in the United States. However, access to health care is easier to obtain in Mexico.

These dynamics generate various health challenges for Tunkaseños. In Tunkás, people are generally less healthy but have better access to medical attention, while in the United States migrants are healthier but have a harder time obtaining regular medical care. In the meantime, in both Tunkás and the United States people are drifting away from traditional health care providers in favor of scientific or Western-style medicine. In the United States this shift can be attributed to a lack of providers, while in Tunkás the government-run medical facilities that offer "modern" care and charge little or nothing for treatment have reduced Tunkaseños' reliance on *parteras, hueseros*, and *sobadores*. As younger generations grow up without the experience of visiting these traditional healers, their popularity will likely continue to diminish and their knowledge may become a thing of the past. However, the Mexican government's provision of information about the importance of proper nutrition, good hygiene, and adequate medical attention is only effective to the extent that towns like Tunkás have access to fresh fruits and vegetables, running water and sanitation, and clean medical facilities.

Tunkás's clinic is well run and is well regarded by town residents, but the persistent lack of healthy foods, compounded by inadequate sanitation systems and enduring poverty, likely means that many Tunkaseños will continue to suffer from easily preventable diseases. Tunkaseños who live in the United States have a better outlook for their nutrition and hygiene. Yet, as the U.S. debates over reforming health care and immigration policy rage on, it is worth remembering the millions of undocumented migrants who need safe and continuing access to quality health care.

REFERENCES

Abraído-Lanza, Ana, et al. 1999. "The Latino Mortality Paradox: A Test of the 'Salmon Bias' and 'Healthy Migrant Hypothesis,'" *American Journal of Public Health* 89, no. 10: 1543–48.

Kaplan, Mark S., N. Huguet, J. Newsome, and B. McFarland. 2004. "The Association between Length of Residence and Obesity among Hispanic Immigrants," *American Journal of Preventive Medicine* 27, no. 4: 323–26.

Oristian, Elizabeth, Patricia Sweeney, Verónica Puentes, Jorge Jiménez, and Maximino Matus Ruiz. 2009. "The Migrant Health Paradox Revisited." In *Four Generations of Norteños: New Research from the Cradle of Mexican Migration*, ed. Wayne A. Cornelius, David Fitzgerald, and Scott Borger. La Jolla, CA: Center for Comparative Immigration Studies, University of California, San Diego.

Prelat, Sonia, and Alejandra Maciel. 2007. "Migration and Health." In *Mayan Journeys: The New Migration from Yucatán to the United States*, ed. Wayne A. Cornelius, David Fitzgerald, and Pedro Lewin Fischer. La Jolla, CA: Center for Comparative Immigration Studies, University of California, San Diego.

Romero-Gwynn, Eunice, and Douglass Gwynn. 1997. "Dietary Patterns and Acculturation among Latinos of Mexican Descent." JSRI Research Report no. 27. East Lansing, MI: Julian Samora Research Institute, Michigan State University.

Romero-Gwynn, Eunice, et al. 1993. "Dietary Acculturation among Latinos of Mexican Descent," *Nutrition Today* 28, no. 4.

Rosales, Rocío. 2009. "Help Wanted: International Labor Recruitment among Los Angeles Fruit Vendors." Paper presented at the Workshop on the Migration Industry, University of California, Los Angeles, May 29.

Sack, Kevin. 2008. "Illegal Farmworkers Get Health Care in the Shadows," *New York Times*, May 10.

Trotter II, Robert T., and Juan Antonio Chivara. 1981. *Curanderismo: Mexican American Folk Healing*. Athens, GA: University of Georgia Press.

Tunkaseños participate in a baseball league in the Los Angeles area.

Los Potros, the baseball team that plays for Tunkás in a Yucatán league. Nearly all of the team's members have been migrants to the United States.

10 Reshaping Community Participation: Tunkaseños in a Binational Context

DAVID KEYES, CRISTINA FERNÁNDEZ, NORMA RODRÍGUEZ,
DIANA CERVERA, AND LUIS MANZANERO RODRÍGUEZ

> *I love baseball so much that I even left a good job once. Back then, you could find another job the next day. My boss said, "If you don't come to work, I'll fire you." I said, "Okay," and I went to play baseball, as he knew full well I would. I don't do that anymore because it's not as easy to find a job.*—Don Alejandro, former migrant

> *It's a beautiful thing to continue sharing our origins and our traditions. I love to participate in something so beautiful that comes from the heart.*—Gerardo, a *jarana* dance teacher in Los Angeles

Walk toward the baseball field at the edge of town and you might hear the crack of the bat and the cheers of the crowd as the hitter sprints to first base. Walk to a house nearby and you will hear traditional Yucatecan music and see a group of students watch their instructor with rapt attention as he demonstrates the steps of the dance form known as *jarana*. A few houses down, a group of older men and women gather to plan out the events of a religious group known as a *gremio*, to which all belong. All three activities are important forms of community participation, ways in which the Tunkaseño community maintains social networks, both in Tunkás and in the United States. This chapter examines these three activities—baseball, *gremios*, and *jarana*—to uncover the patterns of community participation in a relatively new migrant-sending community like Tunkás.

Five questions shape the chapter: How do Tunkaseños participate in their community? Who participates in these activities and who does not? How are these activities translated to the United States? How do Tunkaseño migrants participate in U.S. civic society? And how does Tunkaseño community participation inform debates about civic participation in the United States?

We define community participation as an active process by which individuals spend money and/or time to be involved in a formal, structured, and organized activity that involves people from Tunkás. This definition allows us to consider both those who actively participate in these activities and those who attend them, given that both groups come together in these events to create and maintain their social networks.

Community participation is important in uniting Tunkaseños in Tunkás, and it also plays a role for Tunkaseño migrants in the United States. We find community participation to be crucial for migrants, not only because it facilitates the creation of social networks but also because it fosters and maintains the identity of the migrant community. At the same time, however, the re-creation of activities such as *jarana*, *gremios*, and baseball in the U.S. context can alter them, sometimes making them fundamentally different from their parallels in Tunkás.

Community participation is important for its own sake but also because, as political scientist Robert Putnam has shown, community activities are the building blocks for successful and well-run societies. This chapter begins with an overview of Putnam's work on civic participation, noting how it has changed over the years. We then offer a brief overview of *jarana*, *gremios*, and baseball, explaining the history, organizational structure, and funding of each activity among Tunkaseños in both the United States and Tunkás. There follows an analysis of patterns of participation in the three activities in Tunkás and in the United States. Our data analysis breaks down these participation patterns by various socio-demographic characteristics (age, gender, level of education, and so on) in order to show who is participating and who is not. We complete our findings with a general model, exploring which characteristics are most highly correlated with participation. Our conclusion offers some reflections on Tunkaseño community participation, noting in particular what it can offer to the perspective Putnam has laid out.

MIGRATION AND CIVIC PARTICIPATION

Putnam's most recent writing engages the debate about immigration and civic participation in the United States. This is a continuation of the bottom-up approach he has taken throughout his work, arguing that civic life among average people can have a great effect on society as a whole. Putman posits that building "social capital," which he defines as "social networks and the associated norms of reciprocity and trustworthiness" (2007, 137), makes society as a whole work more efficiently. In *Making Democracy Work* (1993), a study of the relationship between governance and civic life in Italy, Putnam and colleagues rely on Tocqueville's argument that a democratic government is "strengthened, not weakened, when it faces a vigorous civil society" (Putnam, Leonardi, and Nanetti 1993, 182). According to this view, collaboration for shared interests among people is essential for building "civic community." These authors use the example of a choral group to make the point:

> The harmonies of a choral society illustrate how voluntary collaboration can create value that no individual, no matter how wealthy, no matter how wily, could produce alone. In the civic community associations proliferate, memberships overlap, and participation spills into multiple arenas of community life. The social contract that sustains such collaboration in the civic community is not legal but moral (183).

Their argument continues by noting that the strengthening of the civic community is essential to create a society in which people trust each other and work together. The impact of this grassroots-level community percolates up to create strong bonds in society as a whole.

In *Bowling Alone*, Putnam shifts his focus to the United States. He argues that civic society has declined in the United States since the 1950s and encourages Americans to engage in civil activities to ensure that the "Americans of 2010" will be active citizens, engaging in civil activities that will be favorable for democratic life:

> Team sports provide good venues for social capital creation. Equally important and less exploited in this connection are

the arts and cultural activities. . . . Let us find ways to ensure that by 2010 significantly more Americans will participate in cultural activities from group dancing to songfests,
from community theater to rap festivals (2000, 411).

Bowling Alone largely overlooks an important component of many U.S. communities: immigrants. Putnam addresses civic participation in relation to immigration in *"E Pluribus Unum*: Diversity and Community in the Twenty-First Century" (2007). In this work he reviews two opposing perspectives within the social sciences regarding the effects of diversity on social connections. The first is the "contact hypothesis," the idea that "diversity fosters interethnic tolerance and social solidarity" (141). Standing in contrast to the "contact hypothesis" is "conflict theory," which emphasizes that "contention over limited resources fosters out-group distrust and in-group solidarity" (142). Putnam posits that neither of these theories fully explains the effects of diversity on community participation in the United States, and he offers an alternative—"constrict theory"—which suggests that "diversity might actually reduce *both* in-group *and* out-group solidarity" (144). Putnam claims that "immigration and ethnic diversity tend to reduce social solidarity and social capital" and that in the short run residents of ethnically diverse neighborhoods "hunker down" and civic participation is reduced (137). In the long run, however, "successful" communities of immigrants create "forms of social solidarities and more encompassing identities" (137). The key, according to Putnam, is the redrawing of social identities to successfully include immigrants as part of the in-group, to create "one" out of a diverse many (*e pluribus unum*).

Our study has the potential to contribute to this debate, as it explores ways in which community participation in nonpolitical activities such as *gremios*, *jarana*, and baseball can impact civic life in both Mexico and the United States. Paying attention to sending communities as well as receiving communities can yield important information for determining to what extent immigrants will become active participants in their communities in the United States, including their existing social capital and organizational repertoires. This refinement is reiterated by Portes, Escobar, and Arana, who argue against the idea that maintaining transnational ties "retards or prevents political integration among recent migrants to the United States" (2008, 1056). In interviews with leaders of cultural, ethnic, and hometown associations, Portes and his colleagues found that "transnationally oriented groups are as likely to connect to the American political system as those that define themselves as exclusively domestic" (only being oriented toward the United States) (1083). In other words, maintaining transnational ties does not impede integration into the U.S. political system. Based on their interviews and analysis of three immigrant communities, Portes and colleagues assert that the political context of the sending communities from which migrants "exit" has a strong impact on the migrants' political integration in the receiving community: "Distinct contexts of exit affect the organizational life and patterns of incorporation of immigrant groups" (1077).

This chapter builds on the work of Putnam, Portes, and their colleagues, and makes two contributions. First, it expands the field of study to include migrant civic and community participation as it exists on both sides of the border. We explore not only how immigrants are involved in their home communities, but also how people in Tunkás (including many former or future migrants) participate in them as well. Second, it analyzes both the social capital and organizational repertoires that Mexican immigrants bring with them, and explores how patterns of participation shift in the United States. We begin by describing the three activities, including their historical origins, organization, and financing, in order to sketch a background for our later analysis of patterns of Tunkaseño participation in them.

Gremios

On an early February morning, a busy Doña Vera rushed in and out of her house. As she prepared a special stuffed turkey dish called *relleno negro*, she received a continuous flow of people at her home throughout the morning. It was the feast day of St. Thomas the Apostle. Doña Vera was hosting the *gremio de los jóvenes* (the youth *gremio*) this year, an undertaking that entailed many hours of cooking and socializing with *gremio* members, who stayed to drink, talk, and listen to music for most of the day. Fortunately, she was not working alone; other women in the *gremio* helped Doña Vera throughout the day. Later they worshipped their saint and carried his statue in a procession to the church.

Present throughout northwestern Yucatán, *gremios* are associations of townspeople in charge of several of the religious elements in their town's fiestas, which, though related to the Catholic church, are organized independently. *Gremios* traditionally organize around a particular image rooted in the religious traditions of the Yucatán (Fernández Repetto 1995, 57). The core task of each *gremio* is to organize activities to honor its patron saint with a festive meal and a procession in which members convey the saint's image through the town and ultimately return it to the church.

Gremios are syncretic associations, a combination of religious systems brought by the Spanish during the colonial era and elements of the religious systems that predate the Conquest (Farriss 1984, 155). A possible institutional predecessor is the indigenous *cofradía*, a local adaptation of Spanish organizations of the same name that formed to honor local patron saints. The Spanish *cofradías* were primarily urban in character and served to define social identities in a complex society by facilitating the conversion of the indigenous population to Catholicism (156). The *gremios* receded during the Bourbon Reforms in the eighteenth century (Farriss 1984; Loewe 2003), along with other indigenous institutions such as the *cargo* system and the *cofradías*, but they began to reappear around 1925, following the Mexican Revolution.

In Yucatán, *gremio* membership is organized around occupations or other identity categories. Although all *gremios* have an organizational nucleus, people who do not fit the category can still be members, allowing members' relatives and friends to join. There are nine *gremios* in Tunkás, and they make their appearance in the town's fiesta in the following order: *niños* (children); *braceros* (migrants); *rancheros* (ranchers); *antorchistas guadalupanos* (those who honor the Virgin of Guadalupe); *señoritas* (young women); *señoras* (older women); *juveniles* (youths); *ferrocarrileros* (railroad workers); and *agricultores* (farmers). The *gremio* most closely linked with the migrant community in the United States is the *braceros*. Although it shares its name with the mid-twentieth-century U.S. guestworker program, the *bracero gremio* does not comprise former *braceros* but current and returned migrants. Created in 2001 by Tunkaseños in Anaheim, the *gremio* currently has thirty-two members, all men. Even though its members reside in the United States, the *gremio*'s activities have always been conducted in Tunkás by migrants' family members. U.S.-based migrants pay an annual membership fee, but only the few who are able to visit Tunkás during the town's fiestas and those who have returned permanently are able to take part in the *gremio*'s activities.

According to Fernández Repetto (1995), the basic structure of *gremios* has remained consistent for the last century. The main positions are president, secretary, and treasurer, all offices that exist in Tunkás. These are one-year positions filled by a vote of all *gremio* members, and officeholders can be reelected. There are no a priori gender restrictions for positions in the *gremio*, only that the person have a "good" background. The *gremio* president covers some costs of the organization's activities, including food for the celebratory meal, which all members attend, and the banner that leads the procession. The president can remain in office as long as he or she works with other members to carry out the fiesta activities. It is common for the *gremio* presidency to become a family "tradition," with the office being passed from one family member to another.

Participation in *gremios* is voluntary; the only requirement for membership is paying a yearly membership fee. Fernández Repetto identified the ways in which *gremio* activities are commonly financed: membership fees (monetary or in-kind) and donations from members and "honorific members" (1995, 57).[1] Annual membership fees in Tunkás are about 200 or 300 pesos a year (approximately US$15 to $20), except for the *ferrocarrileros*, whose higher fee of 500 pesos (US$40) helps compensate for this group's smaller membership. It is uncommon for *gremio* membership to be denied to someone who cannot pay the membership fee; instead, the person will be asked to contribute whatever amount he or she can afford. Membership fees pay for all activities the *gremio* sponsors, including firecrackers, their saint's Mass, and musicians who play in their procession.

Jarana

It was early February and Tunkás was mid-fiesta. The park was crowded with vendors selling everything from traditional Yucatecan candies of

---

1. We found no "honorific members" in the *gremios* in Tunkás.

coconut and tamarind to piping-hot *marquesitas* (cheese-filled and rolled pancake-like concoctions). Friends and relatives were arriving from Mérida and even from the United States, an indication that the *vaquería* (the annual celebration in which the *jarana* is danced) would soon begin. The townspeople had erected a bullring of wooden poles and palm leaves in front of the government offices in the town's center. The bullring, funded by the fiesta committee of the local government, was to be the site of the most exciting fiesta event: *la corrida* (the bullfight). *Jarana* also plays an important role in Tunkás's fiesta; and the *baile del ceibo* (the dance of the ceiba tree) opens the bullfight each year. A dancer carrying a branch of a ceiba tree, which in Mayan belief represents life, leads a group of dancers whose eloquent footwork keeps rhythm with the *jarana* orchestra of clarinets, trumpets, trombones, and percussion instruments. The procession culminates when the lead dancer plants the branch in the center of the bullring, an offering to Juan Thul, the Mayan god of livestock, so that he will protect the bullfighters.

Jarana is a product of cultural mixing, a combination of the Spanish dance form known as *jota* and traditional Mayan dances. The cultural blending is evident in the dancers' clothing. Women wear the *terno*, a fusion of indigenous women's garb (the *huipil*) and the clothing style of wealthy Spaniards of the colonial period. Today's *terno* consists of three pieces—*huipil, jubón,* and *fustán*—each decorated with cross-stitch embroidery in a pattern known as *shoc bi chuy* in Maya and *hilo contado* in Spanish. The *huipil* is a white cotton dress that extends to mid-thigh and is decorated with brightly colored flowers. The *fustán* is a skirt worn under the *huipil*; it begins at the waist and ends in lace trimmings just below the ankle. The *jubón* is the most intricate piece of the *terno*; it is a square collar embroidered with bright flowers and embellished with jewelry and a headpiece of ribbons and flowers. The women's shoes have nails in the heel to keep time with the music. The men's clothing is much simpler: sandals known as *alpargatas*, cotton pants, and *guayaberas*, the shirts that were originally imported from Cuba in the 1800s and were later appropriated as a trademark product of Yucatán.

Jarana has long been an important part of Yucatecan cultural life and a way in which Tunkaseños on both sides of the border participate in their communities. In Tunkás, there are three main *jarana* groups, organized,

Participants in jarana dance during Tunkás's annual fiesta.

respectively, by the city government, the schools, and other community groups (such as older women in *gremios*).

Dancing *jarana* is a more recent phenomenon in the United States. One group, Kini Motul, was begun six years ago to benefit the victims of Hurricane Isidore. But those who joined found that the dancing brought them great enjoyment and pride, and they continued, participating in the Mexican Independence Day festivities in Los Angeles. Gerardo, a leader of the group from nearby Kini, described the event:

> As we were dancing, you could hear people yelling, *"héchense una bomba, Yucatán!"*[2] From that day on, I loved that atmosphere and being able to demonstrate our culture to all of the people that day. They even followed us to the end of the parade to tell us how beautiful it was, because there had never been a group from Yucatán in that parade.

2. The phrase refers to the common Yucatecan practice of publicly reciting verses with double meanings and comical innuendos.

People who want to dance *jarana* in the United States face many challenges, including the cost of costumes and equipment. *Jarana* outfits cost
between US$40 and $50, and they must be brought from Yucatán by someone who has returned home for a visit. In addition, practices demand a
substantial time commitment. For example, parents typically drive their
children to practices once or twice a week and then wait till the sessions,
which can last up to three hours, end.

Jarana can take on a very different meaning when performed in the
United States. The location of *jarana* dances is a major point of difference.
While *jarana* plays an important role in the fiesta in Tunkás, there is no
similar outlet for *jarana* in the United States. Instead, *jarana* is danced at
festivals, parades, and parties, and in churches, at events that are often
sponsored by non-Yucatecans. Partially because of the change in venues,
participation in *jarana* in the United States becomes more performance oriented and a way to showcase and share a piece of Yucatecan culture with
others and to inspire fellow Yucatecans. A *jarana* instructor described the
dances as "presentations," noting that he enjoys participating "because
it's a beautiful thing to continue sharing our origins and our traditions."

Participants in *jarana* also differ in the United States. Groups in Tunkás
are exclusively composed of Tunkaseños, but those in the United States,
like Kini Motul, also have members from other parts of Yucatán, other
parts of Mexico, and even El Salvador. As Gerardo was describing the
diverse membership, he proudly noted: "we have opened the door to
everyone, so that everyone can get to know our Yucatecan culture."

Jarana in the United States is no longer simply a traditional dance that
brings community members together; it has become a way for Tunkaseños
to demonstrate Yucatecan pride. Thus, though *jarana* serves to bring people together in both the Tunkás-based and U.S.-based communities, it
does so in very different ways and with very different results.

Sports

Sports are extremely popular among Tunkaseños, who are often seen
playing basketball, soccer, softball, and baseball. We focus particularly
on baseball as an example of community participation in sports because
it is the most popular game among Tunkaseños in both Tunkás and the
United States.

Baseball is ubiquitous in Yucatán, from the professional Leones in Mérida to amateur teams in small towns across the peninsula, and its popularity spans gender and age. But in Tunkás in 2009, baseball was noticeably absent. The men's baseball team and the women's softball teams had disbanded in recent years, leaving only the boys' team. The baseball and softball fields are largely empty, sad reminders of a proud sports history. Some locals lament the decline in sports activity. One former softball player proudly produced an old newspaper clipping announcing that the Tunkás team had won the local championship. She said she would love to continue playing if there were a team, and she added that it was "a shame" that there are no teams now. A man in his sixties who had played and coached baseball for years told us that Tunkás is the only town in the area without a team, and he travels to other towns on weekends just to watch games.

In a country known for its enthusiasm for soccer, it may be surprising that people in Yucatán refer to baseball as *el rey de los deportes* (the king of sports) (Joseph 1988, 29). This most American of sports came to Yucatán by way of Cuba, where U.S. sailors had introduced it in the mid-nineteenth century and locals had taken it up with a passion. When Cuban nationalists rose up against Spain in their battle for Cuba's independence in 1868, many fled the island and headed to nearby Yucatán, bringing baseball with them. There are accounts of games being played on the peninsula as early as 1890 (Joseph 1988). Originally centered in the port city of Mérida, baseball quickly spread throughout the state and achieved the popularity it enjoys today.

When Tunkás still had baseball and softball teams, games were played on weekends on fields built specifically for these sports. Indeed, the softball field was renovated in 2006 with migrant remittances and matching funds from Mexico's Tres por Uno program.[3] Tunkás was known for the success of its teams; its softball and baseball teams both won league championships in recent years. No single factor can account for the loss of these teams, but funds clearly played a key role. In our interviews with former softball team members, all mentioned the decline in remittances as one reason for their team's breakup. Doña Teresa, a team organizer, told us

---

3. Under Tres por Uno, the local, state, and federal governments match funds given by migrants for development projects in their hometowns.

that players contributed around 200 pesos (US$15) per month for uniforms, equipment, umpires, and other team needs. But after the economic downturn, many could no longer afford the expense. Doña Teresa had often used money her husband sent from the United States to help the team. "There were players who couldn't afford the fees, so my husband would send 100 pesos (about $8) for those who couldn't afford it, and I would pay for them." But when her husband lost his job, he could no longer send money for this purpose. Doña Teresa also mentioned that previous Tunkás mayors had supported the team with government monies (even bringing a star pitcher from Cancún and paying her $50 a week), but the current mayor took no interest in the team and offered little assistance. With these two sources of funds cut off, the team eventually disbanded and several of the players left Tunkás to look for work in Cancún.

Sports are also an important part of life for Tunkaseños in the United States. Cam Mukul, a leader of the U.S.-based migrant community, said that sports are one of the main activities that bring large groups of Tunkaseños together. Indeed, community leader Manuel Pech also told us that Tunkaseños celebrate the Fourth of July and Thanksgiving by organizing a baseball game and picnic at a local park. Today there are three organized baseball teams that play year-round (there are no softball teams for Tunkaseña women in the United States). Each has about five Tunkaseño players on the roster; the other players are other Yucatecans, Mexicans, Mexican Americans, and even a few native-born Anglo players. Interestingly, this team makeup leads to a mix of Mayan, Spanish, and English being spoken on the field, sometimes simultaneously. The teams play in leagues in the Los Angeles area, and Sunday games attract a sizable contingent of Tunkaseños, many of whom remain at the parks after games to socialize with each other. Until recently, there was also a team in Orange County, but personality clashes led to its disbanding. Asked why he did not join one of the Tunkaseño teams in Los Angeles, a former Orange County player told us the driving distance was an impediment. There has been some talk of reconstituting the Orange County team; Cam Mukul told us that many people have asked him to help organize it but this has yet to happen.

Distance is one barrier that limits Tunkaseño migrants' participation in baseball in the United States. Money can be another, given that both baseball and softball have associated expenses—for uniforms, bats, balls, gloves, travel to away games, and umpires—and this obstacle affects players in Tunkás as well. In Tunkás these costs are typically covered by the players themselves, local business sponsors, and the local government, though the latter's support can vary depending on who is in power. In the United States, funding for baseball teams falls more heavily on the players. As the coach of a team with several Tunkaseño players told us, team costs run to $350 per season (about ten games) plus $50 per week for the umpires. Dividing this amount among the eighteen team members means that each player must pay about $50 each season. This is in addition to the equipment the players furnish, including uniforms, gloves, and bats. The cost may not appear exorbitant, but nor is it insignificant, especially for Tunkaseño migrants, who typically earn relatively low wages.

Sports, especially baseball, provide an important opportunity for Tunkaseños to participate in their community. Although the costs of participation can be high, Tunkaseños' passion for the game converts to high participation levels. Yet baseball, like *gremios* and *jarana*, is more than a pastime. All are important ways in which community members come together to build social capital. To better understand community participation in these three activities, we consider who participates in them, and who does not.

PATTERNS AND EXPLANATION OF PARTICIPATION AMONG TUNKASEÑOS

What sociodemographic characteristics are associated with Tunkaseños' participation in *jarana*, *gremios*, and sports? How is participation in these activities affected by internal and international migration? It is fairly apparent that being younger, male, and having more years of education all correlate positively with participation. However, the relationship between migration and participation is more complex. Migration to other parts of Mexico decreases the likelihood of participating, but migration to the United States appears not to influence the likelihood of participation. Even though Tunkaseños migrate largely for economic reasons, receipt of remittances by family members in Tunkás shows little correlation with participation.

Our definition of "participation" includes those who participate in the activities directly, as well as those who contribute money for them or attend *gremios*, *jarana*, and sporting events. Thus individuals who have done any of the following are classified as participants: (1) participated in a *gremio* in the last ten years; (2) given money or time to support a *jarana* group; (3) given money or time to support a sports team; (4) played in or attended a sporting event more than twice in the last year; or (5) danced in or attended a *jarana* performance at least once in the last year. This broad definition covers any kind of participation that serves to bring Tunkaseños together. Because the definitions of participation differ by activity (because some occur more often than others), we do not compare participation rates across activities.

Using this definition, three out of four Tunkaseños whom we interviewed are "participants." Participation rates vary by age, gender, religion, and wealth, as discussed in detail below. Fifty-five percent of males are participants, compared to only 34 percent of females. Level of education is positively associated with participation: 92 percent of individuals with more than ten years of schooling are participants, versus 67 percent of those with fewer than ten years of education. Excluding *gremio* participation (which, by definition, has ties to the Catholic church), Catholics are far more likely to participate than are evangelical Christians and the nonreligious (figure 10.1). It should be noted that for all three groups, rates of participation are highest in sports, the most secular activity of the three.[4]

Jarana, *gremios*, and sports require financial outlays from the participants. Therefore, it is not surprising that those with more economic resources participate more. The average wealth index score of participants is 15 percent higher than that for nonparticipants. Tunkaseños often talk about wealth as a barrier to participation. This is especially true regarding participation in *jarana*; the handmade *terno* is often far out of reach for many Tunkaseños. Doña Nana, a resident of Tunkás and a *jarana* dancer, noted that if a woman does not have a *terno*, she cannot dance in official events like the *vaquería*.

One way for Tunkaseños in Tunkás to accumulate wealth is through remittances from friends and family in the United States. We expected that remittance recipients might participate more than non-recipients, but the difference was marginal: 77 percent of those who receive remittances

---

4. *Jarana*, while not officially Catholic, is often associated with the town fiesta, and many evangelicals choose not to participate in it for that reason.

are participants, compared to 72 percent of those who do not receive them. It should be noted that formal contacts between Tunkaseño migrants and officials in Tunkás have been strained in recent years, leading many migrants in the United States to withhold remittances to which local authorities might gain access. This contrasts with the situation several years ago; relations between the local government and the migrant community were good then, and migrants pooled their money to help refurbish a softball field in their hometown. But given the current distrust, migrants are sometimes choosing not to send remittances through the government.[5] However, several Tunkaseño migrants mentioned that they sometimes send money through intermediaries in Tunkás, who distribute the funds directly to people in need in the town. Yet without official and sustained contact between the migrant community and people in Tunkás, the potential impact that migrants can have on community participation in their hometown is limited.

Figure 10.1. Participation in *Jarana* and Sports, by Religious Affiliation

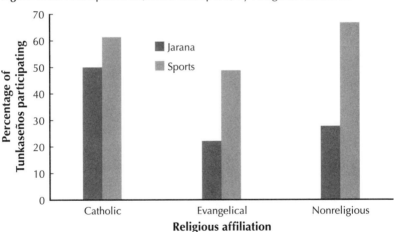

N = 1024

Patterns of participation clearly vary based on these sociodemographic characteristics. What, then, is the relationship between these patterns

---

5. Of course, others are not sending remittances because the economic crisis has brought a reduction in their earnings.

and migration? Do participation patterns change as Tunkaseños migrate to other parts of Mexico and to the United States? We find that overall rates of participation are nearly identical for Tunkaseños whether they live in Tunkás, elsewhere in Mexico, or in the United States. The participation rates are 73 percent of those in Tunkás, 78 percent for those residing in another part of Mexico, and 79 percent among those in the United States (figure 10.2). However, once the appropriate controls have been applied in a multivariate model, domestic migration becomes a negative predictor of participation while international migration is not.

Figure 10.2. Participation Rate, by Place of Residence

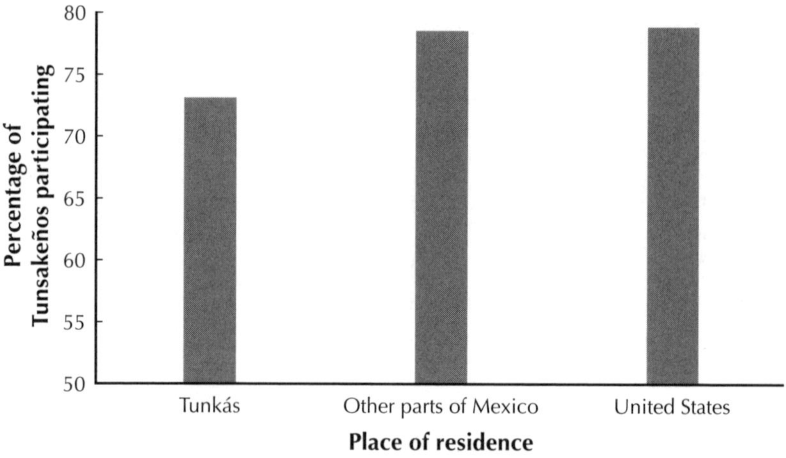

N = 1021

While overall patterns of participation remain largely consistent for Tunkaseños no matter where they live, some differences do emerge if we focus on gender and place of residence (figure 10.3). For example, participation rates are much lower for females in Tunkás than in other parts of Mexico or the United States. The gender differences that pervade Tunkás appear to break down with migration, such that female migrants participate at rates similar to those of male migrants. This may be due to the fact that Tunkaseña migrants see participation in communal activities as a way to re-create a Tunkaseño community away from home and ensure contact with others from Tunkás. Whereas in Tunkás, one need only step outside to interact with other Tunkaseños, activities like *jarana, gremios,* and sports offer migrants some of their few opportunities to encounter other Tunkaseños, and this may explain why Tunkaseño migrants, both male and female, participate in them in higher numbers.

Figure 10.3. Participation Rates, by Gender and Place of Residence

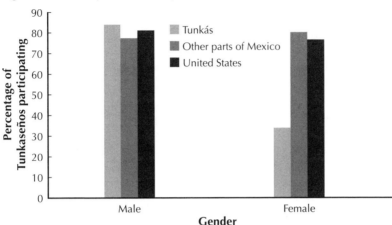

N = 1009

Other differences also emerge when Tunkaseños migrate, and these are largely related to the changing meanings of these activities. Elías, a dance instructor in Tunkás, told us that the "North American influence" was causing boys and young men in the hometown to see traditions such as *jarana* as less "cool." He said that as a result of the close connections migration had established between Mexico and its neighbor country to the north, boys in Tunkás "want to be like people in the United States," and this does not involve dancing *jarana*. The fact that only 8 percent of males in Tunkás and only 6 percent of Tunkaseño males in the United States dance *jarana* supports his assertions. While people like Elías strive to maintain what they see as an important tradition, many Tunkaseños view *jarana* in a different light, due in part to the influence of migration.

When considering education level and place of residence, we find that higher levels of education are strongly correlated with participation rates in all three residence categories (figure 10.4). However, the correlation is stronger in Tunkás than among Tunkaseños residing in other parts of Mexico or in the United States. Ninety-seven percent of Tunkaseños in Tunkás who have ten or more years of education participate in at least one of our three activities. The number drops to 86 percent for those with the same level of education who are residing in other parts of Mexico, and to 81 percent for those in the United States. Thus education level appears to be a more powerful predictor of participation for those who do not migrate. Among those who do migrate, the farther one is from home, the weaker the correlation seems to be between level of education and propensity to participate.

Figure 10.4. Participation Rates, by Education Level and Place of Residence

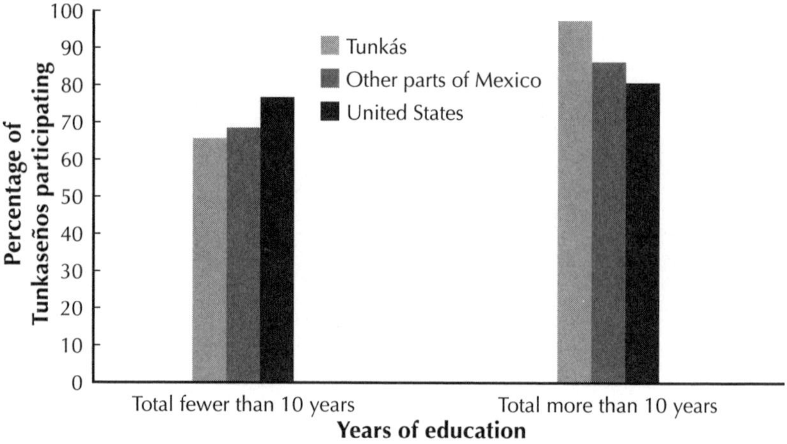

N = 1009

   In sum, the overall impacts of internal and international migration on patterns of participation appear to be mixed. Female migrants are clearly more likely to participate than women in Tunkás. At the same time, having more years of education becomes less important as a predictor of participation among migrants than nonmigrants. The multivariate analysis presented below allows for consideration of these characteristics simultaneously.

GENERAL MODEL OF PARTICIPATION
In order to determine which social characteristics predict participation, we constructed nested multivariate regression models (see table 10.1). Using participation as the dependent variable, Model 1 finds that being male, Catholic, having more than ten years of education, and living elsewhere in Mexico are associated with greater participation at the 99th percentile

confidence level. Being younger, not having children, and being wealthier are associated with greater participation at the 95th percentile confidence level. In Model 2, we added a variable: whether the respondent received remittances. In this model, we find that remittance receipt is not significantly correlated with participation and that all of the factors that were significant in Model 1 retain their significance, with the exception of age. In Model 3, we add international migration as a variable. We find that migrating to the United States is not correlated with a greater or lesser likelihood of participating, but living in another part of Mexico is associated with a lowered probability of participation, at the 95th percentile confidence level in all three models.

Table 10.1. Community Participation among Tunkaseños

	Model 1	Model 2	Model 3
Hours worked per week	−.001 (.004)	−.008 (.004)	−.001 (.004)
Age	**−.086*** (.042)	−.071 (.043)	**−.085*** (.042)
Age-squared	.001 (.001)	−.008 (.001)	.001 (.001)
Male	**.831*** (.224)	**.791*** (.242)	**.834*** (.224)
Catholic	**1.214*** (.174)	**1.289*** (.186)	**1.216*** (.174)
Ten or more years of education	**1.407*** (.282)	**1.701*** (.323)	**1.402*** (.282)
Married	.111 (.213)	.117 (.235)	.109 (.213)
Has children	−.553 (.287)	**−.723*** (.316)	−.556 (.286)
Lives in Mexico, outside of Tunkás	**−.825**** (.294)	**−.989*** (.307)	**−.829**** (.291)
Wealth	**.012*** (.005)	**.014**** (.005)	**.012*** (.005)
Remittance receipt	—	.204 (.221)	—
Lives in United States	—	—	−.059 (.361)
Constant	1.226 (.729)	.826 (.761)	1.212 (.726)
N	937	840	936
Chi-squared	117.49	126.13	123.57

* *p* < .05; ** *p* < .01; *** *p* < .001

Robust standard errors in parentheses.

Indeed, as an overall pattern it appears that characteristics such as age, gender, religion, and education level that are associated with participation in Tunkás continue to be important for Tunkaseño migrants in the United States. It is perhaps most interesting that while internal migration is associated with lower rates of participation, international migration is not. This is despite many obstacles to participation for Tunkaseño migrants in the United States: limited money and free time, the difficulty of obtaining needed materials, long distances to activities, and so on. We hypothesize that it is precisely *because* migrants in the United States are so far from home that they make greater efforts to seek out other Tunkaseños or activities in which Yucatecos are involved. Being far from home makes many Tunkaseños seek any available reminder of home. This enthusiasm is evident in the baseball games that they organize every Fourth of July and Thanksgiving. On those days, a migrant told us, Tunkaseños fill the park, happy to be around friends and family from home.

CONCLUSION

This chapter has examined the ways in which Tunkaseños practice three particular forms of community participation. Our analysis of the patterns of community participation among Tunkaseños shows that while migrating to other parts of Mexico is associated with lower likelihood of participation, there is no significant disparity between the rates of participation in Tunkás and the rates of Tunkaseño participation in the United States.

There are many obstacles that Tunkaseño migrants who want to participate in *jarana, gremios,* and baseball in the United States must overcome, not the least being the expenditures of time and financial resources that are required. However, Tunkaseño migrants are overcoming these obstacles and finding ways to remain involved with their community. As migrant community leader Cam Mukul told us, baseball games are important not only as sporting events but also as spaces for Tunkaseño migrants to come together socially. The same could be said of *jarana* and *gremios.*

It should be noted, however, that though rates of participation remain steady, the nature of the activities themselves can change when they are practiced in the United States. For example, *jarana*, which is so closely tied to the fiesta in Tunkás, becomes much more of a performance activity when practiced in the United States and a way for dancers to express pride as Tunkaseños and Yucatecans. *Jarana* becomes an expression of Yucatecan-ness. Through dancing, Tunkaseños are able to establish a degree of "cultural visibility" in the United States, carving out an identity for themselves in their new homes. This new identity, however, is broader than it would have been in Tunkás, now being part Tunkaseño and part Yucatecan.

The activities of the U.S.-based *gremio de braceros* also differ from those of a typical *gremio* in Tunkás. Migrants' participation is limited to sending financial support for their *gremios* in Tunkás. They can start new ones, as is the case with the *gremio de braceros*, and participate from a distance by paying the annual fee, but they cannot participate as they would if they were in Tunkás. However, the *gremio de braceros* does have the potential to take on a larger role within the Tunkaseño community in the United States. Perhaps because Tunkás is a relatively new sending community, its migrants have yet to organize a fiesta in the United States to coincide with the one in the hometown, as has happened with other migrant communities. As the Tunkaseño community in the United States grows, it may well be that the range of *gremio* activities expands as well.

Returning to Putnam, let us reconsider his main argument in *E Pluribus Unum*. Putnam writes that "in the short to medium run . . . immigration and ethnic diversity challenge social solidarity and inhibit social capital" (2007, 138). Diversity leads people, according to Putnam, to "hunker down" and not reach out to those around them. But "in the medium to long run . . . successful immigrant societies create new forms of social solidarity and dampen the negative effects of diversity by constructing new, more encompassing identities" (138–39).

This case study of community participation on both sides of the Mexico-U.S. border indicates, however, that the establishment of "more encompassing identities" is happening quite quickly for Tunkaseños. Putnam's theory that greater diversity due to immigration will, at least in the short run, lead to a "hunkering down" and lowering of participation rates seems inconsistent with the findings in the Tunkaseño study. For Tunkaseño migrants, greater diversity does not reduce levels of participation. The fact that participation rates in the activities we identified remain roughly the same suggests that Tunkaseños make an extra effort to re-create forms of associational life when they are in the United States. In fact, it may be precisely *because* of the diversity that Tunkaseños find in the United States that they so adamantly strive to re-create activities from their hometown. Perhaps it is more accurate to say that the Tunkaseño case does not contradict Putnam's assertions, but simply that the broadening of social identities is happening at a much more rapid rate than he envisaged. Tunkaseños are expanding their social identities by expanding their community to include fellow Yucatecans, Latinos, and others. With this expansion comes a change in identity and, subsequently, greater access to the social capital that comes from community participation.

It is this rapid broadening of social identities to include Yucatecans, Mexicans, Mexican Americans, Anglos, and others that enables patterns of participation among Tunkaseño migrants to remain similar to those of Tunkaseños in Tunkás. The key to continued associational life is, as Putnam suggested, to expand social boundaries. This is exactly what occurs in the Tunkaseño case, but at a much faster pace than Putnam imagined. Diversity does not lead Tunkaseños to "hunker down" but instead to seek out ways to participate in their community, even when—or perhaps *especially* when—they are far from home.

REFERENCES

Farriss, Nancy M. 1984. *Maya Society under Colonial Rule: The Collective Enterprise of Survival*. Princeton, NJ: Princeton University Press.

Fernández Repetto, Fernando. 1995. "Celebrar a los santos: Sistema de fiestas en el noroccidente de Yucatán," *Alteridades* 5: 51–61.

Joseph, Gilbert. 1988. "Forging the Regional Pastime: Baseball and Class in Yucatán." In *Sport and Society in Latin America: Diffusion, Dependency, and the Rise of Mass Culture*, ed. J. L. Arbena. Westport, CT: Greenwood Press.

Loewe, Ron. 2003. "Marching with San Miguel: Festivity, Obligation, and Hierarchy in a Mexican Town," *Journal of Anthropological Research* 59: 463–86.

Portes, Alejandro, Cristina Escobar, and Renelinda Arana. 2008. "Bridging the Gap: Transnational and Ethnic Organizations in the Political Incorporation of Immigrants in the United States," *Ethnic and Racial Studies* 31: 1056–90.

Putnam, Robert D. 2000. *Bowling Alone: The Collapse and Revival of American Community*. New York: Simon and Schuster.

———. 2007. "*E Pluribus Unum*: Diversity and Community in the Twenty-first Century. The 2006 Johan Skytte Prize Lecture," *Scandinavian Political Studies* 30: 137–74.

Putnam, Robert D., Robert Leonardi, and Raffaella Nanetti. 1993. *Making Democracy Work: Civic Traditions in Modern Italy*. Princeton, NJ: Princeton University Press.

Survey Questionnaire Administered to Persons in Tunkás, Yucatán, and in California, January–February 2009

INFORMACIÓN DEMOGRÁFICA

¿En qué año nació usted?

¿Y en dónde?

¿Dónde vive usted actualmente?

¿A qué se dedica usted principalmente?

¿Cuántas horas trabaja por semana?

En comparación con el año pasado, ¿ha cambiado el número de horas que usted trabaja por semana?

¿Cuánto gana en total?

¿En qué año empezó a trabajar por un sueldo?

¿Está usted afiliado actualmente a algún sindicato?

¿Cómo recibe su salario, en cheque o en efectivo?

¿Alguna vez usted se casó o ha vivido en unión libre con alguien?

¿Su pareja vive o ha vivido en los EEUU?

En total, ¿por cuánto tiempo ha vivido su pareja en los EEUU?

¿Cuántos miembros de su familia viven en Tunkás?

¿Cuántos miembros de su familia viven en los EEUU?

¿Cuántos viven en otras partes de México?

[Si la pareja no vive en Tunkás] En los últimos dos años, ¿su pareja ha regresado a verlos?

¿En qué año nació cada uno de sus hijos?

¿En dónde nació (nacieron)?

¿Se fue a los EEUU?

¿En qué año, la primera vez?

¿Dónde vive actualmente?

¿Prefiere usted que sus hijos crezcan en los EEUU o en México?

HISTORIA MIGRATORIA

¿Alguna vez ha salido de Tunkás para vivir o trabajar en otra parte de Yucatán o México?

¿A dónde se fue?

¿En qué año llegó allí?

¿Por cuánto tiempo estuvo allí?

¿Qué fue su ocupación en ese lugar?

¿Cuánto ganó en ese trabajo?

¿Por cuánto tiempo en total ha vivido en otras partes de Yucatán o de México?

En este año 2009, ¿usted piensa ir a vivir a alguna otra parte de Yucatán o México que no sea Tunkás?

¿A dónde?

¿Alguna vez ha ido, o ha intentado ir a los EEUU para vivir o trabajar?

¿A dónde se fue?

¿Cuándo llegó?

¿Cruzó con documentos?

¿Cuántas veces le agarraron en el cruce?

¿Usó pollero?

¿Cuánto le pagó al pollero?

¿Cuánto tiempo duró en los EEUU?

¿Cuál fue su primera ocupación en los EEUU?

¿Cuántas horas por semana trabajó en ese trabajo?

¿Cuánto ganó?

Antes de que usted se fuera a los EEUU por primera vez, ¿cuántos parientes tenía que ya vivían en los EEUU?

Antes de salir de Tunkás por primera vez, ¿a qué se dedicaba?

¿Cuánto ganaba en ese trabajo?

¿Cuáles fueron sus razones más importantes para ir a los EEUU la primera vez que se fue?

¿Se fue de Tunkás porque no le iba bien en el pueblo, o porque en los EEUU había más oportunidades?

Cuando usted se fue a los EEUU por primera vez, ¿tuvo que dejar a sus hijos en México?

¿Quién los cuidó?

En su último viaje a los EEUU o su último intento a cruzar, ¿cómo logró juntar o conseguir el dinero para pagar el cruce?

¿Cuántas veces intentó cruzar la frontera durante su último intento o viaje a los EEUU?

¿Cuántas veces fue agarrado?

Entonces, ¿pudo pasar o no?

¿Por qué parte de la frontera pasó o intentó pasar?

Cuando pasó la frontera, ¿lo hizo con papeles, o tuvo que entrar sin papeles?

¿Cómo consiguió sus papeles (falsos/prestados)?

¿Pasó usted por una garita?

¿Cómo logró pasar por la garita?

¿De qué manera cruzó la línea?

¿En dónde conoció al pollero que le ayudó a cruzar?

¿Quién se lo recomendó?

¿Cuánto tiempo necesitó para pagar la deuda al pollero (o a la persona que le prestó el dinero)?

En los últimos cinco años, ¿dónde ha pasado más tiempo, en Tunkás o en los EEUU?

En los últimos cinco años, ¿cuántas veces pudo regresar a Tunkás, incluyendo visitas breves y vacaciones?

En su último viaje a los EEUU, ¿se quedó más tiempo de lo que tenía planeado?

¿Por qué se quedó más tiempo?

¿Por qué regresó la última vez?

¿Usted piensa regresar a Tunkás este año, de manera permanente?

¿Por qué piensa regresar?

Actualmente, ¿qué tan difícil es evadir o esquivar la migra: muy fácil, algo fácil, algo difícil, o muy difícil?

Actualmente, si uno no tiene papeles, ¿qué tan peligroso es cruzar la frontera: muy peligroso, algo peligroso, poco peligroso, o nada peligroso?

¿Cuáles son las cosas que más le preocupan a una persona que va a cruzar?

¿Conocía a alguien que se fue a los EEUU y que murió al cruzar la frontera?

En el último año, ¿alguno de sus familiares se ha quedado en los EEUU por miedo de no poder regresar a los EEUU si se va/viene a México?

¿Sabe o escuchó algo sobre las leyes de reforma migratoria que propusieron en el congreso americano en 2006 y 2007?

En su opinión, ¿qué es lo que más hace falta para que menos gente se vaya de Tunkás?

¿Cuáles son las cosas que más le preocupan a una persona que vive en los Estados Unidos sin papeles?

¿Si usted supiera de un crimen en los Estados Unidos, lo reportaría a la policía, o no lo reportaría?

En los últimos doce meses, ¿lo ha parado alguna vez la policía, por alguna razón?

¿Qué tipo de documentos le pidió la policía?

¿Qué le pasó?

¿Alguna vez tuvo que dejar a sus hijos en los EEUU?

Para el año 2009, ¿piensa ir a los EEUU?

¿Por qué?

¿Ha solicitado un *green card*/una mica?

¿La recibió?

¿En qué año la recibió?

¿Ha solicitado la ciudadanía?

¿La recibió?

¿En qué año recibió la ciudadanía?

¿Alguna vez ha arreglado papeles para alguien?

¿Para quién?

Si hubiera un nuevo programa de contrataciones temporales, parecido al programa de los Braceros de los años 50's, ¿estaría interesado en participar?

Si hubiera un nuevo programa de legalización o una amnistía para migrantes en los EEUU, ¿estaría usted más dispuesto a ir a los Estados Unidos, o le daría igual?

¿Los trabajadores en Estados Unidos tienen salario mínimo?

¿De cuánto es?

¿Qué tipo de trabajo piensa tener en los EEUU, la próxima vez que se vaya?

En los últimos tres años, ¿usted ha cambiado de trabajo?

¿Qué fue su ocupación en los EEUU en los últimos tres años?

¿En que ciudad trabajó?

¿Cuántas horas trabajaba por semana?

¿Cuánto ganaba?

¿Cuánto tiempo estuvo sin trabajo en cada uno de los tres últimos años?

¿Cómo consiguió su último trabajo en los EEUU?

¿Como cuánto tiempo necesitó para encontrar ese trabajo?

Durante su trabajo más reciente en los EEUU, ¿el patrón le pidió algún documento de identificación?

En su trabajo más reciente en los EEUU, ¿estaba su empleador SEGURO que usted sí/no tenía permiso de trabajar, o su empleador pensaba que usted PROBABLEMENTE sí/no tenía permiso de trabajar?

En el lugar donde usted ha trabajado más recientemente en los EEUU, ¿el jefe o el encargado habla español?

En el lugar donde usted trabaja actualmente en los EEUU, ¿el patrón alguna vez ha amenazado con reportar a un empleado a la migra?

¿Hubo redadas en su trabajo más reciente en los EEUU?

¿Estuvo usted presente cuando la migra llegó?

¿Fue detenido?

¿Tiene usted algún familiar o amigo que ha sido agarrado por la migra en una redada en el trabajo?

¿Diría usted que es más difícil, menos difícil, o igual de difícil encontrar trabajo en los EEUU ahora que hace un año?

¿Alguna vez usted ha estado afiliado a un sindicato?

¿En dónde?

En los EEUU, los trabajadores tienen derechos laborales como un salario mínimo, pago de tiempo extra, y el derecho de organizarse. ¿Los migrantes con papeles tienen estos derechos?

¿Y los indocumentados?

¿Usted piensa que los sindicatos en los EEUU protegen los derechos de los trabajadores y ayudan a mejorar su situación en el trabajo?

MIGRACIÓN DE JÓVENES

¿Cree usted que los jóvenes nacidos en Tunkás pueden progresar en la vida sin salir del pueblo, o tienen que salir de Tunkás para superarse?

¿Cuándo cree que está bien que una muchacha se va a los EEUU?

¿Y cuándo cree que está bien que un muchacho se va a los EEUU?

En los últimos doce meses, ¿dónde ha escuchado con más frecuencia algo sobre la migración?

¿Cuántos de sus amigos de Tunkás han emigrado a los EEUU?

Para el año 2009, ¿cuántos de sus amigos piensan ir a los EEUU?

HISTORIA EDUCATIVA

¿Sabe usted hablar inglés?

¿Sabe usted leer español?

¿Sabe usted hablar maya?

¿Habla (o hablaba) usted maya en los EEUU?

¿Con quién lo habla (hablaba)?

¿Alguna vez alguien en su lugar de trabajo le ha dicho que no debe de hablar maya en los EEUU?

¿Está bien que se siga hablando maya en los EEUU?

¿Cuántos años de escuela pudo terminar en México?

¿Y en los EEUU?

¿Por qué dejó de estudiar?

Hoy en día, ¿cuántos años de estudio necesita una muchacha para conseguir un buen trabajo en Tunkás?

¿Y en California?

Hoy en día, ¿cuántos años de estudio necesita un muchacho para conseguir un buen trabajo en Tunkás?

¿Y en California?

¿Cuáles materias de escuela le han servido más en su vida diaria en Tunkás?

¿Y en su vida diaria en otra parte de México?

¿Y en su vida diaria en los EEUU?

LA VIDA FAMILIAR

¿Cuántas personas (esposo, padres, suegros, hijos, hermanos, abuelos, nietos, cuñados, tíos, primos, yernos/nueras) viven con usted?

En su hogar en Tunkás, ¿es un hombre o una mujer quien toma las decisiones sobre cómo se usa el dinero, la mayor parte del tiempo?

Y en su hogar en los EEUU, ¿es un hombre o una mujer quien toma las decisiones sobre cómo se usa el dinero, la mayor parte del tiempo?

En su hogar en Tunkás, ¿es un hombre o una mujer quien prepara la comida, la mayor parte del tiempo?

Y en su hogar en los EEUU, ¿es un hombre o una mujer quien prepara la comida, la mayor parte del tiempo?

En su hogar en Tunkás, ¿es un hombre o una mujer quien hace las tareas domésticas como lavar y planchar, la mayor parte del tiempo?

Y en su hogar en los EEUU, ¿es un hombre o una mujer quien hace las tareas domésticas como lavar y planchar, la mayor parte del tiempo?

En su hogar en Tunkás, ¿es un hombre o una mujer quien cuida a los niños, la mayor parte del tiempo?

Y en su hogar en los EEUU, ¿es un hombre o una mujer quien cuida a los niños, la mayor parte del tiempo?

En su hogar en Tunkás, ¿es un hombre o una mujer quien cuida a las personas mayores, la mayor parte del tiempo?

Y en su hogar en los EEUU, ¿es un hombre o una mujer quien cuida a las personas mayores, la mayor parte del tiempo?

¿Alguna vez ha tenido usted que regresar a Tunkás para cuidar a un pariente mayor?

En su opinión, ¿una buena esposa debe de obedecer a su esposo en todo lo que él ordene?

En su opinión, ¿una persona cuya pareja no le obedece, tiene el derecho de pegarle a esa persona?

En la casa donde usted vive, ¿hay alguien que tenga teléfono?

¿En dónde hace o recibe usted sus llamadas, la mayor parte del tiempo?

¿Cuántas veces al mes hace llamadas a sus familiares que viven al otro lado?

¿Y cuántas veces al mes recibe usted llamadas de sus familiares que viven al otro lado?

¿Tiene usted correo electrónico?

REMESAS Y GASTOS FAMILIARES

En su último viaje a los EEUU, ¿mandaba dinero a sus parientes en Tunkás?

¿A quién se lo mandaba?

¿Cuánto dinero mandaba?

¿Con qué frecuencia?

En comparación con el año pasado, ¿el monto promedio que usted envía ahora ha cambiado?

¿Como cuánto mandaba hace un año?

¿Con qué frecuencia?

¿Por qué manda más/menos ahora que hace un año?

¿Alguna vez ha participado usted en el programa Tres por Uno?

¿Alguien en su hogar recibe dinero de alguien en los EEUU?

¿Con qué frecuencia se recibe el dinero de allá?

¿Como cuánto dinero se recibió la última vez?

¿Diría usted que se recibe la misma cantidad que hace un año?

¿Para qué se usa la mayoría del dinero enviado de los EEUU?

¿Alguna vez ha invertido usted en un negocio?

¿Qué tipo de negocio?

¿En dónde?

¿Cuáles de las siguientes cosas tiene su hogar en Tunkás –televisión, estéreo, refrigerador, computadora, lavadora, vehículo, agua potable, electricidad, estufa de gas, suelo de concreto, baño?

¿Y la casa en los EEUU?

¿Cuánto paga cada mes en alquiler, renta, o hipoteca por su vivienda en los EEUU?

¿Tiene alguna propiedad (casa, condominio, terrenos) en los EEUU?

¿Tiene usted algún préstamo pendiente (pago de carro, et cétera) en los EEUU?

Favor de indicar si alguna vez ha usado los siguientes servicios públicos: Welfare, Medicaid/Medicare/Medi-Cal, Food Stamps, WIC, desempleo.

¿Alguien en su hogar tiene u ocupa terrenos en Tunkás?

¿Quién los trabaja?

¿Para qué se usan los terrenos?

¿Cuántas hectáreas tiene?

¿Cuántas colmenas tiene?

¿Cuántas cabezas de ganado tiene?

¿Usted perdió parte de la cosecha por la sequía del año pasado?

¿Usted recibe ayuda del gobierno por haber perdido la cosecha?

¿Cuánto dinero trajo consigo cuando regresó a Tunkás la última vez?

LA SALUD

Cuando usted se enferma, ¿prefiere ir al doctor o al curandero?

¿Cuál es la razón principal por la que usted prefiere ir con el doctor/ curandero?

¿Por qué no va al doctor/curandero?

¿Cuántas veces ha visitado al doctor en los últimos doce meses?

¿Cómo paga por este servicio?

¿Cuántas veces ha visitado al curandero en los últimos doce meses?

¿Alguna vez un médico le ha dicho que padece de una de las siguientes enfermedades—alto colesterol, anemia, asma, cáncer, diabetes, hipertensión, problemas de corazón, problemas del estómago, parásitos?

¿En qué país lo diagnosticaron?

¿Dónde recibió tratamiento?

¿Usted o algún familiar se ha enfermado en los EEUU y regresó a México para que lo atendieran?

¿Cuántos días por semana come usted comida casera, comida congelada o pre-preparada, comida rápida (como de lonchería o McDonalds)?

¿Alguna vez ha usado programas o servicios que lo ayuden con su nutrición?

¿Ha podido seguir las recomendaciones dadas por el programa?

¿Por qué?

Durante su estancia más reciente en los EEUU, ¿tenía/tiene algún tipo de seguro médico?

¿Quién pagó el seguro?

PARTICIPACIÓN COMUNITARIA

¿A qué iglesia pertenece usted?

En el mes pasado, ¿cuántas veces asistió a misa o a culto?

En los últimos diez años, ¿cuántas veces ha podido usted contribuir con dinero a la fiesta anual en Tunkás?

¿Y ser miembro del comité organizador de la fiesta?

¿Y ayudar a organizar la fiesta en forma voluntaria, sin ningún pago?

¿Y participar en algún gremio en la fiesta?

¿Y asistir a la fiesta en Tunkás?

¿Diría usted que su participación actual en la fiesta es mayor o menor que hace diez años?

¿Alguna vez ha usted jugado con un equipo de deporte no-profesional en Tunkás?

¿Alguna vez ha usted jugado con un equipo de deporte no-profesional en los EEUU?

En los últimos cinco años, ¿ha usted podido contribuir con dinero para un grupo de jarana?

¿Y apoyar de forma no-monetaria a un grupo jaranero?

¿Y contribuir dinero para un equipo deportivo?

¿Ha apoyado de otra manera para un equipo deportivo?

¿Cuántas veces asiste usted un partido de deportes?

¿Cuántas veces juega en un partido de deportes?

¿Cuántas veces asiste a un baile de un grupo jaranero?

¿Cuántas veces participa en un grupo jaranero?